# PRISONER
## OF SOUTHERN
# ROCK

**MERCER**
UNIVERSITY PRESS

*Endowed by*
**TOM WATSON BROWN**
*and*
**THE WATSON-BROWN FOUNDATION, INC.**

Praise for *Prisoner of Southern Rock*

Great stories, well written and heartfelt. *Prisoner of Southern Rock* is an engaging and entertaining celebration of Southern music, musicians, and characters.
—Chuck Leavell, musical director, The Rolling Stones

From the first time I heard about Michael Buffalo Smith, I've been impressed with his dedication to preserving and promoting Southern music. His book is an interesting and insightful story of the musicians he's come to know and how he's enjoyed his journey.
—Johnny Sandlin, producer
(The Allman Brothers, Elvin Bishop,
Capricorn Records)

Michael Buffalo Smith as a musician, writer, critic, and Southern music historian really gets it. His taste and deep appreciation for the real thing are qualities that inspire all of us in his wake. And it's a big wake.
—Billy Bob Thornton

At last, a memoir from Michael Buffalo Smith who has lived and breathed Southern Rock since the genre's inception! Lock me up and throw away the key!
—Marshall Chapman, artist, songwriter, and author

If you think you know about Southern Rock, you might want to read Buffalo's book. Here's a guy who lives and breathes the subject. He not only listens to and studies the genre but is personally acquainted with most of the artists he writes about. He knows everything from their first musical notes to what they have for breakfast. Put on some Marshall Tucker and pull up a copy of *Prisoner of Southern Rock*.
—Paul Hornsby, producer (Marshall Tucker Band, Charlie Daniels, Capricorn
Records)

Michael is a witty, soulful writer with a true love for the music and artists that are his subjects. His writings are truly stated and helpfully insightful to all readers. Michael fills a space that is sorely needed in these times of miscommunications and rumors disguised as facts.
—Tommy Talton, Cowboy / The Tommy Talton Band

Michael Buffalo Smith serves up a heartwarming yet candid look at his rise to become one of Southern music's most beloved journalists, musicians, and radio personalities, with an inside look at some of the stars he's interviewed, played with, and befriended over the years. From cult heroes, to the brightest stars, stadiums to smoky bars, Michael delivers firsthand, some of his most memorable encounters along the way, in the true, down home fashion he is known for. *A must read* for any music fan!
—John Galvin, Molly Hatchet

Buffalo interviews the stars, and they're human. He talks with the regular folks, and they're stars. That is the heart of Buffalo's rare talent, to see, value, and celebrate all of the extraordinary people who cross his path, regardless of their packaging. At his core, he is a tireless fan, not only of the stars and big shots, but mostly of true human gifts, dressed in dusty overalls or rhinestones and sequins. It's easy to understand why so many feel at home with Buffalo. He shines the spotlight of his generous appreciation wherever his truth compass points. It is refreshing, encouraging, and empowering to remember the gift of authenticity lies within us all. It's wonderful to know there are folks around like Buffalo who notice and appreciate and write about it.

—Tom Wynn, Cowboy

# MICHAEL BUFFALO SMITH

# PRISONER

# OF SOUTHERN

# ROCK

## A MEMOIR

Mercer University Press | Macon, Georgia

MUP/ H847

© 2012 Mercer University Press
1400 Coleman Avenue
Macon, Georgia 31207

First Edition

Books published by Mercer University Press are printed on acid-free paper that meets the
requirements of the American National Standard for Information Sciences—Permanence of
Paper for Printed Library Materials.

Mercer University Press is a member of Green Press Initiative (greenpressinitiative.org), a
nonprofit organization working to help publishers and printers increase their use of
recycled paper and decrease their use of fiber derived from endangered forests. This book
is printed on recycled paper.

Library of Congress Cataloging-in-Publication Data

Smith, Michael Buffalo.
  Prisoner of southern rock : a memoir / Michael Buffalo Smith. -- 1st ed.
     p. cm.
  Includes bibliographical references and index.
  ISBN-13: 978-0-88146-381-1 (hardback : alk. paper)
  ISBN-10: 0-88146-381-7 (hardback : alk. paper)
  1. Smith, Michael Buffalo. 2. Rock musicians--Southern States--Biography. 3. Music
journalists--United States--Biography. I. Title.
  ML420.S6719A3 2012
  781.66092--dc23
  [B]

2012021950

*Dedicated to the memory of my sweet sister—*

*Patsy Smith Harvey,*

*September 17, 1955—June 19, 2012*

*"Love you honey. I'll see you in the Light."*

# CONTENTS

# FOREWORD

A friend of mine told me recently that he once heard Gregg Allman say that since rock and roll music was born in the Southern United States, using the term "Southern rock" is like saying "rock rock." I couldn't agree more.

I used to do a one-man show in the theatre and in my introduction I would say to the audience, "Okay, you've heard my name and you know I'm from the South, so you're probably thinking, 'Okay, this guy's some ignorant bigot who sleeps with his sister.' Well, let me just remind you of something. If it weren't for the southern part of the United States of America, you guys wouldn't have a substantial number of your great authors and you wouldn't have any modern music. We'd all be listening to Irish lullabies, classical music, etc. So, you're welcome!"

The blues, country, and jazz married up and gave birth to rock and roll. Gregg Allman, Dickey Betts, Toy Caldwell, Dru Lombar, Ronnie Van Zant—all these legendary guys grew up listening to Elvis, Little Richard, Otis, Jerry Lee, Hank Williams, Jimmy Rodgers, Howlin' Wolf, Muddy Waters, Chuck Berry, and a host of great rock and roll, country, and jazz artists. Then when they all started forming their own bands and playing their own versions of the music by all of these influential cats, it came out the way it came out; the Allman Brothers Band, Marshall Tucker, Lynyrd Skynyrd, Wet Willie, Grinderswitch, and (yes, I know they're from Texas) ZZ Top, just to name some of the big boys.

So, to label these legends "Southern rock," like it's a little boutique category, really blows a mule johnson. Most pseudointellectual "experts" need labels to prove they understand things. They may not know that the Allman Brothers are as much jazz as they are blues, as they are rock, but these self-proclaimed "experts" certainly do know what a mule-johnson-related esophagus bruise feels like.

This book is written by a musician from the South who calls a lot of the aforementioned artists friends, idols, and heroes. Michael Buffalo Smith knows and loves the music that was born in his territory. And he is acquainted only with the *topside* of a mule.

Read and enjoy. God bless Memphis, New Orleans, Muscle Shoals, Spartanburg, Macon, and a lot of heavy-aired, soulful, crazy, magical places in between. Hope you all keep food on the table and clean clothes to wear. Saw you here 'while back and hope to see you again directly. I'm gonna put the headphones on now and lean back and listen to some Boston, some Aerosmith, and Bruce Springsteen, cause every now and then I like to also listen to a little Northeastern rock.

Billy Bob Thornton
From a couch in "Southern" California, 2012

# PRISONER
## OF SOUTHERN
# ROCK

# INTRODUCTION

There comes a time in everyone's life, if we are blessed to live long enough, when we find ourselves looking into the mirror and asking, "How did I end up here?" At that moment in time, we realize that the years somehow managed to sneak up on us while we were busy living our lives.

Recently, I found myself in just that position. I was fighting a string of seemingly endless health problems and struggling day to day to keep my head above water. All the while, I was establishing a name for myself as a music journalist and performing artist. I really didn't know just how I got from point "A" to where I am now, which was a good excuse for reliving the events of my life. Writing them down on paper would most likely shed some light on myself as a person, as well as being what Bonnie Bramlett once told Phil Walden that I was "the torchbearer for Southern Rock." If nothing else, it would be good therapy.

Sure, I grew up under questionable circumstances, and have found myself knee-deep in some pretty tumultuous situations during my life, but hey—all's well that ends well, right? After all, I have kind of lived the rock and roll dream here over the past fifteen or so years, and I feel downright blessed to have had the experiences. All of them. The good, the bad, and the ugly. After all, without the bad, how could we truly embrace the good?

Most of my hobnobbing with the stars began after the creation of *GRITZ Magazine* in 1998, so we are really talking about quite a short period of time here. Prior to *GRITZ*, I had been fortunate enough to conduct some pretty hefty interviews, including one actual Beatle, George Harrison back in 1992; the great Chet Atkins in 1994; and Gene Simmons and Peter Criss of KISS around the mid-1990s. But it was *GRITZ* that brought be back home to my roots. My Southern Rock roots. The Allman Brothers. The Marshall Tucker Band. Lynyrd Skynyrd. And those are just the tip of the iceberg. During the thirteen years since the online beginnings of *GRITZ*, I have met and interviewed almost every Southern star that I idol-worshiped back during my heady high school days. Who would have thunk it?

So here it is. It's just my life so far, or at least the highlights, spread across paper for all to see. No secrets. No lies. No alibis. As for some of the situations described in this tome, all I can do is quote my old buddy, the late Bill Hudson in saying, "it seemed like a good idea at the time."

Michael Buffalo Smith, Spartanburg, SC, 2012

# THE AMBASSADOR OF SOUTHERN ROCK

I was standing center stage in front of several thousand screaming fans in Tampa, Florida, singing with the Marshall Tucker Band. Lead singer Doug Gray had invited me to sing with them before and it had always been a rush, but today, well, today was special. The stage was full of friends and stars like Danny Shirley from Confederate Railroad, Mark Emerick from the Commander Cody Band, longtime Charlie Daniels Band guitarist Tommy Crain, wrestler Hulk Hogan and his pop-star daughter Brooke, and many more. My buddy and traveling companion Scott Greene was even onstage singing backup, I believe for the very first time.

Doug pointed to his mic at center stage and told me to have at it. It was a comfortable situation for me, being onstage with Doug, who had become a friend back in 1996, and standing up there with old friends Stuart Swanlund and Pat Ellwood, both of whom I had known since the early 1980s, along with more recent friends B. B. Borden on drums; Dave Muse on sax, flute, and keys; and the amazing Chris Hicks on guitar.

I had grown to love all of these guys, as well as the players that preceded some of them, like Toy and Tommy Caldwell, George McCorkle, Paul T. Riddle, Jerry Eubanks, Franklin Wilkie, Ronnie Godfrey, Tony Heatherly, Tim Lawter, Ace Allen, Frankie Toler, Ronald Radford, and Rusty Milner. It goes without saying the Marshall Tucker Band has been a part of my life since the formation of the original band in the early 1970s. When asked who my all-time favorite bands are, I will inevitably answer the Tucker Band, the Beatles and the Allman Brothers Band.

My love for Tucker was peaking, and now, in a serious dream come true, I found myself onstage jamming with them. In the past, when invited to sing with the boys I eagerly accepted but didn't really think too much about what was happening at the time. This time was different. It was the event that Charlie Daniels stages every year to benefit the

Angelus home for nonambulatory people. Lots of kids live there, but plenty of adults are residents as well, many of whom live with cerebral palsy. Every year thousands gather for four days of music, a golf tournament, and lots of just plain fun. This was my sixth event and in my mind they only get better and better each year, due largely to the management of Gar and Tammy Williams.

Playing for the kids and all the concertgoers is always a thrill, but today it was even more special. Maybe it's because this year I had come to realize just how fortunate I am to have met, performed with, and befriended so many music stars I had admired during my life. Maybe it was the love I felt for all of my pals in the Tucker band and other friends gathered around the stage. Maybe it was looking over at the 50-foot screens on each side of the stage and seeing myself larger than life, and for just a moment feeling like a rock and roll star. Or maybe it was simply the realization that a lifelong dream was at hand, and the bottled-up soul of a performer who was born to play was at long last being uncorked.

Whatever the reason, I was floating on cloud nine-point-five. Ever since I created the Southern Rock webzine *GRITZ* back in 1998, I had been blessed to be known as an authority on Southern Rock. Some have even dubbed me "the Ambassador of Southern Rock." It has been a lot of fun.

I was getting into all the shows for free, having the red carpet rolled out, getting all access backstage at shows, meeting all the performers, and generally having the time of my life. On the other hand, I became exposed to the seedy underbelly of rock and roll, the drugs, the backstabbing, the lies and deceit. Don't get me wrong, there wasn't a whole lot of that bad stuff for me to see, but there was enough. Still, the good far outweighed the bad and I have always been one to write about the good and not the bad. My mother taught me, "If you can't say something good about somebody, just don't say anything at all."

I had been a lover of Southern rock since it first became a genre in the early 1970s, and I truly dove headlong into the music after founding *GRITZ Magazine*. But hey, before we delve into Southern rock, we need to go back to the beginning. Back before Marshall Tucker Band. Before *Eat a Peach*. Before I called Jakson Spires my friend. Before I recorded a duet with Bonnie Bramlett. Before the reunion of Cowboy. Back to the beginning. Fifty-some-odd years ago. Some more odd than others.

# BORN UNDER A (NOT SO) BAD SIGN

I was born the same year as the greatest automobile in the history of automobiles was created, the 1957 Chevrolet. Thank God only one of us had tail fins.

June 24, 1957. Cancer, Aquarius rising. Cherokee-Irish.

If I only had a dollar for every time I heard my mother tell the story of my birth, I'd be rich. Well, perhaps not rich, but I'd at least be able to buy another guitar.

Seems when I was born, the umbilical cord was wrapped around my tiny throat like some sort of hangman's noose. Apparently it was so bad that the doctor asked my father to choose which one he wanted to live if a choice were required. Thank God he didn't end up having to make that decision—I kind of think I know which one he would have chosen. About ten years later, he was probably reliving that that moment over and over in his mind. Not that I was a problem child. No, not at all.

So they cut me out, and my face was as blue as the Southern sky. To compound matters, my arm was somehow lodged in my rib cage, and at first they thought I was going to look like a character from a Lon Chaney movie when I grew up. Then along came a creative health practitioner there at Spartanburg General Hospital who reached over and, with a chiropractic-style twist, popped the old arm out. I was normal. Well, other than being a ten-and-three-quarter-pound chunky baby boy. So I was healthy. What of it?

Dorothy Elizabeth Sorrells, a beauty from Tucapau (Startex), South Carolina, had met Junior Lee Smith of San Jose, California, while he was stationed at Donaldson Air Force Base in Greenville, SC, where he specialized in airplane engine repair. They were married in December 1954, and on September 17, 1955, they had their first child, Patsy Lee Smith.

There were only two kids in our family. Me and Patsy. Funny how I remember she always took pride in telling everyone that she was my older sister. Somehow that changed when we hit adulthood.

I grew up somewhere between middle class and abject poverty. My dad worked all the time it seems. When I was a kid he was employed by Lyman Printing and Finishing Company. I have no idea what that job entailed. All I know is that Daddy changed jobs a couple of times. Once he was a transfer truck driver. I remember riding in the cab of a big Peterbilt and thinking how cool it was.

He landed a job with Community Cash grocery stores when I was ten years old or so and started working in the produce department. He stayed with that job until retirement, some thirty years later. I recall him working at the Lyman, SC, store first (*the same store I spent one summer standing in front of selling Grit newspapers as a kid*), and later he was transferred to Spartanburg where he worked at two or three locations. Somewhere in there I myself worked at the same store as my dad. I bagged groceries and stocked shelves, unloaded trucks, and such. I even spent one year working with him in the produce department. Lots of excitement. Like the day I opened up a box of lettuce to trim and a huge tarantula spider crawled out.

But the one thing that sticks out most in my mind is that I never felt like I belonged in that job. Well, not just that one. I didn't feel like I belonged when I worked at the cotton mill in Spartanburg, or at the fish camp as a fry cook, or moving toilets and bathtubs at Kohler, or working temp jobs for Manpower, or cooking burgers at Hardees.

Now there's a memory. It was the summer between tenth and eleventh grade. I was cooking during the day and then coming in late at night to clean the restaurant with soap and chemicals. And then there was the day I came to work after smoking pot with a friend and put the meat on the bun warmer and the buns on the grill, which ignited a grease fire in the hood over the grill and nearly burned the store to the ground. Another short-lived job. "Just say no."

There were a handful of jobs I enjoyed, like being the projectionist at the Camelot Drive-In movie theater in Spartanburg during the summer that *Star Wars* (the first one, 1977) came out. We only changed movies one time that summer. From *Star Wars* to *Smokey and the Bandit*. I still have both scripts embedded in my memory.

Before the movies started I would play music through the speakers that the customers lifted off the stand and placed in their car. Remember those? For you kids reading this, think "prehistoric iPod."

When I started the job there were a couple of cassette tapes that we played through their speakers. One was classic country and the other was like Sinatra and stuff. Well, I made my own tapes to play. Lynyrd Skynyrd, Marshall Tucker, Waylon Jennings, Charlie Daniels. Rest assured I influenced the musical tastes of a few hundred teens who will always remember "Heard It in a Love Song" playing through the speaker at the drive-in while they made out in the back seat of their dad's Chevy.

The other jobs I enjoyed were the various radio jobs, which all began after my friend Tony Pearson and I got into the radio club in high school and the Junior Achievement radio club. More on that later. But as far as jobs go, I just always felt like I had a higher calling, that I should be doing something huge and creative.

Back to my childhood. It was a time of escape. I always wanted to escape because we were so poor, and it seemed all of my friends had everything they could ever dream of. Of course, this was far from true, but at the time it seemed that way.

In some ways, not having money seemed to make me more creative. I could play for hours in the red dirt with a toy shovel and a cardboard box. At times I got a little *too* creative, though. Like the time I discovered matches, and how cool things looked when they were burning. I guess I was a junior pyromaniac, which inevitably lead to the unfortunate "accident" my sister's Barbie and Ken dolls had in their Barbie dream car—burned to a pile of molten plastic.

Cardboard boxes were the enemy compound. Twigs rubber-banded together were planes shot down over the beach. All of this from a kid who would grow up decidedly antiwar. Same with hunting. Later, in my teenage years, I would go hunting with my friend Larry, and shoot doves, squirrels, all sorts of animals. These days I could never kill an animal. We grow and we change.

I was a big fan of escapist television shows like *Batman*, *Dark Shadows*, *Lost in Space*, and *Star Trek*. I always wanted the official *Star Trek* toys, but they were too expensive. Still, my parents managed to buy me a Major Matt Mason and a couple of his space buds. One of them was a green alien with a large head. I must have had quite an imagination to pretend that the green alien was actually Mr. Spock, and Matt Mason was James T. Kirk.

I had a lot of fun as a kid, even with no money. My imagination ran wild. My Batman cape was one of mom's towels, until the day I decided to make one out of Daddy's suit coat. That didn't fly to well, if you know what I mean. Childhood was filled with riding my bike, playing basketball and kick ball, reading comics, *Famous Monsters of Filmland* and *Model Car Science*, and getting into trouble. Some of the happiest memories I have are the memories of my mother's parents, Hoyt Ashmore and Edna Epton Sorrells.

# 3

## GRANDPA AND GRANDMA SORRELLS
## AND MY SOUTH CAROLINA FAMILY

I was walking through the Bi-Lo grocery store one day recently when my eye caught a big-ol' slice of watermelon, laying up on some ice there in the produce section. There were plenty of whole melons lining the floor underneath like some kind of backyard garden had moved inside. The watermelon slices triggered another of those memory spurts I've been experiencing lately, and for a moment my mind reeled back into the past—to my childhood, to Grandpa Sorrells and his "watermelon slicin'."

You see, life back then was pretty simple—especially for me. I was probably eight years old at the time that I'm remembering. Grandpa and grandma, or "Mama and Papa" as we called my mom's parents, lived in Wellford, SC, not far from Startex—also not far from Lyman. Grandpa grew a lot of vegetables himself, and he'd sell them from his pickup truck.

Every once in a while, Papa would get a hankering to call some of the neighbors over, along with friends and family, and have a watermelon slicin' right there in the side yard. Lots of times it would be grandma and grandpa, mother and dad, Uncle Sonny, my Aunt Jo and Uncle Jack, and all the grandkids. We'd all sit in folding chairs, or on the ground under the magnolia tree, and grandpa would slice the watermelons. He'd cut them long-ways, and each watermelon ended up in eight sections. He always sprinkled table salt on his, and to this day I won't eat watermelon unless it is salted.

Some of the most memorable moments from my youth involve gobbling down watermelon and spitting seeds. It's amazing how much fun an eight–year-old boy can have spitting watermelon seeds. And then there was "seed tweaking." I call it that because I don't know what else to call it. Putting one of the juicy seeds between the thumb and pointer finger and squeezing, resulting in an airborne seed. Fun. Life was so much simpler then.

It amazes me how those little things from the past mean so much to me these days. It's the simple things we tend to remember most vividly. Especially after we become adults, and suddenly come to the somewhat startling realization that life is not as easy as we thought it was going to be. Maybe that's why the good Lord gave us these vivid memory capabilities. When stress hits, we can just close our eyes, lean back, relax and enjoy a game of Tidily-Winks, the sound of a Pete Rose ball card in the spokes of our bike, or maybe a nice slice of watermelon—with a sprinkle of salt.

What I remember most about my Grandpa Sorrells is how he grew all those vegetables in his back yard and drove them all around the community, selling them from the back of his truck. He had a scale that hung in the back, and he'd weigh out the tomatoes, potatoes, and other veggies. In the front seat he always had candy bars and Bazooka bubble gum that he would sell to the kids. Bubble gum was either a penny or two for a penny, I forget which. I sure chewed a lot of it, though, and read the enclosed Bazooka Joe comics. (I still remember collecting the comics and sending them in to get free prizes. Same with cereal box tops.) Candy bars, like Zero, Payday, and Hershey's, were a nickel. Boy howdy, I am really dating myself now.

There were many times when I would ride the truck with grandpa and I have vivid memories of him extending credit to folks all the time. If they wanted some apples or tomatoes, he'd just say "Pay me next time." He was a good man, with a broad smile.

I might not have said that at one particular time, when he chased me back home from a lake down the road, swatting my legs and behind with a switch. I had snuck off to go fishing at this old lake there near Johnson's Hardware Store. I had obtained a cane pole out from under the neighbor's house and found something in Mama's kitchen to use for bait. I guess I was about seven years old. I had no idea how to fish. I also had no idea how dangerous the pier was that I was walking out on. An old shell of a pier, hanging down into the water on one side. When Papa Sorrells caught me there, he became quite upset. It's a wonder I didn't give him a heart attack while he was chasing me home.

Another time, he and I had walked from his house over to the gas station in Startex that sat across the road from Coleman's Grocery. They used to have these little magic tricks and gags hanging over the register, and one time I got the disappearing ball in a cup trick. Hours of entertainment. It was me, always wanting to be an entertainer, whether it was a magician, a ventriloquist, an impressionist. a singer, whatever.

Anyway, Papa had given me some change and I bought two packs of Batman trading cards. On the way home he asked, "Did you get yourself something Michael?" I said, "I got some cards." Well, that little fella turned red as a pickle beet. He thought I meant playing cards, which of course, his strict Baptist upbringing was very much against— gambling and all. Once he saw that they were "picture cards," he just laughed.

I will never forget the day in 1968 I came home from school, got off the bus, and my dad met me at the end of the driveway. "Papa Sorrells is dead." Dad wasn't big on easing into the bad news. I was eleven years old.

Mama Sorrells dipped snuff. Bruton snuff, to be exact. Because of her love of the tobacco product, she would often send me walking down the street to Johnson's Hardware store, a place that sold virtually anything you needed, from screwdrivers to Pepsi Cola. I'd go and buy her snuff and she'd give me a nickel or a dime, which I would always spend on a candy bar or a Coke, or sometimes a box of Cracker Jacks. Remember when 10 cents got you a huge box of that caramel-covered popcorn and peanuts along with a special surprise? Back then the surprises could be anything from a real toy soldier to a miniature racing car or a magnifying glass. As time passed the price went up, the box got smaller, and the prize became a piece of paper with a joke or something else really lame.

Mama Sorrells came to live with us after that and stayed with us until she passed away in 1980, the same year my niece Kelly Michelle Winter was born. I became Mama Sorrells's caretaker for many years. I stayed with her when my parents would go out. I loved Mama. She had these old stories she would tell, like "Bitsy Baker," that made me laugh. In her later years she got a bit confused. In retrospect I am certain it was Alzheimer's. But she could be a lot of fun, even during those years when all we had to heat the entire house was a wood stove in the front of the home. I'll never forget her love of Mac Davis, the pop singer who had his own TV variety show for a while. And she loved Bob Barker and *The Price Is Right*. I had a lot of fun with Mama.

Uncle Sonny Sorrells was my mother's brother. An Air Force sergeant, he was also my bona fide, real-life hero. I loved my Aunt Josephine a lot, my mother's sister, and Uncle Jack and their kids Beth and Jackie. But Uncle Sonny was my hero. He was a hero to all of us.

Sonny always brought us the coolest gifts on Christmas, and I'll never forget him playing and singing music with his wife, my Aunt Becky, whom he married in 1968. It was so sad that they had such a short time together before cancer took him home on 17 September 1972. My sister Patsy's birthday. Again, my dad delivered the news without a chaser, waking me up at 7 A.M. from a dead sleep and saying, "Well, your Uncle Sonny's dead."

What I remember most about Uncle Sonny was going to visit him in Ocean Springs, Mississippi, near Biloxi. He was stationed down there for a few years, and one weekend he took us to the base for an air show starring the Blue Angels, the US Air Force precision flying team. It blew my young mind, and I will never forget that weekend. I recall Sonny being very skinny and completely bald from all of the chemo treatments, but he still had that broad smile he inherited from his dad.

Our family Christmas parties were always great. Early on, we would have them at Mama and Papa Sorrells' house, then later at Aunt Jo's. Sonny was the life of the party in the early days, and those Christmas parties are all very special memories for me. I can still see Uncle Sonny handing out presents and smiling. Happy memories for sure.

As the years passed, I would watch my cousin Beth marry a great guy named Harold Brock and give birth to two wonderful children, Ryan and Katie. Then Jackie would marry Pam and have a son named Justin. The parties became a lot less fun as the years brought the passing of my Uncle Jack, Aunt Becky, her brother Russell, and my own precious mom. Then in 2010 my Aunt Jo left us.

As I got older it seems the only time I would see my Aunt Jo and her family was at those Christmas parties, but I do have a lot of happy memories of going over to their house in Lyman as a kid, especially on birthdays, when we would play Red Rover and Ring around the Rosie out in the front yard. It's funny what kids remember most. I recall the side porch on Aunt Jo's house was brick red. It wasn't brick, but red paint. The thing was, if you touched it, the red, powder like substance would come off on your skin. I recall having nightmares that I rolled around on the porch and was covered in red and my mom was going to give me a "whoopin'."

It seemed like Beth and Jackie got all kinds of neat toys as well. I remember how blown away I was over Beth's slideshow projector, a plastic toy that displayed slides of *The Jetsons* and *Underdog* on the wall. Then one year she got a little film viewer. I believe it used a cartridge with 8mm film, and you put it to your eye and turned a crank to view the cartoons. Now that I think about it, I have always been obsessed with film and moving pictures.

One unforgettable incident I recall happened after Aunt Jo and Uncle Jack had moved into a new house on the other side of Lyman. My cousin Jackie, just a kid at the time, was playing on the steps that lead into the back door and fell over the rail onto the carport, landing on his head. We were all scared to death as he went into surgery and it was pretty touch and go for a while. Thank God he came out of it all fine, and in the coming years marched in the Byrnes High School band at the Macy's parade, got the call to become a minister, attended the seminary, and became the coolest Baptist preacher on the planet. I have always been proud of Jack. He's just a great guy.

# 4

# WASHED IN THE BLOOD OF JESUS

There were two major churches in my young life: Tucapau Baptist Church in Startex, SC, where I went when I was a young tyke, and Mt. Zion Baptist Church in Spartanburg, where I was a member from the age of eleven until I left in my early twenties.

My most vivid memories of Tucapau are of my Grandpa Sorrells's funeral; Vacation Bible School; Reverend Irwin, whose son would later teach me a course in Civics at Byrnes High School; and those little earphones that hung on the back of the pew for the hard of hearing. They resembled a doctor's stethoscope, and I used to always play with them. In fact, I was always getting into something and getting taken outside by my Mom for a good "talking too," as in "talk to the tune of a hickory stick."

I remember Dad rarely went to church back then. I think he took us and dropped us off. I recall he was always tired from working at Lyman Printing and Finishing Company, and I remember him smoking Winston cigarettes. In later years he would ditch that nasty habit, and I myself would pick it up for about ten years' time.

Sometimes, my Mama Sorrells would be in church with us, and I used to play with the loose skin and fat that hung from the bottom of her arms. I can remember studying with great interest the paper-thin skin around Mama's hands and arms.

One time in Vacation Bible School, we were given these white plaster plaques to paint. Mine was a relief-sculpted picture of a Scottish Terrier. I painted it black and added a few drops of paint coming out of the doggie's mouth. When asked what that was, I always said, "The dog is spitting." Well, my teacher and my Mom kept justifying it by saying, "he just spilled a little paint, that's all." But that just wasn't true. I painted that intentionally. It was my way of trying to bring some life and reality to the art. Even on the night following Bible School when all of our art was displayed, my Sunday School teacher stood there telling someone, "Mike spilled some of his paint on his project." A blatant attempt at stifling my creativity. Come on, people!

Mt. Zion Baptist Church in Spartanburg I remember a lot more vividly. It was in that church that I was saved and gave my heart to Jesus. Rev. Hazel Whitfield was the pastor, along with his wife Ethel, daughter Louise, and son Larry, who would become my best friend for many years. Louise had gone to Dorman High School with members of the Marshall Tucker Band, and years later I remember bugging her to get me their autographs when they came in to see her at the Toyota dealership where she worked.

Some of my random memories of the church included the old sanctuary, which was the second one built on the site. It dated back to Revolutionary War days, and the cemetery across the street housed the bodies of many an old soldier. In 1991 my mother would join them, followed by my father in 2006.

I was actually baptized in the old church before they tore it down to build a new one. I was dunked in the baptismal pool there behind the pulpit, in the very same way that Christians had been baptized there since the early 1800s. "Washed in the blood of the Lamb," as Mama used to say.

There always seemed to be a deep-seated spirit in that old building, even on weekends when Larry and I would go in there and sing real loud to hear our voices echo. It wasn't a scary thing at all. It made me feel wrapped up in love. Singing with the Angels.

When I was first making an attempt to learn to play guitar, I had an old Teisco Del Ray my sister had bought for my birthday at K-Mart, along with a cheap little plastic amp. I recall taking the rig into the old church and playing the two or three riffs I had learned, like the introduction to "Smoke on the Water" by Deep Purple and "Eighteen" by Alice Cooper. Somehow, at that time, I felt guilty playing rock and roll in the old sanctuary. To me, though, rock and roll was the ultimate "joyful noise." Some people called rock the "devil's music," but like Mavis Staples was quoted as saying once, "the devil don't have no music. It's all God's music." Amen, sister Mavis. Amen.

Later I went through this phase where I wanted to sing bass. I started singing with Larry in the church choir. We both gave it our all, but a friend of ours named Artie Allen was the king of the bass, and we eventually moved on to the next project—but not before I actually took a shot at preaching my own sermon. My first flirtation with the "stage."

I remember sitting in church in Spartanburg the night of the big tornado of 1973, as it ripped across the county, tearing roofs off of houses and driving 2x4s through the roofs of cars. It was pitch dark outside, and the preacher kept on preaching. When all was said and done, there was a great deal of damage to the community. That event gave me nightmares for years on end.

The Sunday School classes and activity rooms were housed next door in a new, separate building. When the new sanctuary was constructed, it was built onto the front of the existing activity building. As a kid, I remember sitting at the top of the stairs, where the classes and nursery were, and sliding down to the bottom floor on my butt. Thump! Thump! Thump! It was fun in those days, and all the other kids followed suit. Of course, that could be one reason why my chiropractor Dr. Cynthia Horner just looks at me sometimes and shakes her head in disbelief.

There are a lot of happy memories of Mt. Zion, and I remember a lot of really good people who went there. People I will never forget. Charles and Betty Staggs, Monroe and Dot O'Shields and family, the Settles family, the McCalls, the Crowes—so many nice people.

One of the jobs I had during my teen years was cutting grass with Larry. He was good at getting us jobs and seemed to always have a good business head. During the summer we were hired to cut the grass in the cemetery and around the church. It paid well and gave us money to go to concerts and trips to Myrtle Beach. We cut lawns for several other people as well, and I remember blowing my money on *Creem* and *Circus* magazines, 8-track tapes, and Cokes and peanuts. I always poured a pack of salty Tom's peanuts into my Coke and put a little crunch in my soda. Larry always had to stay on me to focus on the job at hand, as my mind was always drifting off to a place where I was a rock and roll star or a famous artist. One memory that stands out in my mind is that when we would get set to cut, whether it was Cleveland Gosnell's yard or Mrs. Dodd's or the church yard, Larry would always shout, "Haul ass! Cut grass!"—which was our call to arms.

We had the coolest Halloween parties at church, and more often than not I was chosen to provide the entertainment, whether it be a spirited game of "Gossip" (one person whispering to another and passing the quote around the room until it came out on the other side completely different); setting up a mini haunted house with a headless body; telling the story of John Brown's Body, in the dark, while passing around items in the dark like peeled grapes ("eyes"), cooked spaghetti ("brains") and unpopped corn ("teeth"). It was always a blast. My dad was asked to play the clown several years after the regular clown, James Tweed, took ill.

Similarly, Christmas was always great. I recall being in the Christmas nativity play, and the church always had a huge Christmas tree. To a kid it looked as high as the moon. Every Christmas following the service, we would be given a big paper sack filled with fruit, candy, and nuts. My Dad played Santa a few times, and when I got older, I myself donned the familiar red suit.

During my high school days I was approached by my friend Bill Hudson who asked me to visit a club called Young Life. He told me that it was a group of young people who got together one night every week to talk about the Bible, God, and life through the eyes of a teenager. The part that really drew me in was his mention that there was lots of music at the meetings. Folks played acoustic guitars and sang. Cool.

I went to my first meeting and had a blast. The songs they were singing were of a spiritual nature, a kind of contemporary Christian music. The people were great and we just had a lot of fun. I went back many times.

My biggest young-life memory was our trip to Disney World. The whole club, including Bill, went down to Orlando on a pair of chartered Greyhound buses. The only bad part was that I got lost in the Magic Kingdom and was on my own the whole day. I finally met up with some recognizable faces about an hour before time to return to the bus. Still, I had fun in the magic shop, Country Bear Jamboree, Hall of Presidents, Small World, and, my favorite of all, the Haunted Mansion.

During my senior year at Byrnes High School and for a couple of years thereafter, Tony Pearson and I became interested in singing Southern gospel music. This was around the same time we were doing the radio disc jockey thing. He and I sang duets at a few churches. I remember Tony singing a tune called "The Lighthouse." He really nailed that one. We were listening to the Happy Goodman Family, Johnny Cook, the Gaithers, the Rambos, the Kingsmen, and other groups for inspiration, all the while still digging the Allman Brothers, Peter Frampton, KISS, and other rock and roll bands. Just a couple of guys in search of an answer.

While attending Spartanburg Methodist College in 1982, I met a guy named Greg Yeary. The guy was a monster on guitar. His style was somewhere between Chet Atkins and Johnny Rivers, but he could play lead in the style of Mark Knopfler, John Fogerty, and even Albert Lee. Besides performing together in our band the Buffalo Hut Coalition, we also performed gospel music. Greg's parents were gospel singers, and they inspired us to do a gospel duet. I remember our regular gig at this Auction Barn where they would hold gospel singings on Saturdays and pass the bucket around for tips. Greg had a blues version of "Swing Low, Sweet Chariot" that was really cool. We also did songs by the Hinsons like "Sea Walker" and other popular gospel tunes of the day. Then on Saturday night we would gig at the honky-tonks, playing "Gimmie Three Steps" and "Free Bird."

# 5

# LYNYRD SKYNYRD AND FAMILY

*"To me, it [the high point of my career] was me and Allen and Ronnie had this dream to make it big, and we were gonna try to make it until we died. That dream came true for us. I remember us three talking about it on the way back from England the first time, 'We did it, you know?'"*
—Gary Rossington, interview with Buffalo, June, 2003

I only saw Lynyrd Skynyrd, the original Lynyrd Skynyrd, in concert one time. It was October 19, 1977, and sadly, it was to be the very last concert for Ronnie Van Zant. I was backstage the night of Skynyrd's final concert. One of my teachers in high school knew Artimus Pyle and had introduced us, and I used that leverage to worm my way backstage. The concert was a benefit for the Marine Corps Toys for Tots campaign, and Artimus, being a former Marine, was very excited, running around backstage at the old Greenville Memorial Auditorium introducing people.

That night I met all of the band members. They were all great guys. Steve Gaines, Cassie Gaines, Leslie Hawkins, Gary Rossington, Billy Powell, Allen Collins, Leon Wilkeson, Artimus, and, of course, the iconic Ronnie Van Zant. It's really hard for me to comprehend the fact that Gary and Artimus are the only survivors of the band living today.

Among the fondest memories of that evening are the few minutes I spent speaking to Ronnie. I told him that I expected him to be some sort of roughneck hell-raiser, judging from the stories in the press. He said, "Michael, I am a peaceful guy. I only fight when someone messes with me, my family, or my friends." It made sense to me.

Allen Collins was very nice to me that night as well. We sat and talked for just a while, and he was trying to introduce me to Gary Rossington, who at the time was surrounded by beautiful girls. I would have to wait over twenty-five years to finally get some serious face time with Gary, when I interviewed him and his wife Dale Krantz for *GRITZ Magazine*.

People often ask me what Ronnie Van Zant was like. Judging from my brief meeting, all I can say is that he was a good Southern boy with a heart as big as Dixie and more talent than almost anyone I ever knew. If he had lived, I am certain the world would have enjoyed many more years of his great songwriting and singing. I would have loved to have seen how his plans to do a country album with Merle Haggard turned out.

When I heard the news of the plane crash, I was shocked. At first, we all thought the entire band was dead. I was upset and shaken. Just three months earlier on August 26, one of my true heroes, the King of Rock and Roll, Elvis had died. Now this tragedy. Even to this day I find myself unable to shake the feeling that came upon me after hearing the news that the Free Bird had fallen to the ground. A few years ago I was called upon to appear on a CMT special called *Country's Most Shocking: Outlaw Country and Southern Rock*, helping to tell the stories about Marshall Tucker and Lynyrd Skynyrd. As I sat in the studio being interviewed on camera, even after all those years, I had to fight back the tears.

In 1982 I met with Artimus Pyle within the smoky confines of the old Andiron club on Highway 29 in Spartanburg, South Carolina. We both had a few beers in us, and Artimus got really emotional while discussing the crash of the Free Bird and the loss of his friend, Ronnie Van Zant. Artimus and I would chat every chance we got, and I was a fixture at all his Artimus Pyle Band shows. He would always ask me how my friend, songwriting-collaborator, and future brother-in-law Steve Harvey was doing. Pyle had jammed with Steve on many occasions and remembered him from the band Dallas Alice which also included future Marshall Tucker members Pat Elwood and Stuart Swanlund as well as Terry Collins and Mindy Harvey, Steve's sister who was killed just a few years ago while driving her Moped home from work. I lost touch with Artimus for a few years while he was fighting bogus allegations of evildoings brought on by some greedy, bad people. In 2006, Artimus would set the record straight with some heavy lyrics on a solo album appropriately titled *Artimus Venomous*.

In years to come, I would conduct interviews with Gary and Dale Rossington, Ed King, Artimus, JoJo Billingsley, and subsequent members of Skynyrd like Randall Hall and Mike Estes. I would have the opportunity to play an acoustic duet with Ed King at one of the annual Winters Brothers Band Summer Jams, and JoJo Billingsley would honor me by appearing on my *Something Heavy* album and in various *GRITZ*-sponsored CD parties and benefits. I sat in with Artimus on various occasions and even sang a duet with him on "Free Bird" during an APB show at the Handlebar in Greenville.

One special occasion was the Celebration of Life, a show Artimus and his wife Kerri put together in St. Augustine, Florida, on October 20, 2001. It promised to be a great show, and the funds raised would go to preserving the ultra-cool amphitheater where the show was being staged. Both of Arti's sons' bands would play, as well as the APB (Artimus Pyle Band, AKA: All Points Bulletin), which at the time included Randall Hall, Barry Rapp, and Tim Lindsey. I myself was also on the bill, which included a guy named Lee Bogan and his band the Rockits.

Lee had grown up just a few miles from me in Union, SC, yet I had never met him. For a while Lee played guitar with country star Joe Diffie and co-wrote one of Diffie's biggest hits, "Honky Tonk Attitude." Lee is a fantastic songwriter, and in 2007 he and I co-wrote our first song together, "Good Ol' Boys Ain't All Bad." Bogan also played with Ronnie McDowell, "Ray Sawyer and Dr. Hook" and others. He's a great guy with way too much talent.

At the Celebration of Life, Lee played several of his songs that just hooked me, including "No Thanks, Drinking Makes Me Nekkid" and the beautiful "The Good Lord, Family and Friends." Lee would later play guitar on Pyle's *Artimus Venomous* release.

Artimus Pyle's oldest son Chris played, as did his other son Marshall Daniel Pyle (named after Marshall Tucker and Charlie Daniels—how cool is that?) I performed acoustic, doing mostly originals, and invited my friend Sharon "Litlwing" Whitten to play with me on several songs and sing one of her original tunes to a great audience response. Later that night there was a huge jam and candlelight vigil. The "Sweet Home Alabama" and "Free Bird" jam featured several drummers and a ton of guitarists. According to one of the Skynyrd family, it was kind of a "cluster fuck," but it sure was fun, and everybody had their heart in the right place, especially Artimus.

When I interviewed Gary Rossington and his wife Dale for a *GRITZ Magazine* cover story in 2003, I did it by phone while they were in Glasgow, Scotland. Pretty weird, since the Rossingtons live only two hours down I-85 in Atlanta. Well, the publicist had tried unsuccessfully half a dozen times to hook us up, going as far as scheduling a face to face in Atlanta during rehearsals for the world tour. It was a good idea on paper, but they changed all of the plans at zero hour. When I finally did speak with Gary and Dale, it was very enjoyable. Well, except for not getting my call directed to the right room.

When a guy on the other end of the line answered, I told him I was Buffalo from *GRITZ Magazine,* and he began cursing to beat the band. Turns out the girl at the front desk had patched me in to the wrong room. Rap star Eminem was in the same hotel, and I had been directed to his room. I am not sure if I actually got cussed out by Slim Shady himself or by one of his posse. Either way, it was one for the books.

A month after the print issue of *GRITZ* with a smiling Gary and Dale adorning the cover came out, Skynyrd was playing down the road in Clemson, SC. I hooked up with the record company, the publicist, and two of the band members, and everyone assured me that my passes and backstage credentials for me and my friend Scott would be at will call. Of course when I got there, they weren't. This is of my biggest nightmares in the business, and it has happened to me about four times.

I finally convinced a Clemson employee to let us into the show, but no backstage access. All I wanted to do was meet the folks I had interviewed, maybe recall the 1977 backstage story with Gary, get a photo, and get out. I watched as hundreds of radio contest winners filed into the backstage area. I sent a note to Gary. I never heard back, and I never got backstage. Bummer.

I had become pen pals via e-mail with guitar god Ed King in 2000 and found him to be a truly funny guy with a real dry wit. I did two different interviews with Ed over the course of four years, and when I heard he was to be the special guest at one of the Winters Brothers Band's annual Southern Summer Jams in Nolensville, Tennessee, I dropped him a line and asked if he would join me on acoustic guitar during my set at the jam. I was blown away when he accepted.

We had a short but sweet set together that was plagued by feedback and lack of monitor, but the sound man was doing his best outdoors under the blazing summer sun. Ed smoked on his stogie and played some tasty slide over a few of my original songs. Pretty cool.

That night Ed joined the Winters Brothers Band and Barry Lee Harwood on a rocking set of Skynyrd classics. Everyone in the audience left with a huge smile on their face, including Southern George and Cici, a couple who come over for the jam every summer from Vienna, Austria. George is the ultimate Southern Rock fan, illustrated in tattoos that tell the history of the genre. Now *that* my friends is a fan.

Speaking of former Rossington-Collins Band guitarist Barry Lee Harwood, Scott and I had met up with Barry Lee earlier in the day at his home near Nashville, and if I remember correctly, he even rode with us to the Winters Brothers show. He had become friends with both Scott and me, and we remain friends to this day. In 2010 he would release his first solo album, *The Southern Part of Heaven*, an amazing multigenre CD.

Not long after the passing of Skynyrd bassist Leon Wilkeson, some folks put together a memorial concert at the Norva in Norfolk, Virginia. I was invited to play on the bill, which included the Rhythm Pigs, Jimmie Van Zant, and Randall Hall. Hall was the guitarist Allen Collins personally chose to fill in for him on the 1987 reunion tour, and he's a hell of a player. Later on I had the opportunity of playing several times alongside Hall and also Mike Estes, who was a member of Skynyrd during the *Last Rebel* tour. Estes played a lot with the Southern Rock Allstars, and it was always fun gigging with him. He would later take centerstage in Blackfoot before settling in with his own band Skinny Molly.

Tragedy just seems to follow Skynyrd. In 2007 former Outlaws front man turned Skynyrd guitarist Hughie Thomasson died at his home in Florida, and then in 2009, pianist Billy Powell died from heart issues. Just weeks later, Ean Evans, the bass player who had replaced Leon, died from cancer. The Southern Rock world was again heartbroken.

JoJo Billingsley was a real sweetheart. After I did a *GRITZ* story and interview with her, JoJo, (Deborah Jo Billingsley White) and I began emailing and speaking on the phone. An ordained minister, JoJo provided much-needed inspiration for me during some of my rougher times. She was an angel and always showed up for our benefit concerts, even recording with me on my 2006 CD *Something Heavy*. What a voice. In 2007 she released her first ever solo album, *I Will Obey*, and it is phenomenal. In November 2007, following the tragic passing of my friend George McCorkle of the Marshall Tucker Band, we staged a Jam 4 George in Spartanburg, and I got a chance to sing with JoJo again. Tragically, in 2010 Jo contracted cancer. She passed away on my birthday, June 24th. Another special friend had gone on to be with the Lord. I will miss her terribly.

It has been quite a journey from the day a friend at church loaned me the *Pronounced Lynyrd Skynyrd* 8-track, to the final show of the original band and meeting Ronnie, to the Skynyrd of today, still selling out shows and keeping the music alive. Great music, great memories.

# 6

## WILLIE AND ME

The preacher's son from Mt. Zion Baptist Church, Larry Whitfield, became one of my closest friends for many years. While we got into our share of mischief together, the fondest memories are of his helping me make money by cutting grass, as I wrote about earlier, or picking up trash around the Bi-Lo complex in Inman. That and teaching me to drive.

My Dad tried. God knows, he gave it a shot. The day he put me behind the wheel of his Buick with the gearshift on the steering column and told me to take off down Highway 129, I nearly killed us both. By the time I managed to pull off of the road one mile later, Dad's face was blood red and he was yelling at me. So much for learning from Dad.

Larry's Grandma had bought him a Chevelle Malibu for graduation from high school. The "Screamin' Demon," he called it. Orange with a black vinyl top, fat Road Hugger tires, and chrome reverse wheels. Oh, and a Thrush muffler that sounded louder than three Harleys cranking at once.

We went everywhere in that car, to the lake, to the beach, everywhere. Sometimes just me and "Willie" (a knick name we had for Larry, who called me "Michelob," because that was my beverage of choice at the time and was kind of a play on the name Michael), and sometimes Dennis and Curtis Smith would road trip with us.

Larry wasn't the least bit afraid to let me behind the wheel, and those long nighttime drives really helped me learn the skill of operating a motor vehicle. We drove down to Myrtle Beach with the 8-track booming and camped, or we went to the lake where someone in his family had a cabin and sat around drinking beer and looking at *Playboy* magazines and playing cards.

Some of my fun memories of Larry are going to rock concerts like KISS, the Edgar Winter Group, Johnny Winter, Black Oak Arkansas, and more; camping in the chilly woods near the church with only a small campfire to keep warm; going hunting for squirrels, doves, rabbits, and such; riding around late at night drinking Boone's Farm wine, smoking cigarettes (Winchester cigars or Kool cigarettes in my case), and just plain "raising hell," playing pool, and bowling—and of course eating, we both did our share of that, and his mom could downright cook up some food. Her breakfasts were to die for, and I remember that being the first time I ever had red-eye gravy and biscuits. I was a health freak even then.

Yeah, there was a lot of crazy stuff we got into in those days, and some of it we will just file under "What happened back then stays back then." We hung out a lot with Dennis and Curtis Smith, the sons of Frank Smith, the minister of music at our church, and his wife Martha. Man we had some good times. Got into a little trouble here and there but learned from the experiences. We listened to a lot of great music, smoked way too many cigarettes, drank way too much cold beer, and each had our fair share of experiences with the opposite sex. Oh boy, did we ever.

There are a few memories of my time with Larry I had just as soon forget, not the least of which is one particular night at the Spartanburg Phillies baseball park. Me and Larry and Dennis and Curtis Smith went to the game on a beautiful summer night and we were just having a great time when we noticed something happening about four rows down on the bleachers that disturbed us. A man and his son had been sitting watching the game, and I suppose the five-year-old had to pee or something, so they left, and the kid left his program book and right on top of it, his full size, beautiful catcher's mitt. Well, as luck would have it, a young black kid, about twelve or so, saw the glove and snagged it, sticking it under his shirt and taking off. I can't remember which one of us it was, but it wasn't me, who took it upon himself to tell a cop who was walking by. The officer grabbed the kid, retrieved the glove, and set everything right as the dad and son returned from the bathroom.

About thirty minutes had passed when these four huge guys in their twenties and thirties came over to pay us a visit. They informed us that because we had ratted out their nephew, they would be meeting us outside after the game. They were not happy campers.

On the way out of the park that night, I reported what had happened to another police officer. He assured me there was no need to worry; they would be on the lookout. Right. When we got outside, we were met by a mob of about fifteen guys, some with clubs, others with chains, intent on beating our asses. I was not going to stand there and get killed, so I took off running to find the policeman. I ran around the outside wall that ran around the park and behind the outfield. One of the guys was now chasing me, and when he caught up to me I turned to face him and said, "You better run back the other way, buddy," and I reached in my pocket like I had a pistol. He must have bought it because he took off running the other way.

I had run completely around the field before I finally found that rent-a-cop who had told me he would be watching. We went outside, but everyone was gone. It was a couple of hours before we found out that my friends were all at Spartanburg General Hospital, where they had all received stitches in their heads and been bandaged up after being beaten. The crazy thing is that the guys really gave me a hard time for running away and trying to get help. I really think they thought I should have stayed and gotten my head bashed in as well. Not me, man. I have always been a lover, not a fighter.

One of the places Larry and I used to go quite often at the time was Smith's Store. A literal hole in the wall, it was located off the main drag in Jackson Mills, not far from the old Boy Scout hut.

Smith's was a kind of dimly-lit place that had several pool tables, along with three authentic pinball machines. The kind of exciting pinball machines you could find everywhere before the advent of computer games. The kind of machines you had to bump and hit, with just the right amount of pressure, to avoid a tilt. The owners would pay off wins in cold, hard cash, which I think was illegal at the time. That made it even more exciting.

The pinball room doubled as a blacklight room, with walls adorned by posters of Alice Cooper, a "Let's Boogie" poster, and one of those famous orange-colored posters of Leon Russell wearing a top hat and a Holy Trinity T-shirt. In the corner was the juke box, into which I was always pumping quarters. I'd play "Band on the Run," and "Jet" by Paul McCartney and "Wings" or "Ramblin' Man" by the Allman Brothers Band.

Even then, I was drawn to the music of the Allmans. There was a guy who came in every so often, on weekends mostly, looking to sell off one of his possessions in order to buy pot. I'll never forget the time he had one of those seventies mod-style Panasonic cassette players and a box full of tapes. I gave him $20 for the whole deal. That night, as I lay in bed in my Wellford home, I listened to the tapes. Cream, Janis Joplin, Deep Purple, James Taylor, and one of my favorites, the Duane Allman *Anthology*. That was my introduction to a great band called Cowboy, and also to the Allman Brothers Band, which would ultimately become my all-time favorite group, even surpassing the Beatles. Well, to be fair, around the same time there was a guy at school named Mark Davis who turned me on to *At Fillmore East*. The Allmans would be burned into my brain forever.

Seems like Larry and I were always betting at pool. If it wasn't for a couple of bucks, it was for tapes. We used 8-track tapes almost like poker chips. I mean, we were buying them every weekend, and each one of us had our favorite tapes. One that stands out in my mind was a bootleg ditty that we referred to as "Ed-All-Led." It had four songs each from the Allmans, Edgar Winter, and Led Zeppelin. What a prize that one was. We must have lost it back and forth to each other a dozen times. Of course, as long as my Marshall Tucker Band *A New Life* tape remained in my possession, I was doing quite alright, thank you very much.

One cold November day in 1974 I found myself driving my '65 Ford Galaxy over to Smith's on a solo mission. I thought I would find one of our Jackson Mill acquaintances or one of the old Byrnes High boys around, and I'd have me a little pick-up pool game.

On the way into the place, I ran into this guy who used to come in sometimes to shoot pool. I can't remember his name, but he had bad teeth and he was always high. He did, however, make me an offer that day that would go down in my book of firsts, something I can't say I'm really all that proud of, but hey, it happened.

He came up to me and said, "Hey Mike, you got any papers?"

Well, I wasn't completely stupid. I had never smoked pot before, but I had certainly read about it, seen it, and smelled it at concerts.

"No," I mumbled, and kept walking.

"I've got some grass if you want to get high."

"Well..." I stumbled a bit. The timing was perfect. A typical teen, I wasn't all that happy at home. I seemed to be the only guy on the Byrnes High campus who didn't have a real bona fide girl friend, and I was looking for some new experiences.

We sat in my white Ford Galaxy, fumbling around for a can to fashion a bong out of, or maybe something we could rig and use as rolling papers. Then we hit on it. There was a BC headache powder in the glove box. He opened up the paper, and sucked the BC into his nostril like it was coke. He picked up a notebook I had lying on the seat and pulled a baggie out of his jacket. The smell of the marijuana as he opened the bag permeated the interior of the car. To be honest, it smelled great.

He was meticulously careful in rolling the joint. I reached over and turned on the radio. WORD was playing the Marshall Tucker Band's "Can't You See." I saw my future, for a brief instant, and I was playing guitar with the Tucker boys. Dreams can come true, fellow babies.

My friend put the makeshift reefer into a roach clip, and we smoked it. Strangely enough, I don't recall it having any effect on me whatsoever. But for a few months I harbored the taste and smell of the pot in my mind. Sweet smelling, but with a distinct aspirin flavor.

# 7

## THE MARSHALL TUCKER BAND

*"We wanted a place to go on Friday and Saturday night, so we figured if we formed a band we could get into all the places without having to be a member of a club or stuff like that; that was the only thing that we knew. We knew we liked to listen to music so we turned it from listening into being a part of it. Showing off was basically the original reason for starting it all."*
—Doug Gray, interview with Buffalo, June, 2004

My association with the Marshall Tucker Band has been, in the words of Robert Hunter, "a long, strange trip." It has also been a trip I wouldn't have missed for the world.

Growing up in the same hometown of Spartanburg, SC, it was inevitable that we would cross paths. The very first Tucker connection I recall occurred back in the very early 1970s, before the band was even formed.

One of my favorite clubs to visit during the early seventies was the Midnight Sun, located near the spot where McDonalds now stands on Heron Circle in Spartanburg. It was there that I'd enjoy bands like Beeverteeth, Nantucket, Mother's Finest, the Swingin' Medallions (themselves a Carolina export out of Greenwood), the Spontanes with their alter egos Harley Hog and the Rockers, and others. I was under age during most of my excursions to the Sun, but because I was gifted with being a big boy, I was seldom carded. I recall seeing some of the Tuckers at the Midnight Sun a few years before they formed the MTB. Those memories are as faded as my old KISS T-shirt, but I know for a fact that Paul T. Riddle was playing. He was about fifteen at the time and had a head full of red hair.

The first time I saw Toy Caldwell play was at a bar called Uncle Sam's on Asheville Highway in Spartanburg. A friend and I went to see Toy Factory perform. I guess it was 1971. I was fourteen years old but easily passed for eighteen with a fake ID. I sat at a table near the stage and just watched that guy play with his thumb instead of a pick. It blew my mind. He was amazing. I'll never forget Toy was wearing a leather jacket with his name emblazoned across the back in silver studs. He was ready to be a star, and even then it was obvious he had all the makings of one.

Another place I used to love to visit during the late seventies and early eighties was Arthur's at Hillcrest Mall in Spartanburg. I can remember seeing Matt "Guitar" Murphy jamming his heart out there. One of my fondest memories is of a show featuring the Throbbers. At that time, the jazz-fusion-rock band consisted of Paul T. Riddle, Buddy Strong, Franklin Wilkie, and Ronnie Godfrey. On this particular night, Toy Caldwell showed up to jam out on a few pop and jazz standards, like "The Nightlife" and "Stardust," playing the guitar given to him by B. B. King, a beautiful hollow-body with B. B.'s name spelled out in mother-of-pearl inlays between the frets. Artimus Pyle was there that night as well, sporting a brand new haircut and beard trim. I can remember just sitting there savoring the music. Toy could play it all.

In the early 1990s I managed to see the Toy Caldwell band play a couple of times at Al's Pumphouse in Greenville. The band featured Pick Pickens on guitar, Mark Burrell on drums, and Tony "Smoke" Heatherly on bass, and boy howdy were they ever good! Those two shows are fond memories. Future MTB guitarist Chris Hicks and his band Loose Change opened one of them, and some years later I got a VHS tape of the Toy set from a guy from Macon named Dave Peck. That night I was backstage hanging out and watching as everyone filled their noses with white powder. I was offered a bump but turned it down. At the time I had done just enough drugs to realize that they hurt me much more than helped me.

Shortly after Toy's death, his friend Al Crisp threw a big benefit show for Abbie and the kids at Al's. My band, the Buffalo Hut Coalition, was there to pitch in. Every local Southern rock and country player imaginable performed, with Marshall Tucker covers mingling with rock and country originals and the stray Hank, Jr. cover. A good time was had by all, and Toy's memory was once again given a booster shot.

The first I had heard of a band called Marshall Tucker was in 1972. I was a student at James F. Byrnes High School in Duncan, SC, and someone had brought a copy of *The Spartanburg Herald* newspaper in, showing everyone an article that had been written about the band and their impending success. As I recall, it was only a week or two later that I heard the debut Capricorn Records album played in its entirety on WORD radio in town, following the annual countdown of the top 100 singles of the year. A disc jockey named Billy Mack spun the album and spoke with some of the band members. It was the beginning of a tradition that would repeat with each new MTB release throughout the years.

One of my favorite Marshall Tucker Band memories is the 1977 Homecoming Concert at Memorial Auditorium in Spartanburg. It's been over thirty years, but I still remember it like it was yesterday.

Friends, family, and neighbors as well as folks from Atlanta, Charlotte, New Jersey, and all across the USA packed into the auditorium for what would turn out to be almost a four-hour-long benefit show, filled with some real honest-to-God Southern rock and roll. This was the first in a long line of backstage experiences, and I was hooked. There was just something special about hanging backstage with the band. This was also the only time I can recall going backstage without writing about it. That is, until now.

My first meeting with Charlie Daniels was in the stairwell at this show. He wore the biggest grin I'd ever seen and was so friendly, he made me a fan for life. His *Fire on the Mountain* LP, produced by Paul Hornsby at Capricorn Studios in Macon, Georgia, remains in my "top ten" and always will. At that same show I stood nervously just off stage right after the concert as Toy Caldwell came walking by. I was such a fan. I couldn't even speak. It would be a few more years before I would meet Toy. When everyone went downstairs for a photo with a couple of Mid-Atlantic wrestlers and an interview for *Rolling Stone*, I was in hog heaven but still too shy to say anything to anyone. That was the first time I met Tommy Caldwell. He spoke first. I guess I looked lost up there. He was real nice and shook my hand. We would meet a few more times in the coming two years, mostly at the grocery store where I worked, but I would have grown up a bit by then and lost a great deal of my "star struck" attitude.

Spartanburg's Marshall Chapman—now a successful singer-songwriter in Nashville—opened the festivities with her own set of infectious rock and roll, playing songs from her new Epic debut, *Me I'm Feelin' Free*, and when the Tuckers hit the stage with their huge "Long Hard Ride" mural hanging in the background, they found an auditorium jam packed full of fired-up hometown fans. With Jaimoe from the Allman Brothers Band playing drums alongside Paul T. Riddle, and Charlie Daniels sawing some mighty tasty fiddle, the Marshall Tucker Band never sounded better. They were hot. From their rocking "Fly Like an Eagle" to what was at the time a major radio hit, "Heard It in a Love Song," those Tucker boys could do no wrong. The band smoked through "Long Hard Ride," with Toy Caldwell delivering some of the hottest thumb picking on that Les Paul that he had ever played. Tommy drove the band through jam after jam, from "Take the Highway" to "Can't You See" to "Blue Ridge Mountain Skies." At one point, Toy took center stage to play a moving "Ab's Song," a tune from the band's debut album that was hardly ever performed in concert.

"Desert Skies," "Never Trust a Stranger," and "Ramblin" brought down the house, with Doug Gray singing in peak form. Paul T. Riddle was amazing as always on the drum kit, and George McCorkle played with all the passion and fire he could muster. Jerry Eubanks's smooth sax and flute, as well as keyboard work, underscored the rest of the band, blending their magical mix of rock, blues, jazz, and country into the sound that we all adored. Before the evening was over, the band was joined onstage by Charlie, who had already joined in on several tunes including the scorching "24 Hours at a Time," along with Jaimoe on congas and Marshall Chapman on backing vocals.

Mayor Frank Allen, at twenty-eight the youngest mayor in Spartanburg's history, presented the band with the key to the city. WORD's Billy Mack was on hand to aid in the presentation of a check for $23,500 from the proceeds of the show to Shriner's Hospital for Crippled Children. Everyone was so pumped that even the news of a bomb scare couldn't sway them.

"Someone called and said they've planted a bomb in here," said Tommy Caldwell from the stage, as cool as a mint julep. "But we ain't goin' nowhere if y'all ain't!" The crowd went wild.

We weren't about to leave this show. No way, baby.

The concert lasted a good four hours at least, and when it was all over, we walked out of the auditorium, sweat soaked and smiling. I made my way over to speak to Tommy Caldwell.

"Great show, Tommy," I said.

"Glad you liked it, man!" He said, grinning from ear to ear.

I shook hands with Toy and Charlie and headed off toward home, knowing that I would remain a Tucker fan for the rest of my life.

I had run across Doug Gray a few times in my life. I remember seeing him at Pic-A-Book in Spartanburg once. I tried to speak to him, but there were a lot of folks around him and I gave up too easily. Who would have ever imagined that he would one day be a close friend of mine. While writing *Carolina Dreams: The Musical Legacy of Upstate South Carolina* (Marshall Tucker Entertainment) in 1996, I was interviewing the past members of the MTB and fell into the trap of listening to the wrong people. Some self-proclaimed "friends" of the band advised me against talking to Doug, stating that he was hard to talk to and didn't like to be bothered with things like interviews. They said a few nasty things about him that I just found hard to believe. Boy howdy were they ever wrong. I ended up becoming fast friends with Doug, who even helped me get *Carolina Dreams* into print via a company he and his manager Ron Rainey had started. Doug remains a good friend today, and he is still carrying the MTB banner all around the country, doing hundreds of shows each year.

In 1980, the band released their second Warner Brothers album, *Tenth*, which proved to be an overall excellent album. From the rocking show opener, "It Takes Time," to George's "Gospel Singin' Man" and the thunderous "Cattle Drive," which featured Paul T. and Tommy driving the drums and bass like cowboys rounding up a herd, the record, again produced by Stewart Levine, was a major hit. Tragically, though, it would be the last one to feature brother Tommy.

The band came back home to Spartanburg on April 21, 1980. The night before, they had recorded one of their hottest shows, live in Long Island, New York, for broadcast on the King Biscuit Flower Hour. The tour had been going extremely well, but everyone was ready for a little time off back home.

On April 22, Tommy Caldwell was in his Land Cruiser on his way down Church Street to work out at the YMCA when the unthinkable happened. Someone driving a 1965 Ford Galaxy had come to a complete stop in the lane directly in front of Caldwell. Tommy's Jeep had been modified for off-road driving, with huge tires that put the vehicle high in the air, so when he hit the stalled vehicle, the Jeep flipped over.

Tommy was taken to the ER at Spartanburg General Hospital, treated, and admitted, but he was in a coma. For the next six days, prayers and well wishes came in from all over the country and the world. Everyone waited. Tommy's mother and father waited. They had just lost their youngest son Tim in an auto accident a month earlier. Tommy's brother Toy waited. The Marshall Tucker Band waited. As for me, I was getting updates every day from my sister Patsy, then a nurse at Spartanburg General Hospital.

On April 28, 1980, Tommy Caldwell passed away. Friends and family and fans alike were grief stricken. The world had lost one of its finest treasures, and the Marshall Tucker Band had lost its leader.

The obvious choice for a replacement came in the form of Franklin Wilkie, a onetime member of The Toy Factory and a lifelong friend of the band. Later that year, WORD radio DJ Sgt. Rick McAlister hosted a contest, asking listeners to write an essay describing why they loved the Marshall Tucker Band. I was among the winners who were treated to a smoky ride by bus down to Columbia for a Marshall Tucker and .38 Special show, along with backstage passes and a visit with the band after the show.

During the early 1980s, three MTB members, George McCorkle, Jerry Eubanks, and Doug Gray, owned a recording studio in Moore, Spartanburg County, SC, called Creative Arts. Because of my association with Silver Travis, I ended up spending quite a lot of time at the studio. I remember being in the studio with engineer Randy Merryman when Doug Gray was putting vocals on some songs for the album *Tuckerized*. It was an exciting experience for me. I had never seen anything like it. I received quite an education on studio work during those days. The studio was a great place to hang out, and while working with Silver Travis, I got to spend a lot of time there.

The original Marshall Tucker Band broke up in 1984, but Doug Gray and Jerry Eubanks chose to continue on. At first they hired Nashville session men but later brought in guys like Rusty Milner, Ace Allen, Tim Lawter, and Stuart Swanlund, all road veterans of local bands.

When Toy Caldwell died on February 25, 1993, I was devastated. Toy was my all-time inspiration for playing guitar, and his death shattered my world. I remember it was snowing outside when I received word, via a friend at WSPA-TV, that he had passed. Over the years, I have joined Tony Heatherly, Toy's bass player, a couple of times to visit Toy's grave on the anniversary of his death. On one occasion, Tony, myself, and Mark Emerick of the Commander Cody Band stood over the grave playing Toy's songs. Then Tony sang the song he wrote for Toy that I recorded on my *Southern Lights* album, "Ride On My Friend." It was a beautiful memorial.

Right after *Carolina Dreams* was published, I began work on Doug Gray's biography. One of the ideas we had was to have me follow Doug around to some gigs and observe. During summer 1998, I met up with Doug and the band in Hickory, North Carolina, on a beautiful summer morning at the Holiday Inn. I was driving a rental car from Greenville, SC, to Hickory. It had been a smooth ride, and I was ready for some fun.

The group had just gotten in from Indianapolis, Indiana, and everyone was relaxing and doing their own thing. Rusty Milner was laying out by the pool, and Stuart Swanlund was taking a nap before he and I descended upon the Subway sandwich shop mid-afternoon. I was told that Doug and Tim Lawter had hit the road on foot in the direction of the only strip mall close by, which was about a mile and a half down the frontage road. Oh, and by the way, the temperature outside was hovering around the 95 degree mark.

The rooms in the Holiday Inn were nice. Lots of elbow room. I had a desk and a large TV with tons of channels and a Nintendo hooked in, although I never once used any of it. I did however make use of the desk.

The lady downstairs had given me a list of band and crew names and their corresponding room numbers and informed me that Mr. Gray asked that I call him upon arrival, which I did. That's when I found out he was out walking.

I discovered later that Doug had checked into the hotel at about 11 AM and had been working on paperwork and making phone calls for a couple of hours. It seems he does a lot of business from his hotel room and handles a lot of the arrangements for the shows, making sure everyone has what they need and everything is flowing smoothly.

After about an hour, my phone rang, and it was Doug.

"The crew's going on over to the stadium," he said. "You want to go, or wait and ride with us?"

It was a generous offer. I could go over and watch them set the stage for the MTB, or wait and go over with the band. After due thought and consideration, I opted to wait and go at 5:30. It was hot outside, and besides, I wanted to interview some more band members.

I made my way down to Doug's room and dropped in for a quick visit. He had invoices, contracts, and various other important papers placed in small, neat stacks across the bottom of his bed. He was lying across the center of the bed, cell phone in one hand, a note pad in the other.

"Make yourself at home, Michael," he said. "I'll be off the phone in a minute."

I couldn't help but notice that this guy was extremely organized. I mean, I try to keep organized, but sometimes, more often than not, I fall short of that elusive goal. Well, at least I learned early on to make checklists, and I took note that Doug does the same thing. The only difference is that my checklist is usually two pages, and his is more like half a notebook.

I asked Doug if he had eaten, and he said no but that he wasn't hungry. Now, in the past, every time we've met for interviews or to chat, it's been over lunch. That's why it kind of amazed me to see how little Doug eats on the road.

"I'll just have a banana," he said with a grin.

He had already made his daily phone calls to say hello and check on his daughters Gabrielle and Mariah.

After about twenty minutes, I left the room so that he could conduct more business and returned to my own room. I was beginning to get a bit sleepy, but then I remembered I had promised Stuart I'd drive him down to the Subway in the rental car.

He got his order to go. I had already attempted to eat some Chinese food right after I arrived in town, but the chef had gotten a little heavy on the hot and spicy end on his version of General Tso's Chicken. Three bites and four glasses of iced tea, ice and all.

We returned to my room, where Stu lit into his sub-sandwich, and I hit the record button on my cassette recorder. We talked for about forty-five minutes, hitting the pause button here and there when the conversation drifted toward our fifteen-year friendship and away from the Marshall Tucker Band.

After the interview, I had about an hour until 5:30 PM, when I would meet the gang at the bus to ride over to the gig. I shut my eyes for about ten minutes, and then I found myself wide awake. I made some notes, wrote a couple of pages in my spiral notebook, and brushed my teeth. By then it was time to go downstairs.

That's when things started really hopping.

Doug came downstairs right behind me and introduced me to about six people in five minutes. Heading out the door, a small-framed man dressed in black carrying a black tote bag walked by. He was very thin, but his arms looked like Popeye's arms. All muscle.

"Michael, you've met B. B., right?" asked Doug.

"No, I don't believe I have."

I shook B. B. Borden's hand and made a mental note that he seemed to be quite a likeable guy. I would later find that I was absolutely right.

Riding on the tour bus was like riding in a private jet, except I felt more comfortable being on the ground. The ride is as smooth as Tennessee whiskey. Beautiful leather seats up front, as comfortable as it gets.

There was a kitchen area with a refrigerator full of sodas, water, and O'Douls nonalcoholic beer. A few Budweisers here and there for those who still drink a beer. Up front was a huge television with a satellite hookup and VCR. There was a drawer under one of the seats filled with tons of movies. A restroom with a shower was located across the hall. There were bunks for each band member, each with its own privacy curtain and an individual TV.

I took a seat up front with Doug, B. B., Tim, and his wife Mindy. Other band members wandered toward the back of the bus. Dave Muse stood up front with the driver for a while before taking a seat.

Doug and I chatted for a minute, and then his attention was diverted by some segment of the movie playing on the TV. It was the old Cheech and Chong chestnut, "Up in Smoke." Doug made one of his quick-witted comments, but it went right over my head because B. B. spoke to me at about the same time. It is easy to see that this is the beginning of their favorite time. The ride to the venue, just before show time. Everyone seemed to be in high spirits, and the weather looked perfect for an outdoor concert.

Tim Lawter is just a lot of fun. He and Doug have a "comedy bond" that is obvious to anyone who's around them for more than thirty minutes together. When one of them is not cutting up, the other is.

On the way to the gig in Hickory, Lawter got right in my face with those wild eyes of his.

"Let's get drunk tonight," he said, sounding dead serious. "Just me and you. What do you say?"

I stood there dumfounded for ten seconds, and he laughed out loud. "I'm just kidding!"

When the bus pulled up at the stadium and we all got off, Doug was greeted by several of the local police officers, one of whom used to play in a band in Spartanburg. I followed Doug around like a shadow as he walked down to the stage area looking for our stage passes, which we eventually found.

Then we headed toward the field house where dressing rooms had been set up for the band in the locker rooms. We found the one marked off for the Charlie Daniels Band, but we kept circling—me, Doug, and some of the band and crew, looking for the MTB dressing room.

We made our way back to the bus, where we drank some water before heading back down to the stage for sound check. Today things had been running behind, so there was no time for the usual sound check. Instead, the band and crew conducted a line check for about twenty minutes.

During this time Doug was talking to crew and venue people, making sure the microphone cables and lighting were all in working condition. Meanwhile, I was being more nosy than Lt. Columbo, walking all around the stage, looking at Rusty's and Stuart's guitars, the Hammond B-3 organ, and the whole back line setup.

Across the back of the stage was Charlie's band equipment. I found myself gawking at the scuffed stickers that covered the road cases. Bumper stickers from venues across the USA and around the world. Harley Davidson stickers, festival stickers, and more.

There was a case sitting open, stage left, just this side of the drum riser, and in it there were two violins—that is, fiddles. There were also several bows. Charlie's arsenal.

Momentarily, Doug walked by and said "We're going back to the bus; you want to go?"

Well, of course I did. I was watching his every move on this trip. I had a job to do. No time for daydreaming today.

There were twenty or thirty fans gathered outside the bus now. Doug smiled and said "Hello" and kept moving. The air-conditioned comfort of that big rolling motel awaited him.

Inside, there were trays of meat and vegetables. I looked over at Doug, motioned to the food, and gave the international "You want some?" signal. He smiled and shook his head, "No."

For about ten minutes, Doug just sat and stared, thinking about the upcoming show. Every night is different, as is every audience. Today things were running a little behind, and he was somewhat concerned that there was no time for a sound check. But he is quite good at "rolling with the punches." After twenty-five years, you learn to be.

Doug headed out for the locker room to change into his stage clothes. A couple of the guys had already changed and were back on the bus, so I just stayed there to speak with them for a while.

About fifteen minutes passed and it was time to head for the stage. Ten minutes after that, the band was introduced to an enthusiastic round of applause and launched into their biggest hit, "Heard It in a Love Song." For the next fifty minutes, the Marshall Tucker Band ruled the ball park. During the extended jams, Doug turned to face drummer B. B. Borden, laughing and beating away on his tambourine.

The minute Doug said "Good night," the MTB road crew began rushing the stage, tearing down the equipment and loading it onto the trucks. The Charlie Daniels Band crew began positioning their equipment, and the Tuckers came down to meet fans in and around the stage area.

Doug was still onstage, talking briefly to Charlie's keyboard player Joel "Taz" DiGregorio. When Taz came down the steps to the field, Doug was caught by a member of the press, and Taz went walking across the field with Stuart for a smoke. Tim Lawter had hooked up with Charlie Hayward, CDB bass player.

A few minutes later Doug was off the stage chatting with friends and fans and with CDB guitarist Chris Wormer. I followed Doug around as he was surrounded by adoring fans. He talked, joked around, and signed autographs on everything from CDs to copies of my *Carolina Dreams* book to T-shirts and bare skin.

"Hey, it's a job!" he said at one point, to no one in particular.

Doug seemed to like the children most of all, and anyone who brought a kid up to him received the star treatment. He always has time for the children.

And then he began his walk toward the bus. Security men were all around, and I found myself swept up in the momentum, like some sort of amateur security policeman.

Halfway to the bus Doug yelled to someone, "I gotta go get these pants off and put on some shorts and tennis shoes so I can come hear Charlie."

A handful of mostly female fans were gathered near Charlie's limo, waiting with Sharpies and photos in hand. When we walked by, they recognized Doug and started squealing, asking him to pose for photos and sign their albums, creating another five-minute delay in getting him back to the bus.

There were now ten or more fans gathered outside the bus door, and Doug assured them that if he could get on and change, he'd be right back out to greet them.

On the bus, Doug took a cold beverage from the refrigerator and made himself a peanut-butter-and-banana sandwich. He then changed into his shorts and proceeded to keep his promise to the fans outside the bus door. In the meantime, I followed Tim Lawter and his wife down to the stage area to listen to Charlie Daniels, who kicked off his show with

"The South's Gonna Do It Again," then announced, "Before we go any further, let's have another round of applause for one of my all time favorite bands, the Marshall Tucker Band!"

The applause was booming as Charlie segued into "Drinkin' My Baby Goodbye." After about five songs we had to head back to the bus. Apparently, working bands aren't afforded a lot of time to just hang out and enjoy the other entertainers.

"Charlie sounds great," Tim said as we walked toward the bus.

"He is great, ain't he?" I added, watching Mindy nod her head in agreement with Tim.

About five minutes after we got back to the bus it was time to pull out and return to the hotel.

I had a choice. We had discovered that if I turned in my rental car anywhere besides the place we got it, Greenville, there would be a rather hefty fee for them to recover it and bring it back. So I could either follow the bus when they pulled out at 2 AM or I could stay overnight and leave early in the morning on my own.

When I awoke at 6 AM, I packed and headed out of Hickory for the five-hour drive to Myrtle Beach.

It was Bike Week at the beach, and as luck would have it, I ended up lodged in traffic just the other side of Conway, where I would creep along over the next three hours. That's right, three hours. When I finally made it to the beachfront hotel, I checked in and went up to see Doug. He was getting ready to take a nap, so I called B. B. Borden's extension. He had told me the day before that he'd be more than happy to do an interview. B. B. appeared in my doorway about ten minutes later, and we talked for about an hour. I learned about all of the bands he'd played in prior to MTB, including Mother's Finest, The Outlaws, and Molly Hatchet.

Today the band had been enjoying some time on the beach and just resting up for the night's big show.

At about six o'clock, it was once again time to meet at the bus and head over to the Palace Theatre. The bus was going to leave right after the show to head home. I opted to stay overnight, and drive home on Sunday morning.

I got into my Tracer and followed the bus through the crowded streets of Myrtle Beach, finally arriving at the Palace.

Backstage, a buffet was being set up for Charlie Daniels' class reunion as we made our way to the dressing rooms. There was a star bearing the band's name on the door, which led into a comfortable waiting area just off of two different dressing rooms. In it were trays of food, bowls of M&M's, bottled water and sodas, and a TV playing old Warner Brothers cartoons.

Old friends dropped in to visit Doug and security people wandered around, mingling with backstage guests and band members. Some people were dipping into the deli trays, drinking cold beverages, and such. David Muse walked by me on his way into the dressing room, followed by Rusty Milner. Doug headed for the stage area to check things out.

"We got it set up with Charlie to drop by and say hi," Doug told me. "Right after we finish playing."

Every few feet, it seemed, Doug was stopped by fans, road crew, or fellow band members. Finally, he made his way back to the dressing room, where he was able to sit for at least a few minutes and chat with friends.

Close to show time, the backstage area of the Palace was buzzing like a beehive. Band members were checking their instruments, the roadies had tuned everything, and B. B. sat down behind his drum kit. Doug peeked out from behind the curtain to get a look at the sold-out crowd.

"Looks real good," he said with a smile.

A group of bikers approached the side of the stage, and Doug greeted them with hugs.

"It's about time to start," he told them. "We'll talk right after the show."

Two minutes later the band was introduced, the curtain rose, and "Heard It in a Love Song" bellowed out of the PA speakers for the bizzillionth time, sounding as fresh as spring air.

Standing in the wings, it sounded terrific. Doug's voice was soaring and taking flight like an eagle. B. B. was pounding the drums with a fervor, while Tim rocked along on the bass in perfect time. Stuart and

Rusty were playing melodic guitar one minute and pumping out dirty blues the next, while David switched between sax, flute, and Hammond B-3 organ with the expertise of a Major League pitcher changing up pitches for each batter.

An hour later, the band concluded the show, bringing the audience to their feet with a rocking retelling of "Can't You See." As the curtain closed, Doug scurried over to me in a semi-trot.

"Let's go," he said. "Charlie's expecting us."

I followed him through the stage hands, then through the fans, as he assured each one, "I'll be right back." He made a beeline to a room where Charlie Daniels was seated, signing autographs, and speaking to former classmates and fans.

"Oh, we didn't know he was busy," Doug told the man in charge. "We don't want to interrupt."

The man took Doug by the arm and led us past the line.

"He'll want to see you," said the man.

Sure enough, Charlie's smile was as broad as the Tennessee River as he hugged Gray and then spoke to me about the *Carolina Dreams* book. Doug and I posed for a photo with Charlie, shared a few brief minutes, and then left him to meet with his fans.

As we turned, a forty-something man stood holding a four-year-old girl. The beauty was dressed from head to toe in cowgirl attire and looked as pretty as a Georgia peach.

"She'd like your autograph," the man said to Doug.

"Well, aren't you just the prettiest girl," Doug smiled, signing her picture. "Now you always be a good girl, and always hold on to your dreams. Remember, you can do or be anything you want to be, as long as you believe."

The father looked stunned that such spiritually uplifting words had just come from the mouth of one whose reputation as a rowdy Southern rocker has always preceded him. Of course, things were different these days. Doug himself was a family man.

Making our way back through the hall, Doug was stopped by a fan known as "the cornbread woman." She was dressed in jeans and a Charlie T-shirt and hugged Gray like a long-lost friend. She told him that she had brought the band some more of her famous homemade cornbread, something Doug and Tim especially, along with the rest of the band, look forward to with salivating pallets.

David "Dibby" Warren told Doug that it was time to head for the lobby to sign autographs, and I once again got sucked into the entourage vacuum that weaved its way through the corridors and across the back of the auditorium to the MTB merchandise table, where Chris stood, talking to fans who were purchasing everything from *Face Down in the Blues* towels to MTB panties and T-shirts. Rusty was already out, surrounded by three or four fans.

Charlie was on stage now, kicking into "The South's Gonna Do It Again." In the lobby, there were forty or fifty fans circling around Doug holding album covers, books, CDs, and caps, all wanting autographs. Gray greeted each person with a smile, and everybody had a story for him. Some eternal MTB memory that meant something special to them. Doug listened, smiled, and talked to them all while he signed their memorabilia.

There was a small group of bikers behind us now, and I recognized them as the group that had approached Doug prior to the show. Patiently, they waited for a moment to talk to him, and after about twenty minutes of signing, they got their time. Doug came up to the bikers, hugged each of them, and shook their hands, trading comments and laughing.

In all, Doug was out front meeting and greeting fans for over an hour while the Charlie Daniels Band rocked inside the theatre. With a signal from his road manager, Doug bid his final "bye byes" to everyone, and we were again on the move, on foot. We were lead through the back of the venue, and out to the bus, where Doug and I said our goodbyes. He was back on the road headed for the next venue, and I was in the rental car headed back to the hotel.

The next morning I left out from Myrtle Beach heading back home to Greenville. Riding down the virtually empty roadways, I made notes about the weekend on my tape recorder.

Arriving back in town at about four o'clock, I took the rental back to the place where I got it and met Doug there. It was at that moment that I realized the true duality of this man. On the road, he is 100 percent professional, constantly watching everything around him. Back home, he is able to let his hair down and just "be Doug." He joked around with me, and I thanked him for a great time. He stepped outside and waved to my wife Jill as I got into our car to head back home. In my head, I could still hear the strains of "Can't You See" and "Heard it in a Love Song." The familiar music I had grown up with. The music that I love.

I had been working on the aforementioned *Carolina Dreams* book for a couple of years. It was to be a book about all of the great musicians to come out of our South Carolina Upstate. People like Artimus Pyle of Lynyrd Skynyrd, jazz guitarist Hank Garland, and of course, the Marshall Tucker Band.

After pitching the idea to a few publishing houses, Doug Gray offered to publish it through Marshall Tucker Entertainment, a company he owned with his manager Ron Rainey. After several stops and starts and a few bumps in the country road, the book was published in 1997. We had a book signing party at Pic-a-Book in Spartanburg with MTB friend and store owner Jane Hughes, which was ironic since that was the first place I ever saw Doug offstage, years earlier. I had planned for Doug to be there but his schedule didn't allow it, although several local favorites did show up, Barney Barnwell, Franklin Wilkie, and Mark Burrell among them. We had another signing event at Barnes and Noble in Greenville, and Doug came out for it. Then we did a smaller signing at Books-a-Million in Columbia, SC. A published author. I was thrilled.

In the years to come I would write the as-of-yet unpublished biography of Doug Gray, the voice of the Marshall Tucker Band, and in doing so meet many of his old friends and family, including his dear mother Peggy, whom I just loved. Sadly, Peggy was killed in an auto accident just prior to the Volunteer Jam Tour of 2000. Marshall Tucker bowed out of the Greenville show, and Charlie Daniels dedicated "How Great Thou Art" to her memory. The day of the Greenville Jam, we all found ourselves at the Floyd's Greenlawn Chapel in Spartanburg for Mrs. Gray's funeral. It was truly a heartbreaking day.

For a few years there, I was working as editor of a weekly newspaper in Inman, SC, not far from where Doug lived. During those days we were getting together for lunch all the time, usually Mexican, and having fun talking about everything from politics to rock and roll.

Around this same time the band had a little recording studio called Studio 151 in Spartanburg that sat beside Smith Music, the place where we all bought our instruments and supplies over the years. I can remember visiting the studio several times, like the occasion when the band was recording *Face Down in the Blues*. I always enjoyed watching as the songs were assembled, layer by layer.

I have now been blessed to sit in and sing with Tucker over twenty-five times, and it is always fun. Most of these jams took place at the annual Angelus Benefits down in Clearwater and Tampa, Florida. Those events are always the highlight of the year. There are late-night jam sessions, the all-day country and Southern rock concert, the golf tournament, and lots and lots of face time with old friends. Besides all of the MTB jams, Angelus has afforded me opportunity to sing with the Charlie Daniels Band; play guitar with Montgomery Gentry (thanks to Chris Hicks, who simply handed me his Les Paul one night and told me to "go for it"); and play countless jams with Tommy Crain, Steve Grisham, Dangerous Dan Toler, members of Little Texas and Trick Pony, Bonnie Bramlett, and many more.

To some folks, hanging out in the recording studio for two days would be just plain boring and tedious. For me it's more fun than watching the Super Bowl with four of my buddies and a keg of cold beer. I love to watch the magic that takes place in the recording studio, and I especially love it when that magic is being created by my friends and one of my all-time favorite groups, the Marshall Tucker Band. In spring 2007, I was back in the studio with the guys.

The first track they were working on was a song written by James Copeland called "Cold Steel." It has a real MTB feel, similar to "Silverado," except with its own unique story about motorcycle riding. I sat and watched Chris Hicks add some guitar parts while talking to all of my other buddies, including Doug Gray, Stuart Swanlund, and sound man Keith Glenn.

They were recording at Southeastern Sound Studio with Buddy Strong, who runs the place, engineering the project. Buddy is a helluva guitar player himself and was a member of the early 1980s band Garfeel Ruff on Capitol Records with Rickey and Ronnie Godfrey, Frank Wilkie, and Allen Pearson. Buddy knows music.

During a break I said my hellos to drummer B. B. Borden and bassist Pat Elwood. We caught up for a while and then they were called back into the studio.

The next day I returned to observe some more studio magic. Doug's daughter Gabrielle dropped by for a while and ran over the words to a song she would be singing with Chris Hicks. It's a beautiful country song written by founding Tucker member George McCorkle, who contributed a lot to the release. The song is called "I Love You that Way," and it is amazing.

Former MTB drummer David "Ace" Allen came in to lay down drum tracks for the tune, with Hicks playing acoustic and Ellwood on bass.

I was talking with the guys on break and reminiscing about the days in the late seventies and early eighties when Stuart and Ace were in a band called Lightnin' West, while Elwood was in one called Dallas Alice. Ah, the good ol' days. I had to wonder if they ever dreamed that in the future they would play with Tucker.

I spoke with some of the band about the upcoming Volunteer Jam Tour that would put them back on the road with the Charlie Daniels Band and the Outlaws. It seemed everyone was very excited about those shows, as well as the many other concerts that are always on the board for the band.

A few days later I got a call from Doug telling me to bring my guitar and come to the studio. When I arrived it was just him and me and Buddy the engineer, and Doug invited me to play guitar on "Cold Steel." What a rush. I was at long last on an album with my heroes. The dream never dies, baby!

In summer 2007, the Volunteer Jam Tour was back on the road. The Tour kicked off in style at the Bi-Lo Center in Greenville, SC. Going in, I expected a great evening, but I really had no idea whatsoever that it would become a homecoming for the MTB.

It all began when my buddy Scott Greene and his son Steve, along with Pastor Cliff Marshall (the ultra-cool leader of my church, Freedom Fellowship), picked me up in the Suburban (a vehicle that has logged many a mile on the rock and roll highway). We made our way over to Sticky Fingers for a pre-concert meal and some fun conversation.

At the venue we separated, as I had to be backstage while my friends took seats out front. The first person I saw backstage was my pal "Smoke," Tony Heatherly. Smoke was the bassist for the Toy Caldwell Band, and most recently had spent a few years thumping the four strings for the Marshall Tucker Band. It was indeed great to see ol' Smoke again. We made our way back to the MTB dressing room, which was filled with Doug Gray's children and their friends, all chilling out. It was at about this time that the familiar faces started popping up in rapid succession.

The second familiar face I saw was that of Clay Cook. I was so happy to see him at the show, as I believe he really adds a lot to the band. Not only is he great instrumentally but he has pipes reminiscent of Uncle Doug.

Chris Hicks and his wife Jenny came in and I was surprised and happy to see the band's manager, Ron Rainey, had flown in from California. It was great speaking with Mr. Rainey again. It was also nice to see Paula and the others from the CDB office in Lebanon, Tennessee. Paula has helped me out so much over the past eight years—she is a "superstar" in my book.

Doug Gray came in, followed by his wife Rene, and we all caught up for a bit. Soon Stuart walked in, along with B. B. Borden, David Muse, and Pat Ellwood and his wife Linda. Then I saw Buddy Strong from Southeastern Sound Studio and his wife.

I glanced around in the hall only to find founding MTB members Paul T. Riddle and Jerry Eubanks in the house, and my mind began to reel. Would this be an MTB reunion? Everyone was here except the now Nashville-based George McCorkle. I'd always dreamed of seeing all of the surviving Tuckers join with the current band for a jam someday. Unfortunately, George would die of cancer in 2007, and the dream would die with him.

The original Tucker road crew came out to support the band. Moon Mullins, Puff, Blackie, and Stump were all there. Did someone say family reunion? I even got to meet Toy Caldwell's youngest daughter Geneal, a very sweet young lady, and her friends, all nice folks.

Seems like every turn brought another friend. I was really in my element. Tom and Ann Bell were there. I usually only see those kids down at the Angelus in Florida.

The show began with a blazing set from the Outlaws. While I have long been a fan of the "Florida Guitar Army," this was my first ever live experience with them. Hughie Thomasson led his band through an hour of hits, including "There Goes Another Love Song" and their show-stopping jam, "Green Grass and High Tides," with Chris Anderson swapping off on smoking guitar leads with Hughie. It was a great set, and I kept walking between the side of the stage and out front and back to the Tucker dressing room. Somewhere during the show I ran across Charlie Hayward and kidded him about following me. He had been at the Boyer benefit in Muscle Shoals a couple of weeks earlier. I also spoke to Taz DiGregorio and Bruce Brown from the Charlie Daniels Band. We talked about past shows, my online magazine and Taz's new solo album, *Shake Rag*.

Next on deck were our hometown heroes The Marshall Tucker Band, supported by friends, family, and all of Greenville. They kicked things off with "Fire on the Mountain," with Clay Cook playing Toy Caldwell's pedal-steel opening note for note. The band rocked through the title track of Chris Hicks's solo project, *Dog Eat Dog World*, and later played "Georgia Moon," a beautiful Paul Hornsby-penned song from that same record.

Doug led the audience in a sing-along on "Heard It in a Love Song," and at one point Hughie Thomasson snuck up onstage behind former band mate Hicks with a tambourine, goofing for the audience. It was beginning to look like the Volunteer Jams of days gone by and as the night wore on would only become more so.

Everyone got a treat when Doug brought founding MTB drummer Paul T. Riddle to the stage to play "This Ol' Cowboy," and Chris Hicks sang "The Rain" from Tucker's *Beyond the Horizon* CD.

When "Can't You See" started up, Chris signaled for me to come up and sing, and Tony Heatherly came up to play bass, with former MTB drummer Ace Allen on the kit. It was truly an honor for me when Chris relinquished his verse and let me belt it out in front of my home town crowd. A true highlight of my life.

After the Tucker set, Chris Hicks introduced me to Hughie Thomasson and Chris Anderson from the Outlaws. I was once again in Southern rock heaven. Sadly, brother Hughie would pass away just months later at his home in Florida, shortly after recording an incredible Outlaws comeback album called *Once an Outlaw*.

The Charlie Daniels Band was locked and loaded and took absolutely no prisoners, dedicating their show to the memory of Toy and Tommy Caldwell. The band performed "Long Haired Country Boy," "El Toreador," "Simple Man," "The Legend of Wooly Swamp," "In America," and many more popular hits before pulling out all the stops on "The Devil Went Down to Georgia." I have heard the CDB so many times live, but I have never heard "Devil" sound better than on this night.

Charlie stepped up to the microphone and announced that, in keeping with the grand tradition of the Volunteer Jam, he was bring all the members of all three bands out onstage. All of the Outlaws, Tucker, and the CDB joined in for an amazing extended version of "The South's Gonna Do It Again," with smoking guitar solos from Hughie Thomasson, Chris Hicks, Clay Cook, and Chris Wormer. Charlie Hayward held down the bass duties along with three full drum kits going at it. It was a memorable close to a wonderful show.

I said goodbye to as many friends as I could and made my way to the exits to locate Scott, Steve, and Cliff. By all reports, they had enjoyed it as much as I had.

It was June 2007 when we lost the third original MTB member. George McCorkle died of cancer, and we all wept. George and I had become good friends over the past few years, and he was always the first to agree to come out and play at one of our benefit concerts. He drove down a few times from Nashville to Huntsville, Alabama, for an Arch Angel Foundation benefit and again for my *Something Heavy* CD release party.

George had come into Mill Kids Studios to add some great guitar work to an album I was recording with the Crawlers, and we had a great time. He played a lead break on the instrumental "Rocket City Express," and he and I traded off leads on "Everyday Grind," a song I co-wrote with Steve Harvey years ago. George played on several other tracks as well, and when our friend Ray Brand of the Crawlers died of cancer in 2005, George joined us again in the studio to do a song I wrote for Ray called "A Change in the Weather" for an upcoming Ray Brand memorial CD.

It was slightly overcast in Spartanburg, SC, the morning of July 3, 2007, and a bit cooler than it had been. Well, at least until about halfway through the graveside service, when hundreds of these old fashioned cardboard church fans were being used by many of the people in attendance, and my sweat-soaked black blazer was peeled off and tossed over my shoulder.

Doug Gray had called and invited me to ride over to the funeral with him. Attending with Doug was akin to hanging out with the President or something. Virtually everyone was coming up to Doug, shaking hands, telling stories, and cruising down memory lane.

They were burying our brother George today and hundreds of friends, fans, and family members gathered around the tent to pay our final respects.

The tour bus came up, and the pallbearers brought George's casket down the hill to its final resting place. The family made their way to the seating in front of the casket, George's wife Vivienne sitting front and center beside family friend Bruce Wall, along with George's son Justin and his wife Bebe and other family members.

Surviving original Marshall Tucker Band members Paul Riddle and Jerry Eubanks joined Doug, along with former band members Franklin Wilkie, Rusty Milner, Tim Lawter, Tony Heatherly, and David Allen. Toy Caldwell band drummer Mark Burrell and Toy's youngest daughter Geneal were in attendance, as well as all of the original Tucker road crew, Moon Mullins, Puff, Blackie, and Stump.

George's first wife Elaine and her husband were there, as well as musicians Artimus Pyle of Lynyrd Skynyrd, David Ezell, and Mark McAfee. So many friends were there, all brought together by the friendship of the gentle soul that was George McCorkle.

The preacher from the church George attended in Tennessee opened the service, telling a great story about being a Southern rock fan and his first meeting with George.

One of George's longtime friends and co-writers Jay Boy Adams played a beautiful new song he had written about friendship, and another singer-songwriter friend of George's, Monica Perry, sang a breathtaking acapella version of George's song "Peace Stories."

US Navy representatives folded and presented the flag to Vivienne and delivered a twenty-one-gun salute. A lone Navy bugler played "Taps."

A few friends spoke about George, including his stepson, and after the closing prayer, Jay Boy led everyone in a sing-along on "Fire on the Mountain."

It was a very special service to remember a true one-of-a-kind human being and a real honest-to-God Southern rock pioneer. A good man and a good friend. Love you, George.

Now it seems as though everything has come full circle. From the time I bought my first Marshall Tucker Band LP at Record Bar and asked my friend Larry to give it to his sister to get autographed to the early eighties, meeting some of them in town, at work and at the studio, to the writing of *Carolina Dreams*. All of the gigs, bus rides, studio experiences. The Marshall Tucker Band continues to tour and record to this day, keeping the memories of Toy, Tommy, and George alive.

# 8

# THE COLLECTOR

I have always been a collector. As a kid I collected baseball and football cards. I also collected comic books, which I still do today, oddly enough. I collected model cars and Beatles and Batman trading cards. Later, I collected rock and roll magazines, many of which I still have, as well as 8-track tapes, LPs, 45s, Boy Scout event patches—the list just goes on and on. I went through a serious coin and stamp collecting period as well. I had a pile of wheat pennies and some beautiful old silver dollars. I ended up giving my stamp collection to the brother of a girl I had a crush on in 1976. I was trying to impress her. Sheesh.

When I was a teenager I got my hands on a book from the Spartanburg Public Library about autograph collecting, and a monster was born. I began writing to politicians, athletes, and celebrities, asking for their autograph, and I was indeed thrilled when the envelopes began to pour in.

Some of the packages I received were an 8x10 photo of a young Dustin Hoffman (this was around 1972) signed "To Mike" with a peace sign drawn on it; a pen-and-ink drawing of Prince Valiant signed by the artist Hal Foster; a signed photo of Mario Andretti with his race car; a letter and illustration of the Cat in the Hat and signed photo of Dr. Seuss; an original sketch of Snoopy signed by Charles Schultz; autographs and photos and more from the Carpenters, Kenny Rogers and the First Edition, Presidents Richard Nixon, Jimmy Carter, Gerald Ford, George Bush, and Ronald Reagan and Vice Presidents Walter Mondale and Spiro Agnew. Over the years I continued the autograph collection, meeting TV stars like *Star Trek*'s William Shatner, Walter Koenig, James Doohan, and others. I got Ronnie Van Zant's signature on one of my album covers in 1977 and later collected all of the Skynyrd signatures, all of the Marshall Tucker Band, Charlie Daniels, and Molly Hatchet ones as well.

With the advent of *GRITZ Magazine* in 1998, I started asking every interview subject for a signed glossy and boy howdy, they can add up quickly. I am the proud owner of hundreds of 8x10s, most signed with kind personal comments from everyone from Billy Bob Thornton to Bonnie Bramlett, Koko Taylor, .38 Special, Dickey Betts, Gregg Allman, Peter Frampton, KISS, the list goes on.

Over the years I have become a real pack rat. A real collector of way too many things. There are some people who would tell me I should just get rid of a lot of my collection and memorabilia, but that's not my style. I have to have my "stuff." It makes me happy, and I still plan on having my own private museum one day to display everything in. I'll have it too, just you wait and see.

## ALWAYS THE ENTERTAINER

Long about the eighth grade, I had decided I was the next Rich Little and had put together a show featuring the voices of everyone from Richard Nixon to Johnny Cash. I especially liked to try and sound like the country stars of the day, and I put together a show where I did Merle Haggard, Charley Pride, and many others. I premiered my "act" during the talent show at D. R. Hill Junior High School and got my first real applause. I felt like a star that day. Then I auditioned at WSPA-TV for the local TV talent show, "Carolina Country," hosted by Dave Craig.

When I got up there, I really began to get nervous, and when the band asked me what key the songs were in, I freaked. I didn't even know what a key was. But I went on to audition. I knew it was awful so I never even called them back. How embarrassing. My Dad had driven me to the audition, and he made me feel much better on the way home. He said, "You did good, Mike. You just ain't ready yet, but you will be. Keep working on it." That was the kindest thing my Dad ever said to me, and I will never forget it.

Later on, "Carolina Country" featured performances by the talented Daryl Rice as well as other area bands like Kay Crowe & the Tune Twisters and fellow Byrnes High student Pam Knighton.

Oddly enough, my Rich Little act went over like gangbusters during boy scout camporee, where I took home a blue ribbon for first place. I was on my way.

# THE SOUL OF TROOP 144

I paid a visit to my old scout hut a few years back, only to find it boarded up—a decrepit, ancient-looking log cabin. The newer boards that stretched across the windows and the front door seemed to be the only things holding the old place together. All of its life had somehow been drained out of it. The grass and weeds had grown so high that they almost swallowed the petite structure completely, but there was still enough there to recognize, still enough to make a smile come to my face, as I recalled my days in Troop 144.

The scout headquarters was located in Jackson Mills, a small town between Lyman and Wellford.

When I think about the Boy Scouts I remember the merit badges. I got journalism, art, and music first. I got the Golden Quill award for writing, a God and Country award, and a Project SOAR (Save Our American Resources) patch for my uniform. I eventually got the coveted Eagle award. Oh, and I was the troop artist and even designed a bandana/neckerchief for the troop based on the Confederate stars and bars flag design. Of course, this was in the good ol' days, prior to "political correctness." Whatever that is.

We used to play Capture the Flag and other games, and the camporees were a blast. I'll never forget winning that blue ribbon at the Camp Croft event for talent, doing some of the aforementioned "Rich Little wanna-be" impersonations and comedy. Boy, the thought of standing in front of all those people and doing my a capella Johnny Cash is pretty embarrassing now.

I may have never joined the Scouts had it not been for Carl Keffer. Carl and his sister Teresa were two kids my Mom babysat every afternoon for years. Carl was a scout and talked me into joining. I always had a lot of fun with Carl and Teresa, and we'd spend the afternoons playing outside, often with the Mason kids from across the street.

One of the older kids in the troop, Steve, used to bet us all the time that he would do these outrageous acts. At that same Camp Croft weekend, we collected $7 and change for Steve to jump from a 15-foot cliff to the ground below.

He jumped, fell like a rock, and when he hit, he went knee-deep into the soft mud. Well, the ground looked hard to us. We all laughed until we cried.

One time, I was given a job in the scouts. It was the first time I learned to exercise responsibility. I was made "Quartermaster." My job was to take care of the tools, the shovels, the axe, and other things that we scouts used in our camping excursions. I still maintain a certain pride in remembering that job. I was meticulous about those tools.

The troop was lead by Hubert Odom, a good man who later served as mayor of Wellford for many years. I kind of came into the Scouts at a later age than many. Seems like I was thirteen when I got awarded the Tenderfoot status. In years to come I would move on to Second Class, Life, and eventually the much-coveted Eagle. Not that I actually earned them all. Let's just say that in our troop, the rules tended to be a bit more relaxed. I got a lot of merit badges, many I earned, others, well...and I received the aviation badge fifteen years before I ever set a single foot on an airplane. Of course, I made up for it on the journalism and art badges, to be sure—oh, and music.

Camporees were great fun. Many of us would buy, sell, and trade various patches from different events, and my collection began to grow. Unfortunately, none of those patches or my badges or awards exist today. They were all burned by my father as a punishment for doing something wrong. Pretty harsh punishment. He told me I didn't deserve any of the Boy Scout awards I had earned, took them all into the back yard, put them in a metal trash can, and set it afire while I cried. Now there's a memory. Did I learn my lesson? Well, sure. But I would have learned it if he'd sat me down and talked to me as well, and I'd still have my treasured awards, including my Eagle.

I had earned the Order of the Arrow by spending the night alone at Camp Old Indian and learning survival tactics. I was so proud of the white sash with the embroidered red arrow on it because I recalled seeing one my Uncle Sonny had earned when he was a kid. I also had the OA ring.

One of the awards I was happiest to have was the God and Country Award, a beautiful pin that I wore proudly. Sadly, none of that stuff exists today, although I did manage to replace a few items thanks to eBay.

The Boy Scouts taught me quite a lot. I learned how to survive in the woods, cook in the ground, and make a killer vegetable stew. I learned to keep my tools clean and in repair, help out my fellow man, and, like our friend Charlie Daniels says, keep God first at all times. It was a major growth and learning experience, and my troop days stand out as some of the most fun years of my youth.

# 11

## THE CHARLIE DANIELS BAND

*"I don't look at myself as having a role; I feel like I am just an entertainer. I don't see myself as an influence or having a certain image to live up to. I am just an entertainer that goes and plays shows and makes records and tries to entertain people. I have much more of a mature look at my career per se than what I had when I was younger. I have kids come up to me and say "I have been listening to you for a long time and you have had an effect on my music" but I really don't look at myself in that way. I am just a picker, man."*
—Charlie Daniels, interview with Buffalo, December 2003

The first time I ever saw Charlie Daniels in person was on that summer afternoon in 1977 at the Spartanburg Memorial Auditorium that I told you about earlier. The Marshall Tucker Band's Homecoming Concert. It was only two months before the passing of the King, Elvis, and four months prior to the Skynyrd airplane crash. I had been out of high school for one year and was all wrapped up in the local music scene, still trying to figure out which direction to take my life.

By now I had learned a bit about how to get backstage at shows, mostly by acting like I belonged. At twenty years of age, 6' 1" and 265 pounds, I looked like a roadie. I just made my way to the backstage area where Moon, Puff, and Blackie and other members of the Tucker road crew were running about, setting the stage, assembling Paul's drum kit, doing line checks and all. I kind of walked past several important-looking crew people, nodded my head, and kept walking.

Pretty soon I was in the stairwell that connects the loading dock to the stage area and the balcony. I didn't really have a battle plan at this moment, I was just winging it. I heard the sound of what seemed to be cowboy boots on concrete, a little heavy breathing, and the shuffling of saddlebags. I looked down one level to find Charlie Daniels coming up the stairs right toward me.

"How ya doin'," he asked with that famous smile of his.

"Pretty good," I replied. "I'm really looking forward to hearing you jam today."

"Oh, it's always fun with the Tucker boys," he said. With that we passed on the stairs like two ships in the night. But it was a pivotal encounter for me. The beginning of a relationship with Charlie and his band that would last for at least thirty more years.

I remember one fall in the mid-seventies, when Larry Whitfield and I were buying bullets to go hunting on Thanksgiving day, that we heard "Uneasy Rider" for the very first time on the radio. I thought it was hilarious. Wasn't long after that I learned that Charlie had actually attended school right there in Spartanburg as a kid before his family headed up to Wilmington, North Carolina, to set up housekeeping.

Charlie's music took a hold of me, man. There wasn't a song I didn't like. And of course he was always featured on every MTB album that came out. And then there were the famous Volunteer Jam shows, starting in 1975. The first music I ever heard from the Jam was the 45 bonus record that came with his *Fire on the Mountain* album in 1975.

Larry's girlfriend and soon-to-be wife Robin had asked my sister Patsy to ask me to pick up a record Larry would like for his birthday. I knew he'd want *Fire on the Mountain*. I also knew about the bonus single included in the package, and I was about to go into spasms wanting to hear it. In a typical Michael B. move, I took a razor blade and ever so carefully sliced the shrink wrap, just enough to get at the 45 and remove it. I played the record, recorded it to cassette, and carefully returned it to the sleeve of the LP. I then took some transparent Scotch tape and sealed the shrink wrap. Good as new. I remember Larry getting the gift from Robin at the nurse's residence at Spartanburg General Hospital. The first words out of Larry's mouth were, "Hey, this has been opened!" Curses, foiled again!

The 45 was a two-sided jam featuring members of the Tucker Band with the CDB, Artimus Pyle, Dickey Betts, and others. It was classic, man. Major jamming. It grabbed me by the short hairs and slung me around the room. When the first full Volunteer Jam LP came out, I was on it like stink on a skunk's butt. Over the years, there were several other Volunteer Jam LPs, and I devoured each one, always dreaming of attending one of those fabled jams. Unfortunately, I would not attend a Charlie Daniels Volunteer Jam until he took it on the road in the late 1990s with Marshall Tucker, Molly Hatchet, and Hank Williams Jr.

I attended two Volunteer Jams in Charlotte, one with Hank Williams Jr., Marshall Tucker, and Hatchet and another year with .38 Special and Edgar Winter, and both concerts were awesome. I also attended one in Greenville, SC, the same day I attended Doug Gray's mother's funeral. Not a happy memory. Marshall Tucker obviously had to cancel, and Molly Hatchet kicked it all off. The sadness of the funeral earlier in the day, coupled with Jill not feeling well, drove us to return home. There would be no Charlie Daniels for me that night.

I do need to mention here that my first real sit-down meeting with Charlie came on President's Day, 1996. I had driven up to Nashville on business, and one of the main items on my list was dropping by Charlie's office on Central Pike in Lebanon.

Once there, Charlie hooked me up with a cup of coffee and took a seat behind his huge mahogany desk. It was there that I conducted the first of perhaps ten interviews I would hold with Charlie over the years. A lot of this material was for inclusion in my first book *Carolina Dreams: The Musical Legacy of Upstate South Carolina*, for which he kindly wrote the foreword as well.

In years to come, I would interview Charlie many times and attend countless CDB concerts, many with my running buddy Scott Greene. Some of the very best of these shows took place at the annual Angelus Benefit in Florida.

I look forward to this show every year. The annual pilgrimage from Upstate SC down to Tampa for Charlie Daniels's three-day golf and country rock concert to benefit the Angelus House, a home for the physically challenged. The event is a lot of fun, and it has become a big part of my life.

In 2005, I returned to Tampa. This was the second time I drug Scott along for the event. Our ten-hour drive was divided into two parts. We had to wait until Scott got off work on Wednesday at 5:00 PM, load up, and roll. We stopped at the Days Inn just this side of the Florida line and spent the night, hopped back in the vehicle Thursday morning, and made it to the hotel by 1:30 PM. Once again the event was hosted by the

Seminole Hard Rock Hotel and Casino in Tampa, an amazing hotel with an equally amazing staff. All good folks. This place is awesome, with rock memorabilia on display all around, like Duane Allman's guitar, Dave Hlubek's "Rebel flag" guitar, handwritten lyrics from John Lennon, stage costumes, and more.

I was on schedule to perform that afternoon in the bar, so we checked in, took everything up to the tenth floor room, and I got ready for the show, putting on the ol' Buffalo hat and swag. Downstairs, young Aaron Kelly was already entertaining, singing to a prerecorded soundtrack. The kid really has the pipes, I tell ya. (A couple of years later Aaron was on American Idol and made it all the way into the final top ten.) Then I played a few and was joined on my closer, "Will the Circle Be Unbroken," by Chris Hicks of Marshall Tucker.

Next stop, the hospitality room. Adult beverage, anyone? We started running into the usual suspects, so many good friends we see at the Angelus every year—Tom and Anne Bell, Mary Wilson, Tommy Crain, Rick Broyles, and Doug and Rene Gray were among the first. We met up with good friend Mark Emerick of the Commander Cody Band as well.

Thursday night was the "Pairing Party" for the golf teams to be matched up with their country music star teammates. Lots of excellent food was served, including some out-of-this-zip-code and out-of-this-world baked salmon. Once the golf teams were decided, the jam began. Obviously my favorite part of the whole shootin' match, I had no idea just how stellar tonight's jam would be. Tommy Crain and the Crosstown Allstars rocked the house with their own excellent music and were soon joined by the man of the hour, Charlie Daniels, along with CDB keyboardist Taz DiGregorio and backup singer Carolyn Corlew.

Charlie Daniels became a 19 year old that night. Dressed down in his street clothes and military cap, Charlie put a hurtin' on that Les Paul guitar, kicking off with "Every Day I Have the Blues" and following with "Long Haired Country Boy." The group sounded like they had been rehearsing together for weeks. Hard to believe it was all on the fly. Charlie called out "One Way Out," Tommy Crain put the glass slide on his finger, and off they went. I was so privileged to be standing right in front of Charlie and Tommy as they went at it. Charlie spread his legs for a firm stance and went face to face with Tommy, just like in the glory days. Boy howdy, they were smokin'! At one point I saw Charlie look at Tommy and say, "Watch this!" Then he ripped off a riff that would make Dickey Betts envious.

Charlie sings it every night, "I done told you once you son of a gun I'm the best there's ever been!" The guys ripped through "Can't You See," "Sweet Home Alabama," "The South's Gonna Do It Again," and "The Devil Went Down to Georgia." It was amazing.

More jammers took the stage, including local favorites the Trunk Band and members of Ghost Riders, including my pal Steve Grisham. There was a lot of great music played.

On Friday morning Scott and I jumped into the car for the one-hour drive to Sarasota to visit Bud Snyder. I had worked with Bud for years on *GRITZ* advertising but never met him in person. Bud is a veteran of the Allman Brothers Band, having done sound and mixing for the Brothers as well as Gregg's band and Dickey Betts and Great Southern. He was a great guy. very spiritual. I dig that. The studio off from the house is very cool as well. I had just missed Pedro Arevalo (Dickey's bassist and a multi-instrumental genius) but I met his dad, Carlos. We all had a nice visit, then I had to get back to play another gig in the lobby bar.

This time out I played the first set, then turned it over to the other singers. Once I finished performing I had to hightail it to the banquet/auction. As usual, the food was excellent, prime rib and asparagus and stuff. Yum. The live auction was crazy. You have to be sure not to scratch your nose or raise a hand, or you'll find yourself the proud owner of a Wayne Gretzky hockey stick. The coolest item that year was a foal from one of Charlie Daniels's horses named Charlie's Angel. Beautiful animal.

After it was all said and done, we went over to the hotel's huge club Floyd's for another jam. Tommy Crain and the Crosstown Allstars kicked it off before once again adding Charlie Daniels and Charlie Hayward to the mix for "Further On Up the Road" and several others, again ending up with a scorching "Devil Went Down to Georgia." I still say nobody will ever play the guitar on "a band of demons" like Tommy Crain. It was so cool.

Next up came Confederate Railroad with a mini-set that included "Trashy Women," their biggest hit. Danny, Wayne, Jimmy, and the boys always give 100 percent, and tonight was no different.

Marshall Tucker was scheduled to go on next, but because of whatever reason, Montgomery Gentry took the stage for a set of smoking covers, including "The Midnight Special." After several songs, Chris Hicks, Stuart Swanlund, and B. B. Borden from Tucker joined them. At one point Chris Hicks saw me taking pictures and invited me onstage. I figured it was to sing backup, but as it happened Chris took his Les Paul guitar off and put it around my neck. What a guy! We played "Can't You See" and just had a blast. By now Tommy Crain was onstage along with others. I kicked off "Sweet Home Alabama" and saw Eddie grinning. Fun? You bet! The jam continued for a while, and after a bit I found myself tired out and headed back up to the room.

Saturday was show day, and what a show it was. Local band Wiley Fox opened it all up with talent and major class as always. Several young country acts followed but I was waiting on Trick Pony. When Heidi and the boys took the stage the crowd went nuts. They tore it up big time, ending with one of my favorites, "Pour Me."

Scott and I were both all over the place. I got to spend some quality time with cartoonist Guy Gilchrist (creator of *Nancy* and *The Muppets* comic strips). He's a great guy and a major friend of the Angelus. I spent a little time with Doug Gray, some with Bruce Brown and my friend Mike Proctor, who runs the High Lonesome Saloon in Georgia. It was a big surprise to see another pal, Brad "The Animal" Lesley, former Cincinnati Reds pitcher turned actor. Always great to see him. He's a lifelong fan of Marshall Tucker like me. Oh, speaking of MTB, I just love those cats and look forward to seeing them all every time, along with Dibby, Keith, and the rest of the crew.

Confederate Railroad played a great set as usual, and Tommy Crain sat in. Marshall Tucker Band set up, and Doug announced that it would be different tonight as he was supposed to rest his voice and was going in for vocal cord surgery February 2nd the next month. Still, he sang "This Ol' Cowboy" and Chris did "The Rain." Then Doug brought out Danny Shirley to sing "24 Hours at a Time." The band rocked it up with Tommy Crain sitting in. To close it all out, the band brought me out to sing with them on "Can't You See," with Mark Emerick on guitar and a cast of thousands, or what seemed like thousands, joining us on the stage.

This is when the wonderful security folks started to get nervous. The mass of people sharing the stage was amazing and my only wish was that I could have heard Mark's guitar better, but from where I was standing it was hard to hear anything except the next band to play tuning their instruments.

The backstage area was ridiculously crowded by now, and I just Buffaloed my way through the mass of humanity and out onto the loading dock. I hung out for a bit while the next act played, but then security freaked out on us and started forcing people to leave the backstage areea, including several musicians and guests. I listened to a little of Montgomery Gentry tunes before catching the shuttle back to the hotel.

Back at the Hard Rock I made a beeline for the hospitality room for a refreshing beverage, then hooked up with Doug and Rene Gray and sipped tea while they did the sushi thing. Before long they opened up the ballroom again for more "horse doovers" and a lot of fun conversation with Charlie and Pat Hayward, B. B. Borden, Pat and Linda Elwood, and more. The Trunk Band hosted another final jam, and it was all over but the drivin'.

We said goodbye to all our friends—at least the ones we could locate—and hit the bed at late-thirty in the AM. The next morning, it was breakfast with friends and off we were. Leaving is always the hard part, but it's nice knowing that before long we'll see one another again. And there is always another Charlie Daniels Band concert right around the corner.

Today, *Fire on the Mountain* remains in my top ten albums, and Charlie and his band hold a special place in my heart.

# 12

# THE MAKINGS OF A BOOK WORM

All through elementary and junior high schools, I was resistant to reading. I don't really know why, but the fact remains I read about four books prior to hitting high school. To be honest, I have to credit rock and roll with turning me on to reading. Had I not become such a huge fan of music, I probably would not have started reading magazines like *Creem*, *Circus*, *Crawdaddy*, and *Rolling Stone*. I still remember the first time I ever bought an issue of *Rolling Stone*. 1972. I was at Pic-a-Book in Spartanburg and saw this newspaper quarter-folded with Alice Cooper and his pet boa constrictor on the cover. I had to have it.

The issue was dated March 30, 1972, issue 105. I know because I somehow still have it. The magazine also had great articles on the Mersey Scene (featuring many famous Beatles locations such as the Cavern Club, Penny Lane, etc.), President Nixon in China, John McLaughlin of Mahavishnu Orchestra, the Concert for Bangladesh Money Trail, the 1972 Voter Registration Laws, Paul McCartney, and record reviews of Eddie Cochran, Al Green, the Firesign Theatre, Jimi Hendrix, Neil Young, Family, Manfred Mann's Earth Band, and Little Feat as well as a Captain Beefheart record review by a man I would soon grow to idolize, the king of all rock critics, Lester Bangs.

Lester's writing sucked me in, and soon I was reading with equal fervor the musings of Dr. Hunter S. Thompson and rock writer turned movie producer Cameron Crowe. That same year, a kid named Jimmy Johnson and his friend Moondog were looking over a magazine in agriculture class. It was a rag called *Circus*, and again Alice Cooper was on the cover. The issue included a foldout poster of Alice, apparently naked, wrapped in his boa constrictor. Freaky but intriguing. That day I went out and bought my first issue of *Circus*.

The memories kind of swirl together at this point, but what I do remember is buying every issue of *Circus* and *Rolling Stone*, and especially *Creem*, that I could get my hands on. Once in a while I would also buy *Rock Scene*, a magazine that focused more on the New York City scene and the all-night parties and shows. My dad always loved reading those, and it amused me that he liked to read Wayne County's advice column (Wayne was a noted New York transvestite rocker who later became Jane County). Of course this was during that early-seventies period where I turned Daddy on to Led Zeppelin, Alice Cooper, and the New York Dolls. Shortly after that he would *really* dig the sounds coming from my bedroom stereo—the Allman Brothers Band, the Marshall Tucker Band, and Charlie Daniels.

From those humble beginnings, I began to devour books. Lots of science fiction and fantasy. Everything Harlan Ellison ever wrote. Isaac Asimov. And books like *Heart of Darkness* by Joseph Conrad, *On the Road* by Jack Kerouac, and my favorite, *A Catcher in The Rye* by J. D. Sallinger. Then I began to read Stephen King, and there was no stopping me. I had to read every word the New Englander wrote.

So I credit rock and roll with my love of reading. And I credit *Circus, Rolling Stone, Crawdaddy,* and *Creem* for planting the seed that would one day grow *GRITZ Magazine.* And after I left *GRITZ,* I moved on to create the Universal Music Tribe online, while still harboring a dream of doing my own print magazine again. It's not likely, but hey, the dream never dies.

# 13

# HOW I GAVE UP ON GOING TO THE MOON
# AND BECAME A WRITER INSTEAD

Oddly enough, I would have never even dreamed of becoming a writer during my days in grade school and high school, although I did create my own music magazines and comic books as far back as eighth grade. Back then I was more into rockets and outer space and even dreamed of being an astronaut like Neil Armstrong.

I was just twelve years old in 1969 when I sat glued to the black-and-white TV as Neil Armstrong made that "one small step," which, according to Buzz Aldrin, was actually a 3- foot drop from the bottom of the LEM ladder to the moon's surface. By no means a "small" step.

Considering that I was obsessed with rockets, outer space, and the moon, at that time I was all about *Star Trek* and *Lost in Space*. I dreamed of being an astronaut. My dad, who worked at the grocery store, brought me home a special gift that weekend of Armstrong's "small step." Seems Pepsi was offering a really cool space package if you sent in a certain number of bottle cap corks. Remember those? But the Pepsi man had a few of these items in the truck and gave one to my daddy. I was thrilled. It was a really nice big legal-sized folder that tied shut like a document holder. On it was the NASA emblem and the Apollo 11 insignia. Inside were 8x10s of the Apollo 11 astronauts as well as photos of the moon, Saturn, Venus, and other planets, along with a booklet about the "space race."

I didn't remember John Kennedy's famous "moon" speech from eight or nine years prior but had seen it on TV playbacks. I was sure JFK would have loved the fact that his promise to go to the moon was fulfilled in such short order.

My first real thoughts of writing professionally were spurred by a professor at Spartanburg Methodist College, Dave Shuping, who made me feel as though I had a gift for writing. That encouragement, combined with years of reading Bangs, Thompson, and Crowe, created a desire in me to get serious about writing.

Back in high school I had written music articles for the school newspaper, *The Spotlight*. I had a "top ten" column called "Flipside," and I even had my own "Music Hall of Fame." I remember getting some guys mad at me because I panned the Black Sabbath *Sabotage* album and they thought it was high art. Of course my reviews of the Allman Brothers Band and the Marshall Tucker Band were always glowing. Go figure.

For several years I wrote fan fiction for various sci-fi fanzines including my friend Becky Hoffman's *Southern Star*, even going so far as to create my own 'zine *Paradise One*. I also made my own one-issue rock magazine called *The Coop* (named for Alice Cooper) in tenth grade, and during the high school days I created my own comic books on wrestler Ric Flair (as a gift for my buddy the Weasel) and the band KISS, prior to their first official comic. I must have been ahead of my time.

At SMC, I tried to kick it up a notch. Writing in the school paper about local and national bands and such was commonplace. Somewhere along the line I had my first article published in *The Spartanburg Herald Journal* in my hometown of Spartanburg, SC. It was a profile on local musician David Haddox, who at the time played drums in my band.

After college I worked at various newspapers in Spartanburg County and in North Carolina, always pushing my agenda for rock and roll writing, which doesn't really fly with editors who are trying to cover the city council's board meeting or the latest fender bender out on the frontage road.

While working at *The News Leader* of Landrum, SC, and her sister publication *The Polk County News Journal* of Columbus, NC, in 1990 Stephen Long and some other friends and I started an ecology newspaper called *Utopia*. It was all about recycling, Earth Day, and all of that good stuff. The two pages in the center were all music and all mine. I did CD reviews, commentary, show reviews, and more. Unfortunately, the 500-copy run coupled with the fact that we only published three issues kind of led my efforts nowhere.

Somewhere around this time I started a regular column called "Southern Accents." Modeled after Lewis Grizzard's famous column, I just wrote about whatever crossed my mind. The column ran in the *Inman Times* (Hilda Morrow was the first to give me a break by publishing it), *The Polk Country News Journal*, *The Landrum Leader*, *The Boiling Springs Chronicle*, and later in *EDGE Magazine* and *GRITZ*.

In 1991, I was working at WTYN Radio in Tryon, NC, while at the same time reporting for the paper *The Tryon Daily Bulletin*. I was performing in a play at the Little Theatre when I met James Irwin, and within three months he and I were publishing the first alternative-press newspaper in Greenville, SC. The biweekly tabloid was called *EDGE Magazine*, and for three years we had a blast. This was my first real, honest-to-God forum for editorial commentary. I got to do reviews and music writing on my own terms, and it was a blast. I was given the chance to interview everyone from George Harrison to Gene Simmons, from Paul Riddle of Marshall Tucker to Artimus Pyle of Lynyrd Skynyrd. It was a great training ground.

Those years at *EDGE* were a blast, working with James Irwin, Charlie Bergman, and David Morris (all three of whom are now sadly deceased), along with a staff that included Julie and David Moss, Mickie Ansell, Bethany Williams, Jill Greene, David Windhorst, Gail Gray, Phillip Knighten, Gary X, and many more.

Then in 1994 I broke ties with *EDGE* and started the decidedly more artsy *The Color Green* with folk artist/advertising man Bob Jones. This venture continued along the same lines, bringing interview opportunities with Chet Atkins, Carrot Top, Peter Criss from KISS, and Gregg Allman.

Somewhere along the line a friend named Russell Hall introduced me to his editor at *Goldmine*, the national monthly magazine for record collectors, and I started writing reviews and articles for them. Soon I became their go-to guy for Southern Rock. Besides writing huge 10,000-word cover stories on blues diva Koko Taylor, prog-band Kansas, and "The Motor City Madman" Ted Nugent, I created deep cover stories on the Marshall Tucker Band, Charlie Daniels, the Allman Brothers Band, Lynyrd Skynyrd, Texas rocker Edgar Winter, and Gov't Mule (in their first national cover story) among others.

Soon I was writing for online venues like *Suite 101*, *Y'all Magazine*, and print publications like *Relix*, *Hittin' the Note*, *Blue Suede News*, *Mojo*,

*Discoveries,* and many others. Of course all of those gigs took a back seat when we started *GRITZ* in 1998. *GRITZ* afforded me countless opportunities, including getting up close and personal with the very finest Southern rockers and other musicians on the planet.

Some of the high points right off the top of my head were my three-hour-plus conversation with the late Tom Dowd, a man who went from working on the Manhattan Project to producing the greatest LP of all time, the Allman Brothers *At Fillmore East* album. Talking to Gary and Dale Rossington of Lynyrd Skynyrd while they were on tour in Scotland was cool, as was getting to know so many heroes before they died, among them Dru Lombar, Duane Roland, Little Milton Campbell, Ray Brand, Hughie Thomasson, George McCorkle, Jakson Spires, JoJo Billingsley, and Tommy Crain. Of course it was a thrill to interview Dickey Betts, Bonnie Bramlett, and Gregg Allman—and Charlie Daniels has been great each time we have interviewed, which has been six times in ten years. Meeting and interviewing Capricorn Records alumni like the late Phil Walden and producers Johnny Sandlin and Paul Hornsby were also quite high on my list. Then again, interviewing and getting to hang out with Billy Bob Thornton is up at the top of my "most fun" list.

God knows how much I love playing music and getting onstage and just rocking the house. I love acting on both stage and screen, drawing cartoons, and entertaining. But if you ask me what my true bliss is, the reason I feel the good Lord put me on this earth, it is writing. Writing is my solace. My escape. Ronnie Van Zant once sang, "All I can do is write about it." Me too. If I didn't have that, I'd be one sad bison.

# 14

## SOMEWHERE BETWEEN THE CARPENTERS
## AND BLACK OAK ARKANSAS

Growing up, I tended to look for ways to escape. I knew that the other kids at school looked different from me; I just didn't know how they were different. What it was, I would later discover, was that they wore new, clean clothes to school. I didn't. They were all basically the same size overall, some shorter, some taller, but I was different. I was fat.

During elementary school my escape came in the form of superheroes—Batman, Superman, the Fantastic Four. During those formative years my music was usually whatever my dad listened to—mostly country, Hank Snow, Johnny Cash—or the 45s my sister Patsy played on the small record player in her bedroom. That was my first introduction to the records of four young men who had a style all their own. Four young men who recorded on the Vee-Jay label, the Beatles. I do recall seeing them on the *Ed Sullivan Show* when I was six. One of the records was "Please Please Me." Throughout my elementary years, my sister also had records by Oliver ("Jean"), the Partridge Family ("I Think I Love You"), lots of pop stuff. It would be several years before I learned to appreciate the "bad boys" of rock, the Rolling Stones, the Doors, and later Black Sabbath.

Man, I went through so many phases and stages musically, but no matter whether I was groovin' to Sly and the Family Stone or mellowing out to John Denver, music was always my refuge. Give me a pair of headphones and an 8-track player or a good old fashioned phonograph and some slabs of vinyl and I was in heaven. Rock on, with your bad self.

The first rock concert I ever went to wasn't exactly a rock concert at all but more of a pop concert. It was the Carpenters, Karen and Richard. I went with my sister Patsy and can remember the music being really catchy and melodic, and I remember having a huge crush on Karen. I was about fifteen years old. It was a humble musical experience for one who would soon be rocking to the sounds of Edgar Winter, Foghat, and KISS.

In high school, I was rarely seen without one of my countless homemade rock and roll scrapbooks. It seems all I ever did was play music on my stereo, read about music, or write about music in the school newspaper.

One of my first rock star encounters came at the height of the popularity of Black Oak Arkansas. At the time, they were riding high on the hog with a remake of the old song, "Jim Dandy." My buddy Larry and I had already attended a Black Oak concert in Greenville about two months prior, and before you could say "Hot n' Nasty," BOA was back at the Memorial Auditorium and so were we. Black Oak oozed showmanship with Jim Dandy Mangrum strutting around stage in satin pants and Davy Crocket boots, wielding a washboard like a weapon, and singing in the scruffiest voice in rock and roll at the time. The guitarists drove the audiences into a frenzy by performing their nightly ritual of swinging their guitars high over their heads and smashing them together, then throwing the pieces into the audience. I don't really know why we all felt that was a major cool thing at the time, but we did. That, and Tommy Aldridge's fifteen-minute drum solo. Ah, the staple of the seventies rock concert, the extended drum solo. Well, for what it was worth, it was entertaining.

That night as we made our way out of Memorial Auditorium I looked up to see a double-decker tour bus pulling out. The window was down and Jim Dandy Mangrum was leaning out of the window, smiling and waving. I ran up to the bus and reached up just in time for him to slap my palm with his.

"Good show!" I yelled.

"Thanks!" he replied, as the bus drove off. Not exactly a major encounter, but nonetheless a pivotal point in my Southern rock schooling.

The next time Black Oak hit Greenville they brought along an unusual opening band, a group from New York City called KISS. I had recently seen them perform on ABC TV's "In Concert," and I had read a bit about them in *Rock Scene* magazine. KISS was taking Alice Cooper and the New York Dolls, mixing it with kabuki, sci-fi, and a whole lot of psycho circus. By the time KISS got through with the audience, Black Oak didn't stand a chance. After a handful of songs, Jim Dandy, Ruby Starr, and the band left the stage, never to return. I enjoyed those crazy New Yorkers as much as anyone else that night, but I was really bummed out missing the BOA show.

# 15

## DO YOU KNOW THE WAY TO SAN JOSE?

Some of the happiest memories of my childhood were the trips I took with my sister and my parents across country to visit relatives in southern California. We didn't drive out every year—mostly because my dad's job didn't exactly have us eating like kings—but we did make it out west from Carolina every three to five years.

Those excursions were always a blast. We would leave out on a Sunday morning at 4:30 in the AM and dad would drive up through North Carolina to Interstate 40, straight through the middle of Tennessee, and into Arkansas, where nine times out of ten we would stay over the first night in Little Rock. The whole trip took four good days with dad stopping into the least expensive motel we could find, long about dusk, and returning to the road bright and early the next day. Of all the times we drove out to the west coast, and all of the trials we experienced in order to spend a week with my dad's family, the one thing that sticks out in my mind the most is dad's left arm.

I remember sitting on the sofa at Grandma's house, having just arrived. Dad would try and be in good spirits, but his eyes were blood red from driving too much, and his left arm would be so sunburned from hanging it out the window that it resembled raw meat.

Man, there was a lot of fun in those old trips. My dad had two brothers, Jerry and Johnny, who had families of their own, and three sisters—Marjorie, Dorothy, and Shirley. All the aunts, uncles and cousins were sometimes overwhelming to a kid like me, but they were all great. We had great fun playing together, especially at night as the sun set on the foothills surrounding Fortini Road in San Jose. It was out in the country, and we'd get out on that back road and toss the Frisbee until it got so dark we could no longer see the flying disc. Then there was the time cousin Vic showed up with a glow in the dark disc. The fun went on for hours. When I close my eyes now, I can still smell the cool night air and the apple trees on Fortini Road.

Uncle John turned into a kind of hero to me. I don't know if he knew it, but he was. He was always cool like James Dean or "the Fonz," and in later years he did a lot of work on motorcycles, and he and cousin David De LaVega painted incredible designs on motorcycle tanks. John had a big poster of Easy Rider hanging in his bed room that he later gave me (I had it framed in red a few years back and it hangs in my den to this very day), and I remember him turning me on to Jethro Tull and Joe Cocker's *Mad Dogs and Englishmen* album, as well as Canned Heat, Delaney and Bonnie, and so many others. One summer he was all about the movie *2001: A Space Odyssey* and the soundtrack album. Another summer, I vividly recall sitting in Uncle John's car with him listening to a wild DJ on the radio I had never heard of called Wolfman Jack. A couple of years later that DJ would play host on my escapist Friday night TV favorite *The Midnight Special*.

Another great thing about John was his model car building. John was no casual modeler. He taught me the tricks of award-winning modeling, like how to add extra coats of paint, use thread to create realistic spark plug cables on the engines, and "cherry out" the interior. He got me so hooked on models, I subscribed to *Model Car Science* magazine and built countless models at home with my dad. Everything from cars like the Beatnik Bandit, the Uncertain-T and the Red Barron, to standards like the '55 Chevy and '66 Mustang, along with things like the Batman, Superman, and USS Enterprise model kits. It was one thing dad and I shared that I really value the memory of. Dad always tried to get me to take my time and do it right, but I always insisted on ripping the box open before we even got back home from K-Mart or J. M. Fields. Half the time I would lose some of the small parts that way, fumbling in the darkness in the back seat of the station wagon. Eventually I learned better.

California was always fun. So many cousins. Dennis Hartman was one of the most quiet, but I can now see we had quite a bit in common. He later started playing guitar, and when he came out to visit one summer he and I compared notes. I was still pretty rough and only knew a few chords at the time. Dennis's dad is my uncle Lloyd, and his mom, was my aunt Dorothy, I remember as reminding me of my dad a lot in looks. She had a cute voice, and what an accent! I mostly remember her saying, "Michael, you and Dennis want to go out and throw rocks down the *crick*?" That was her pronunciation of "creek." The creek behind Grandma's house was fun to play in, and it crossed the road in the front of the house, under a small bridge where you could most always find a family of ducks. We used to toss them bread crumbs. I loved Aunt Dorothy, and was deeply saddened in spring 2009 when I heard she had passed away.

The way I got the news was really unusual. I had just joined Facebook online and had heard the news from my cousin Edward Smith, Jerry and Geraldine's youngest boy who was now the father of kids who were much older than I had been the last time I saw him in 1977. Through Eddie I began reconnecting with cousins, Frankie Alves, Buddy Alves, Joey Alves, Aunt Geraldine, and Uncle Jerry and cousins Robert Smith and Diana Smith. We were having a family reunion online. Meanwhile, I had also begun writing my cousin Jack Buchanan from my East Coast family, his sister Beth's son Ryan and daughter Katie, and Jack's son Justin. Wow. Facebook was bringing everyone back together.

Aunt Marjorie was married to Victor De La Vega, a handsome Mexican man whom I remember giving me my very first guitar, an acoustic Spanish guitar with amazingly high action. In retrospect, it may have been set up for slide. All I know is mashing the strings to the frets was virtually impossible and made me believe I just had no chance of learning to play. Still, his giving me that guitar was the seed for me to learn to play, come hell or high water.

Uncle Vic had a huge black velvet painting of a Mexican bandito over the fire place that so impressed me, I would buy one just like it at a pawn shop many years later. The things that shape our lives, huh? Vic and Margie had great kids too. My cousin Victor was a motorbike lover like Uncle John and often painted bike gas tanks. His brother David was a fabulous artist who could draw Captain Hook to beat the band. Deserie I remember being beautiful, as was her younger sister Sabrina. Desi and Beenie. The youngest child was named after Zorro—Alejondro Diego De La Vega. I have nothing but fond memories of all of the cousins. Playing together, having cookouts at Grandpa's. Those were some of the happiest memories of my youth, actually. We had great fun at Grandpa's.

I recall one time having dinner at Vic's house. Aunt Marjorie cooked authentic Mexican food. It took all day long to make real enchiladas in corn husks. Everything was great, and Uncle Vic toyed with me over the chili. I thought of chili as the ground beef and chili powder that we often had on hot dogs. This chili was made of ground chili peppers, including jalapeno, and boy was it hot! Uncle Victor would say, "This is the real chili, Michael. Be careful." I remember sticking a big heaping spoonful into my mouth. Four alarm, baby! Water only made it burn more. All the adults had a good laugh. But what else could they do?

Dad's other sister Aunt Shirley was married to Arthur Alves, and they had a slew of kids as well. My kind and gentle cousin Buddy, his brothers Joey and Frankie, and the quiet, older sister Margaret. Visiting them at home was always fun, and me and the boys shared a love of comic books, *MAD Magazine,* and rock and roll. Cousin Frankie says I was a major influence on him and Joey discovering KISS. Well, I apologize, guys. Just kidding. Aunt Shirley had a heart of gold and always sent us home from California with bags of groceries, pockets full of money for the trip, and lots of hugs and kisses.

Dad's brother Jerry was always kind as well. He always had a hot car, or a "hot rod," as I recall. His wife Geraldine was a beautiful Mexican woman, and they had two boys named Robert and Eddie Smith and a daughter named Diana. I remember vividly watching movies at Jerry's house, especially James Bond's *Live and Let Die.*

The last time I was out in San Jose was way back in 1977. As the years passed, Grandpa passed on, and later my grandmother. Aunt Shirley died, as did her daughter Margret and my Aunt Dorothy. My whole California experience became nothing more than a faded yet wondrous memory.

# 16

## A BAND CALLED COWBOY

*"...a guy named Duane Allman came through while we were living there and he was with Capricorn Records and Phil Walden at that time. We stayed up until early in the morning a couple of times and played together. Duane went back to Macon and I don't know what he said to Phil but we got signed to a contract."*
—Tommy Talton, interview with Buffalo, July 2007

The first time I ever heard the music of Cowboy was when I acquired the aforementioned *Duane Allman Anthology* cassette tape. Their song "Please Be with Me," with Duane Allman on Dobro, blew me away and became one of my all-time favorite songs. I would later purchase each of the Cowboy albums and just loved their harmonies and down-home country rock sound.

In early 2007 a pair of concerts were held to raise money to assist founding member Scott Boyer with major medical bills from recent emergency surgery for an arterial disease. As always, Dick Cooper did a great job promoting and putting the show together, and everything came off like clockwork.

Scott Boyer, Tommy Talton, and Topper Price, along with David Hood on bass, opened the show with Cowboy's best-known song, "Please Be With Me," in an acoustic setting. Boyer was then joined by Mitch McGee for "The Blues Are Flowing Freely" and a few others. All good.

The music just kept coming, including a red-hot set from Microwave Dave and the Nukes and two songs from Canadian soul man Danny Brooks that ran a chill through the audience. Someone commented that Brooks possesses an "ancient" voice. He is definitely one great vocalist.

Dan Penn and Spooner Oldham blew the crowd's collective mind with their piano and guitar duet act, performing many of their huge hits like "I'm Your Puppet," "Dark End of the Street" and the immortal "Cry Like a Baby." Sweet soul music never sounded better.

The Decoys came on next, featuring Boyer, Kelvin Holly (guitarist for Little Richard), Muscle Shoals Swamper David Hood, NC Thurman, Mike Dillion, and guest artists that included legendary FAME drummer Jerry Carrigan and a four-piece horn section. "Shot from the Saddle" rocked, as did the Decoy's entire set.

It was a real treat to see Billy Swan perform again, and he rocked through two of his biggest hits, "Lover Please (Please Come Back)," with Bonnie Bramlett stepping out to sing backup, and the 5-million copy seller "I Can Help."

The Capricorn Rhythm Section—Boyer, Talton, Johnny Sandlin, Bill Stewart, and Paul Hornsby—played an excellent mini-set, and Charlie Daniels bassist Charlie Hayward stood in on a couple of songs as well.

The crowd went wild over a performance by brother and sister Angela and Zak Hacker, recent first- and second-place winners, respectively, of the Nashville Star competition. They each performed some of their songs before closing together with an excellent cover of "Hard to Handle."

Next up was "The Leaning Man of Alabam'," Funky Donnie Fritts, who performed a few of his timeless writings, closing with Bonnie Bramlett and Zak and Angela Hacker singing backup on "Memphis Women and Fried Chicken." It was rocking.

Next came Southern Rock Soul Sister Number One herself, Bonnie Bramlett, singing her heart out on several tunes that included "Atlanta, Georgia," Robert Johnson's "Come On in My Kitchen," her Capricorn hit "It's Time" (originally written and recorded by Cowboy), and a cover of Eddie Hinton's "Cover Me." She, like many of the other acts on this night, received a joyous standing ovation. To close out this magnificent show, Boyer led the band in "Will the Circle Be Unbroken."

Back at the hotel, the rumored after-jam never happened, simply because it was too late. I visited in Tommy Talton's room for a while with him and his wife Patty and her friend, along with Bill Stewart and Charlie Hayward. Later we all made our way to the presidential suite for the VIP after-party, where Tommy Talton's jokes made me laugh so hard I thought I would die. He, Hayward, Stewart, and others continued the discussion of movies we had begun downstairs and had a good time talking to old friends and new ones. By the time I finally crashed back at the room it was 4 AM.

On the way out the next morning at around 11:30, we dropped back by Tommy Talton's room and said goodbye to everyone and thanked them all for a great time. It had been a wonderful show. Now all we had to do was hit the road. We would arrive back home, shaken and stirred but safe, at around 10 PM.

It was only two weeks later on April 18th when I made my way back to 'Bama, this time to Birmingham, for the second benefit show. I had actually driven down to Alabama a day early to meet up with friends, swap road and fish stories, and perhaps snag the stray interview. It was a beautiful drive all the way down, and even my pass through Atlanta was relatively easy. Seems every trip I go on, I am required to strap on my NASCAR helmet and drive through Atlanta.

Tuesday night ended up being a laid-back evening, which was nice because the next day would be a wide-open journey in the fast lane.

Wednesday morning I went over to the Alabama Theatre at about 10 AM. Now, the Alabama Theatre is one of the most breathtaking venues I have ever seen in my entire life. It was built back in 1927 by the Paramount Motion Picture Company and served as the definitive venue for movie premieres in the South. Inside are wraparound balconies, opera boxes, and ornate decor that looks like a cross between the Vatican in Rome and a castle from the Harry Potter movies.

The crew busied themselves getting the stage ready for sound check, and we all hacked around and talked, watched video of Marshall Tucker shot the week before, and drank bottle after bottle of cold water.

Just before sound check, the various artists began to drift in, and before long we were in the midst of a true Southern-fried rehearsal with the Decoys, the Capricorn Rhythm Section, Paul Thorn, Bonnie Bramlett, and many others. Soon we received word that neither Butch Trucks nor Wayne Perkins were going to make it to the show. In losing them, we gained a few unplanned guests, including Allman Brothers Band bassist Oteil Burbridge, himself a Birmingham resident who had just dropped in.

After a few hours of sound check and impromptu jams, it was time for the show.

The Decoys opened and things got to rocking straight away. They rocked the house just like they had two weeks prior. The Capricorn Rhythm Section was next, sounding great as always, churning out "Everybody Needs Love," "Don't Cry Baby," and Cowboy's biggest hit, "Please Be With Me," among others. They were joined by Randall Bramblett on a couple of tunes as well.

It was indeed a pleasure to see Russell Smith and other members of the Amazing Rhythm Aces perform again, and Smith sounded excellent, pulling out the big guns for "The End Is Not in Sight" and "Third Rate Romance."

Zac Hacker rocked the stage, backed by an all-star band. Throughout the night, there was a never-ending cycle of great musicians stepping out to jam, including harp virtuoso Topper Price, former Bama Band member Billy Earhart, guitarist Rick Kurtz, bass legend David Hood, percussionist Mickey Buckins, and another surprise guest, Wet Willie's Donna Hall.

Paul Thorn came onstage and dominated, as always. While I myself have been a huge fan of Paul's for several years now, it still amazes me that many folks don't know who he is. Still, at every show I have attended, I have watched him win over the entire audience, and this short set was no different. Backed by a band that included members of the CRS and the Decoys, and with Scott Boyer III and Kelvin Holly playing lead guitar, Paul ripped into the up-tempo "Rise Up." Scott Boyer and Bonnie Bramlett joined on backing vocals for the whole set.

Rapping between songs and getting his usual laughs, Thorn commanded the attention of the audience, playing "I Have a Good Day Every Now and Then" and following up with a pair of his most popular songs, "Ain't Love Strange" and "Mission Temple Fireworks Stand," the latter of which brought the audience to their feet for a standing ovation. I must add here that it was great to hang out a little with Paul again, along with his road manager/songwriting partner Billy Maddox. Two great cats.

Funky Donnie Fritts repeated the glory of his amazing set from the first benefit two weeks earlier, and once again wrapped it all up with

"Memphis Women and Fried Chicken," bringing to the stage a massive all-star band. I watched as musical history unfolded before my very own, somewhat tired, eyes.

Sweet Bonnie Bramlett took to the stage and burned white hot. She is the best, hands down. One of this writer's all-time favorite singers. The lady had more soul than Don Cornelius at an Aretha Franklin concert. Have mercy! Can I get an "Amen?" Love you, Bonnie.

Next up was truly the man of the hour. A true Southern rock icon and another of God's near-perfect vocalists, Gregg Allman. Scott Boyer introduced him as an "old friend," and Gregg stepped out onto the stage looking happy and healthy. I believe in my heart of hearts that he sounds even better now than he did back in the day. Gregg picked up an acoustic guitar and, backed by Johnny Sandlin, Tommy Talton, and the whole Capricorn Rhythm Section, blew everyone's mind with some ultra-rare performances, beginning with a breathtaking rendition of "All My Friends," a song written by Boyer. After a few minutes of tuning problems Gregg hit the familiar lick to open "Midnight Rider," and the crowd was screaming. Deviating from the set list, Gregg was ready to have some real fun. With a coy smile on his face, he strapped Kelvin Holly's Telecaster on, turned to the horn section, and asked, "Do you guys know 'I Can't Turn You Loose?'" In mere moments, the band kicked into the Otis Redding classic and Gregg was belting out the vocals and having a great time doing it. It was a magic moment. Backstage where I stood mere feet away from Allman, everyone was dancing. It was amazing.

Gregg took over the B-3 duties previously handled by Paul Hornsby and played a magnificent version of the song he once told me in an interview was his favorite song that he'd written, "Queen of Hearts." Boyer thanked everyone for coming, and it was all over. Another page in Southern rock and soul history had been written, to be sure.

In April 2009, Tommy Talton and his band were having a CD release party at the Melting Point in Athens, Georgia, and it was sure to be a stone-cold blast as Talton's gigs always are. They were celebrating the release of his second album *Live Notes from Athens*. Add to this the buzz surrounding his recent appearance at the Beacon Theatre in New York standing in as a guest of the Allman Brothers Band.

A band called Lingo opened the show, and I didn't really know just what to expect. I figured they must be pretty doggone good, being that John Keane (of R.E.M. and Widespread Panic fame) produced Lingo's record and Randall Bramblett appeared on it several times. The four guys put on an amazing show that just blew me away. Tight, melodic, catchy, original tunes that will stand the test of time. At one point they invited Tony G. of Talton's band up for a rousing take on the Meters' "Cissy Strutt." It was a groove. Their whole set was filled with youthful energy combined with the wisdom and musical ability of four "old souls." Oh, and they did a very cool, almost reggae version of Johnny Cash's "Ring of Fire" that was just great.

It was time for the main attraction. Like they used to say when they introduced James Brown, "It's star time, ladies and gentlemen!" The Tommy Talton Band took the stage, and rather than come out "guns a blazin'" Tommy strapped on an acoustic guitar to open with one of my favorite Talton compositions, the beautiful "Broken Pieces." He really surprised us all by inserting a verse of Sam Cooke's "You Send Me" into the middle of the tune.

Next came "Sit Here in the Sun," and boy howdy did it sound great. Brandon Peeples was on bass, Tony Giodano was on keyboards, and, as a special treat, Garrison Bert Elliott was on the sax for this gig. Tommy had just changed drummers, and Scott Phillips was behind the kit for his first gig with Talton. I cannot say enough about how great a job Scott did, especially on the dynamics and jams that came later. Awesome.

And the hits just kept on coming. Many of the songs that were played are on Tommy's CD *Live Notes from Athens*, recorded the year before at this very venue.

The band played great songs like the instrumental "My Baby Don't Shave," the excellent "Getaway Cars," and some eclectic and just plain fun covers like Dylan's "Leopard Skin Pill-Box Hat," Buffalo Springfield's "For What it's Worth," and one I had not heard Tommy perform before, the most excellent Van Morrison tune "Into the Mystic."

Speaking of Morrison, Talton also played his own "Color My Sleep," another favorite of this writer, with its Van Morrisonish-sounding melody.

Another great surprise was hearing "Hard Drivin' Man," a song cowritten by Tommy with John D. Wyker and Tommy Coleman that I actually recorded a version of on my *Something Heavy* album. Tommy rocked it, baby.

Being an old school Cowboy fan, I was of course very pleased to once again hear the band perform "River to the Sea" and "Time Will Take Us."

Talton led the band into slide guitar rockers and ethereal space jams, with every band member adding their own color swatch to the canvas. In the end, it was pure, unencumbered art.

Speaking of amazing space jams, the show closed with a cover of Allen Toussaint's "On Your Way Down." It was an amazing show.

After the show we all hung out and chatted, posed for grip-and-grin photos, and then said our goodnights. I believe I hit that comfortable bed at about 2:30 A.M. The next morning we met with Tommy and Patty and talked a bit and said our goodbyes. I sure love those kids. I feel very blessed to now be friends with the coleader of one of my favorite bands, Cowboy.

In November 2007, I went into the studio with Cowboy for the recording of their all-new reunion album, their first in thirty-six years. The whole session was just amazing. One for the books.

Sitting in Duck Tape Studio in Decatur, Alabama, along with the entire original lineup of Cowboy and their original producer Johnny Sandlin some thirty-five years after the recording of their seminal second album *5'll Getcha Ten*, it became apparent very quickly that these guys have still got it. It was almost like those thirty-five years were a simple blink of the eye and they were simply picking up where they left off. All six of these musicians were locked and loaded, ready to create a brand new Cowboy record. Total professionalism prevailed, and why wouldn't it? Cowboy was one of Capricorn Records' charter bands, and this was not their first rodeo.

Tommy Talton was there, along with partner in crime Scott Boyer, keyboard man Bill Pillmore, currently of Asheville, NC; drummer Tom Wynn (who also played with Talton in the legendary Florida band We the People), bassist George Clark, both of Winter Park, Florida; and guitarist Pete Kowalke, who now resides in Oregon. Johnny "The Duck" Sandlin was there, as was his bright young engineer Jeremy Stephens.

The atmosphere in the studio was nothing short of joyous. Some of these guys hadn't seen one another in thirty-five years, and they were having a blast. The guys were all set up in this open studio with the mixing console smack dab in the middle of the room. Johnny's Duck Tape Studio is like no other I have seen before, more like a living room with soundproofing on the walls. Of course there is a drum booth and a vocal booth, necessary elements for separating the mix. Amps are set up in a kitchen area off the main room. It's all Sandlin's style. He's one of a kind. Unique. Just have a look at the gold and platinum records that line the walls and you get a clear picture of just how huge Sandlin's legacy really is. There are Allman Brothers albums like *Brothers and Sisters*, *The Duane Allman Anthology*, and the Gregg Allman and Cher epic *Two the Hard Way*. Widespread Panic, Col. Bruce Hampton and the Aquarium Rescue Unit, Bonnie Bramlett. So many great records, including the band of the hour, Cowboy.

I sat for a while watching Sandlin as he listened to the band run through a Talton song, his eyes closed in concentration. It's like witnessing a moment few journalists ever get to share. The intimate moment of connection between the producer and the musicians, bonded by the sheer power of a good song.

On day two we all reconvened at Duck Tape around noon, and the guys got right down to business. Boyer contributed a beautiful song called "Maybe Miracles," and the original plan was for George to play acoustic bass on the track. Unfortunately, that plan was not written in the stars, as there were internal wiring problems with the pickup jack, but he did end up playing one of the single coolest bass guitars I have ever seen. A classic bass from Sandlin's collection. Bill Pillmore laid down some smooth pedal steel to the song, which only adds to its ethereal beauty.

Other tunes the guys recorded include "Positive Flow," written by Pete, an up-tempo number that reminded me of the Flying Burrito Brothers, if Toy Caldwell and Dickey Betts were sitting in. Bill turned in a fine tune called "I'm in a Mood," a song reminiscent in some ways of Cream and underscored by a funky wah-wah guitar pedal. And they recorded a Talton tune called "Comfort Zone," another good one that features an infectious repeating guitar riff that sticks in your head and gets you to humming. "Too Many Choices" is great as well, lyrically reminiscent of Eddie Hinton.

On Sunday morning I met George Clark at the continental breakfast and talked a little about the project.

"I thought it would be great to get back together again after all this time," said Clark. "It has really been fun."

Clark and I spoke about the fact that most bands have a central leader—the Allmans had Duane; Marshall Tucker had Tommy Caldwell; Skynyrd had Ronnie Van Zant.

"I think both Scott and Tommy were the leaders in this band," said George with a smile.

I told him about the first time I ever heard Cowboy, and that it was their appearance on the Duane Allman *Anthology*, "Please Be with Me," which became one of my all-time favorite songs.

"It was really quite simple the way that one came together," said Clark. "They asked me to play standup bass on it, and Duane Allman knocked it out in two takes. He was just great."

We were soon joined by Tom Wynn and talked even further about all of the great music Cowboy has created over the years, as well as their new material.

Back at the studio at noon the guys got down to work on "Comfort Zone," adding some simply smoking lead work from Pete. In what seemed almost like a scene from a movie, everyone got really quiet, then Johnny Sandlin raised a hand to the sky and said, "Let's take it from the top."

Next came the adding of background vocals to the song "Positive Flow." Scott, Tommy, George, Bill, and Pete gathered around a single microphone to work up the harmonies. After a few run-throughs, we were all just blown away by the sheer magic of the vocals, prompting Sandlin to utter the words, "Beautiful. Just beautiful."

Bill smiled broadly and said what I feel summed up the entire session. "Wow. It sounds like Cowboy."

On Monday morning we all gathered downstairs for coffee and our final get-together. We sat and talked for about an hour before everyone had to leave for their individual drives back home. Home was seven hours and one time zone change away for me, but at least I didn't have the twelve-hour trek to Florida that faced Tom and George. This had been one for the books as far as I was concerned. A dream come true. Hanging out in the studio with one of my all-time favorite bands and getting to know them and find that they are all just great guys.

As much fun as the whole session has been, this was only part one. Talton and Boyer and Sandlin would be recording a whole other "side" for the album in January, with former Cowboy players Bill Stewart and Randall Bramblett and other outstanding players like Chuck Leavell and David Hood. Unfortunately, the powers that be decided to shelve the project. Then, sadly, bassist George Clark died in October 2008, making a full-on reunion of the original Cowboy no longer possible. Still, it had been a great experience getting to know the band that was one of my favorites as far back at tenth grade.

In fall 2010, Cowboy again reunited. This version was not the band from the first two albums, but everyone in this band was a former Cowboy. Boyer, Talton, drummer Bill Stewart, bassist Stan Robertson, Randall Bramblett on keys and sax, and Bill Pilmore on pedal steel. They returned to Macon, Georgia, on December 17 to play a very special show at Cox Capital Theatre. That concert, which features seventeen of their best tunes as well as a cameo appearance by Bonnie Bramlett, was immortalized on an album called *Boyer & Talton: Cowboy Reunion 2010* by Hittin' the Note Records. It became clear very quickly that this group was one Cowboy that wasn't quite ready to retire its spurs just yet. And that, my friends, makes me a happy camper.

# 17

## HIGH SCHOOL CONFIDENTIAL

Back in 1996, I was driving down a two-lane blacktop through the mountains near Table Rock, South Carolina, with the window down, listening to some Allman Brothers tunes on my newly acquired Walkman. See, my truck, a 1993 Toyota, was a stripped-down model. One that was more in my price range at the time of purchase. No rear bumper and no options—unless you included the cup holder that slid out from under the dash. My stepson Ben always kidded me about that. The most obvious of the missing amenities was a tape deck, or a CD player, or a radio—something to play some music on as I rolled along the highways and bi-ways of this great land of ours. That's why I purchased myself a Sony Walkman at the local Wal-Mart. It was great, but I still wanted a tape deck.

The air smelled especially nice on this night. Have you ever noticed how sometimes the air can just plain smell good? Mama Sorrells used to say she could smell rain. I believed her, too, because every time she'd say it, it would come. Buckets of rain.

It was cool. October night air. God's special time of year. Summer has lots of fans, as does the snowy winter, and there are gazillions of springtime lovers, but as for me, it has always been the fall that has gotten me going. The colors of the trees, the smell and pure cleanness of the air, heading into the holiday stretch.

When you're out on the road near sunset, on long stretches of open road, alone, your mind can really begin to paint pictures. I started thinking, and the pictures began to form. I just freed my mind and let it wander. High school. Yes, high school. I had graduated so many years earlier. Back in 1976. Now it's been over thirty-plus years since I walked the halls of Byrnes High. In a way it seems like a lifetime ago, and in other ways it seems like yesterday. I can almost see my classmates in Ms. Deweese's art class (Rebecca was my first encounter with a feminist. She insisted her name be preluded by the more politically correct *Ms.*). My classmates—pal Tony Pearson; Judy Lawhon, the girl I "double-dated" along with Tony and Kim Jones to the Piedmont Interstate Fair the night I got deathly sick from a lethal combination of fast rides and fast food; and Tammy Rhodes, a sweet little girl with hair, and a heart, of gold. The four of us had the front table, closest to the teacher. We were kind of the teacher's pets I suppose. That class was a lot of fun. It definitely ranks among the best memories of those early- to mid-seventies years.

Tony and I had a lot of fun in the radio club and in the Junior Achievement radio company. That was my first real taste of being in the public eye, and I ate it up. I guess that's why, after about nine weeks, the twelve-member radio club had dwindled down to just two—me and Tony. We were going to take over the radio world. In fact, we used to make cassette tapes for each other of fabricated radio shows, playing records, doing commercials, and just plain talking. It was great fun. That eventually bled over into making our own wacky comedy tapes, which at times bordered on tasteless. After all, we were into *Star Trek*, KISS, Richard Pryor, *National Lampoon* magazine and Cheech & Chong, to name just a few things.

Tony joined me and another good friend in school, Bill Hudson, to do some comedy in the Byrnes High talent show one year. We did a take on Chucky Margolis, a skit that at the time was a popular segment on the Hudson Brothers comedy hour. We also did a lampoon version of the old standard, "It Had to Be You." We were quite a hit. That show was a landmark event. That was the first time I ever heard Doug Hooper play guitar. He had recruited a bass player and a drummer and hit the BHS stage with the Jimi Hendrix version of Bob Dylan's "All Along the Watchtower."

In the years that followed, Doug became a good friend. He often invited me over to his house, and he'd come home from working in the Startex Mill, greasy from head to toe, go wash up, pull out one of his guitars, and play. My sister had given me a Conrad bass guitar for Christmas, and Doug was extremely patient in trying to show me how to play songs by Deep Purple, Black Sabbath, KISS, and other rock and roll bands I was into at the time. I credit Hooper with turning me on to Frank Zappa, Mountain, Tucky Buzzard, Camel, Atomic Rooster, Bloodrock, and Blackmore's Rainbow, among others.

We got into a few serious grooves there once in a while. He could really play. In fact, Hooper was one of the reasons I tried so hard to play the guitar. A combination of his influence and the confidence-boosting of another pal, Stuart Swanlund, later on in the eighties drove me to learn to play.

I can remember being so envious of Donnie Powell, Doug Hooper, and their band. It was 1975, and I was living in Wellford, just off of Highway 129. There was a junk car lot and garage between my house and Donnie and Tim Powell's place. Their dad owned the garage. I can remember being overwhelmed by the machine John Powell brought in one day to crush the used cars. Flattened them like pancakes. Hours of entertainment.

I don't remember how their band got together, I just know they were letting Judy Lawhon sing with them, and at the time I had a crush the size of Texas on her. (I recently learned that Judy passed away a few years back from cancer. So sad. She was a sweetheart, as was her mother. We had spent some time over at her house and her mom and I got along famously.) You know, I don't think I ever heard that girl sing. Not once. But I did hear the band. Almost every afternoon, they were rocking. Playing Peter Frampton's "Show Me the Way" and "Do You Feel Like We Do," and "Rock and Roll All Night" by KISS, among others. I wanted to play too, but there was a small problem. I didn't know how.

Doug had been real patient with me, trying to teach me to play the bass guitar, and I had learned a little. My rocking was, for the most part, all in my mind as I stood in front of a full-length mirror in my bedroom pretending to be everyone from Elvis to Gene Simmons to Leon Wilkeson.

I really don't know if their band ever ended up gigging, but I certainly was jealous. Hey, I was really envious of the guitar players at school too.

There were several other high school musicians who caught my eye as well. This guy named Travis Harvey played the Bellamy Brothers' "Let Your Love Flow" at one of the talent roundups and sounded great, and a guy named Randy who played some guitar for the "Mr. Rebel" contest sticks in my mind. I remember coming up to Randy and asking about playing guitar and he just blew me off with a lot of superior attitude. I'll never forget that, even after all these years.

All of these musical experiences coupled with some early jams with old friends Jeff Corn and Alphonzo Pea, and our "Soul Dog Review" helped to mold my early guitar style. We played "Green Onions" and "Get Ready" by Rare Earth. That was about it, but we had fun. Ain't that what it's all about? Sadly, Alphonzo was killed while in high school and Jeff passed away a few years ago from lung cancer. They were both good guys.

My jams with Doug Hooper over at his house are definitely some great memories, not to mention a major influence. I'll never forget how amazed I was at the sound he got out of his guitar and that big ol' Road amp. One thing he and I had in common—we were never too tired to rock and roll. Amen.

As I get older many of the people and experiences from my days at Byrnes High have faded, but I remember my neighbors across the road at that time, the Mason's, very well. Great folks. They lost their son Dewayne in an auto wreck during my high school years. The oldest daughter Janice was very sweet, and I remember falling for her one school year. I am not really sure she ever even knew. I remember all of us standing out in the cold at the road to catch the school bus and staring at her. Hey, I was a kid. But the whole family were just good people. Happy memories of countless kickball games in my front yard. And I can remember Janice's younger sister Connie as being very sweet also.

I didn't have a whole lot of genuine friends during high school, but the ones I did have were pretty special to me. People like "the California Kid" Lisa Sanders and a few others. We kind of hung together behind the school in the mornings and on breaks, smoking things and drinking things. Lisa was another one of my first major crushes, but we were such good friends I never really let on as to how I felt about her. She encouraged me to play guitar and sing and write. Something about her being from California gave her this hippie vibe that I just loved. I wrote one of my very first songs about Lisa. She was one of the most genuine, kind souls I ever met.

# 18

# BILL AND THE WEASEL

Like I said earlier, I met Bill Hudson while I was in high school, and we became friends quickly. We shared a lot of interests including science fiction, especially *Star Trek*, music, books, comics, and movies. I must have gone to hundreds of movies with ol' Bill. We'd sometimes sit through a movie two times if it was good. Other times we'd sneak from one theater in the Bijou to another, hitting two, sometimes three movies on a Saturday.

Bill read all the time. I do now, but back then I didn't. Bill always had a paperback in his pocket. *Always*. The first time I met Bill, he was wearing a vest covered in various pin-back buttons bearing social and political commentary. He was also wearing sandals with rainbow-colored toe-socks. I remember he always retreaded his own sandals with tire rubber. Pretty cool.

He had a great family. I didn't know his dad too well (except that he had a cool old Cadillac convertible that Bill and I once took cruising in downtown Greenville, and he had boxes upon boxes of Playboy magazines in the garage), but his mom was something else. She was a ball-buster. I heard Bill tell stories, like the time a flasher in Greer opened up his trench coat and exposed himself to her. Mrs. Hudson pointed at his privates and started laughing out loud. If that doesn't break a flasher, nothing will.

When Meat Loaf's *Bat Out of Hell* album came out, Bill's mom absolutely loved it. She liked a lot of our music, from Alice Cooper's *Goes to Hell* album to the four KISS solo records. Like I said, Mrs. H. was one hip mama.

Bill had an older sister I never got to know, but I knew his younger sister Beverly, and at one time Tony Pearson and I both had a crush on her at the same time. Not that either of us had a chance with her. Bev was a sweet girl, with a good heart. Thanks to Facebook, I reconnected with her and her brother Barry as well in 2009, and, yes, Beverly is as sweet and kind as ever. Barry too.

Barry was a genuinely nice kid. We had a lot of fun with Barry. I remember him going with Bill and me to a *Star Trek* convention once. We had a ball. We had lots of fun with Barry and no doubt warped the kid's mind somewhat.

I don't recall exactly how we came to know Rebecca Ross Hoffman, but it was through her that we became involved in the "fandom" universe. We used to go and hang out at her house in Greer almost every weekend. Her husband Joe was often there, as were her boys Ted and Jamie.

She created her own "fanzine" called *Southern Star* and published it out of her home in the days before home computers and laser printers. She typed the pages, designed the layout, and printed them up. Bill and I both ended up drawing cartoons for her 'zine as well as others we discovered because of her. Becky introduced us to a lot of interesting folks like Mac "the Klingon" Carson and a sweet young lady named Faith whom he would eventually marry. Speaking of marriage, Becky's friend Cindy Sirmons would end up married to Bill. We all had a blast attending Trek conventions and local fan club meetings. I credit Becky with turning me on to a lot of the fandom stuff. A few years ago she passed away. She still lives in our hearts. A good-hearted Vulcan. Loads of happy memories.

For a couple of years there, it must have been around 1978 or '79—I was going to Mid-Atlantic Championship Wrestling at Greenville Memorial Auditorium almost every single Monday night. Bell time, 8:15. Most of the time, it was myself and my buddy Eric "the Weasel" Wenzel, now a retired twenty-five-year Navy man I am proud to call my friend. There were a lot of times when we would meet up with some other pals, and on rare occasions we would drag a couple of other guys along to witness the mayhem inside "the squared circle."

Weasel was a died-in-the-wool fan of "the Nature Boy," the one and only Ric Flair, and I can't begin to count the number of "life and death" matches we witnessed featuring Flair at the Brown Box. I found the whole thing quite entertaining, and throughout the years I would find myself "pulling for" such diverse athletes as Flair, Ox Baker, Blackjack Mulligan, Andre the Giant, Ernie Ladd, Ricky Steamboat, Jay Youngblood, and others.

Of course, my introduction to wrestling had come about several years earlier while watching my favorites on television—folks like Argentina Apollo and Haystacks Calhoon, so when the opportunity presented itself for me to attend some real—and I use that term loosely— wrestling, that is "rasslin'" matches, I jumped on it like Superfly Jimmy Snuka off the corner ropes. Heck, I even attended the training camp in Charlotte with high hopes and aspirations of becoming the next wrestling superstar, but once I found out how easily you can get hurt in a "fake" sport I was out of there. I just liked the acting element of it all anyway, and I would later find an easier place to express that particular skill.

Eric and I always looked for parking places off of the main drag in an effort to avoid paying extra for parking. Heck, tickets were a whopping $5.50, and we were lucky to come up with that much. Those matches were great fun, to be sure. I never could figure out just why there was always so much blood flowing in the ring at the auditorium, but when the same guys did the same things on TV, there was never any blood. I would find out later, as I hung out with some wrestlers and even considered a career in the theatrical sport myself, that the guys built up scar tissue on the forehead by scraping it repeatedly with a piece of blade. Then, when the time was ripe for a blood-letting, they would simply slide a finger nail or some other such object across the tissue and the blood would flow freely. And then there were the fake blood capsules that also helped create the effect.

Weasel was also into comics, and I will never forget his "mission" to own a copy of Marvel Comics' *Fantastic Four* issue number one, which he manifested for himself, and most likely still owns. Weasel would accompany Bill and me to movies a lot of times or to the bookstores and record stores. He was a nervous kid back then with his own share of family weirdness, which he eventually overcame. Like I said before, he turned out a great, happily married man with a lot of skills he learned in the Navy. I remember when he first told us he had enlisted I thought he'd last about a week. Shows what I know. You go Weasel. Nowadays

Eric is a member of the Arizona Paranormal Investigation Society in Phoenix. If you knew the Weasel, it would make perfect sense.

I was just thinking about how crazy me and Weasel got sometimes. We were both into KISS and had this ongoing joke about how much I looked like Gene Simmons and he looked like Ace Frehley. Of course, neither of us looked anything at all like Gene or Ace, but we would ride up beside one another while driving through downtown Greenville on a Friday night, and I'd look over and he'd be covering the bottom half of his face with one hand like the KISS guys did before they quit the whole "never seen without makeup" scheme. I would jump and react as if I'd seen Ace. Then I would do the same. Silly, but fun at the time. Driving through Greenville we'd pass the Cline Company (Simmons's real name was Kline) and Gene's Restaurant and blow our horns. Same with the Ace Animal Hospital. Weasel was a lot of fun.

As for Bill, we enjoyed so many great times. Bill is one of the best friends I ever had. I learned a lot from Bill. He was always just a little ahead of his time. Like Howard the Duck, he was "trapped in a world he never made."

Tragedy struck in October 2010. Barry Hudson called to tell me that Bill had suffered a massive stroke. He was in the hospital for a day, but in the end he passed away. I was devastated. I went to the beautiful memorial service and had some time with his family and his wife Cindy, and later that day I spoke with the Weasel at length from his home in Arizona. Talk about the end of an era. I will never forget Bill.

# 19

# KELLY MICHELLE:
## ROCK-AND-ROLL BABY

They say we often lose someone in our life just before someone else comes in. Such was the case in December 1980, when my Mama Sorrells passed away just before my sister Patsy gave birth on December 26 to Kelly Michelle Winter, my niece.

I have nothing but happy memories of my niece as a child, although she had to walk through the fire on her way to becoming the brilliant young woman she would grow into. I have great memories of turning her into my personal photographic model. At the age of one, I was putting new wave wraparound sunglasses on the child, different hats, taking pictures of my little rock baby. Kelly was so sweet, she never cried when I was playing with her. I always had music playing, and she would just laugh and dance around. Well, as much as a one year old dances around.

My parents, my sister, and Kelly used to go to K-Mart a good bit and I remember the tiny child seeing the big store logo towering in the air and screaming "Owie-owie-owie!" It was her Pavlovian training. She knew she was going to get to ride the quarter pony ride outside the front of the store and started getting really excited when she knew we were approaching K-Mart.

Throughout the years I had lots of fun with Kelly, and by the time she was in her early teens she had become as big a music fanatic as me. I decided to take her to Charlotte to the Lollapalooza festival. Man it was fun. Alternative bands like Smashing Pumpkins, Green Day, L7, and Nick Cave and classic bands like Parliament Funkadelic rocked the house. It was about a gazillion degrees, but they had these outdoor showers you could stroll into to cool off. It was a crazy rock and roll day and a truly happy memory.

Throughout school, Kelly never got lower than an A on her report card. Patsy must still have closets filled with accomplishment certificates and awards Kelly won. Pretty smart kid. Smart, yes, but she still carved her "boyfriend" Kurt Cobain's name into her arm with a safety pin. Hey, it was true love. What do you expect?

Kelly went on to college and ended up in Florida where she worked at a major newspaper before returning to college recently. She still loves music and even drives from South Florida all the way to middle-Tennessee for the Bonnaroo Festival each June. I'd like to think that I had something to do with influencing her musical tastes over the years, playing her things like the Allman Brothers Band, David Bowie, Kate Bush, and, yes, even KISS.

# 20

# ROCK AND ROLL AS THEATER

It's no secret that during the early 1970s, my love for Southern rock shared space in my psyche with my love or theatrical rock and roll. Bands like Alice Cooper, David Bowie, and perhaps more than any of those, KISS.

I've given this a lot of thought over the years, and while all of these bands did turn out some pretty rocking music, I was more about the stage shows and the image associated with them. For sheer musical enjoyment I would play *At Fillmore East* or *Layla and Other Love Songs*. When I wanted to escape reality, which was pretty darn often, I would go to see Alice Cooper or KISS, or read about them in rock magazines. Still, I owned every album pressed by all three of these bands. Go figure.

Of all of the trio, it was KISS that I became addicted to. I still watch old videos of their shows and have followed the solo careers of all four original members, the amazing reunion tour in the mid-1990s, and watched as Gene Simmons proved to the world that he can make a buck off of anything and everything, including toilet paper, condoms, and caskets. No matter what you think of Simmons, it is undeniable that the man knows how to make money—millions.

The very first time I ever heard of KISS, I was reading the "new bands" section of *Rock Scene Magazine*. This was in 1973, during a time when I devoured rock and roll magazines like breakfast cereal. While I was heavily into *Creem* magazine, *Circus*, and the more intellectual *Crawdaddy* and *Rolling Stone*, I also loved *Rock Scene*, a decidedly more cheaply made product based out of New York that seemed to focus the lion's share of its attention on the music coming out of the City. I credit *Rock Scene* with teaching me about bands like Wayne County and the Electric Chairs, the Ramones, the New York Dolls, and, yes, KISS.

That first visual image of four guys dressed in all black leather, wearing something akin to kabuki-style face paint, burned its way into my brain, where it remains some thirty-five years later.

That same weekend, I tuned my mom and dad's black-and-white RCA television to ABC-TV, one of the only three choices available back then, for a show called *In Concert*. I had made it a ritual to watch *In Concert* and then quickly switch over to NBC for Burt Sugarman's *Midnight Special*.

On this particular Friday evening, I was introduced to the madness of KISS, live in concert for the very first time. Truth be told, I cannot for the life of me remember who else was on the show that night. All I remember is the four songs KISS played and mishearing the lyrics to "Black Diamond." I thought they were singing a song about the band Black Sabbath. No, really, I did.

The four greasepainted rockers were tearing up the stage, blowing fire, jumping all over, setting off fire lights and sirens, releasing confetti from the ceiling into the audience, and making a fan out of one future journalist and musician in South Carolina.

I had never seen anything like this. Sure, I was pretty blown away by David Bowie's "1980 Floor Show" the year before on *Midnight Special*, and certainly by Alice Cooper's appearance on *In Concert* that same year, a show that was banned in many small towns around the country. I still don't know how Wellford, SC, managed to avoid that Alice blackout.

Still, KISS combined everything my young escapist mind loved about Bowie, Alice, the Dolls, and all the others, then kicked it up several notches. I remember that night vividly. I also remember choosing my "favorite" band member that night. Hands down, it was the man named Gene Simmons. I liked all four musicians and their alter egos, but it was Simmons who combined elements of Hammer Horror films, comic books, and all things shocking into one character, who just happened to also be a hell of a bass player.

My old friend Larry Whitfield was as into music as I was. One day we were at an 8-track store in Anderson, SC, where they sold what amounted to bootleg tapes off all the new albums coming out. I bought the debut KISS album on 8-track, and we wore that thing out. Riding around on weekend nights in Larry's Chevelle Malibu, we blasted "Strutter" and "Firehouse" as loud as we could. Of course, it had to be loud to drown out Larry's Thrush muffler.

I saw KISS in concert a total of eighteen times. The one show that stands out most was 1976, when they came to Greenville Memorial Auditorium. Bill Hudson and I went. I was a senior in high school and a die-hard fan. The stage was amazing. Peter Criss, the drummer, had huge cat statues on either side of his drum kit with glowing red eyes, and the stage was set like a cross between some off Broadway show and the world's biggest rock and roll band. Well, let's face it, at that time it was a little of both.

It was one year earlier when Larry and I had gone to see KISS with openers Styx and Mott the Hoople in Asheville, NC. During the opening band's set, I made my way around to the side of the stage, where I found a group of fans hanging out in front of a makeshift fence. One of the guys said that the band was behind the door in front of us, putting on makeup. About this time, a blonde girl in her twenties smiled at me and said "hi," and I asked if the guys were coming out to say hello to us. She disappeared and just a few minutes later emerged from behind the door with the tallest, thinnest dude I had ever seen. It was obvious he was a member of KISS, but since none of us had seen them without their kabuki-like greasepaint, we didn't know for sure. That is, until he stuck out his infamous tongue and nearly incited a riot then and there. Long story short, we met all four members briefly before they ducked back in to the dressing room to get into costume and makeup. All I remember is that they were all very kind, signing a few autographs and thanking us for coming to the show, and that Gene Simmons commented on my T-shirt. I was wearing a Marshall Tucker Band shirt I had purchased in Myrtle Beach, and Gene pointed to it and said, "Good band."

Years later after I became a journalist, I had the opportunity to meet and interview both Gene Simmons and Peter Criss. I was able to thank both of them for all the years of fun I had enjoyed because of their little ol' rock and roll band.

Nowadays, as I watch the family man that Simmons has become on his reality TV show, *Gene Simmons' Family Jewels,* it's kind of hard to believe they have been doing what they do for over thirty-five years. Time flies when you're blowing fire and spitting fake blood!

# 21

# NEW FRIENDS—TONY, LEON, PAM AND CANDY

I met Tony Brown and his friend Frank Looper at *The Rocky Horror Picture Show* when it was playing in Greenville at Bell Tower Cinemas. It must have been the late seventies. Bill Hudson and I became fast friends with Tony.

Bill and I had been going to *Rocky Horror* every weekend. As an interesting side note, I would find out years later that a certain young girl named Jill McLane worked the ticket booth there at Tower Cinemas for RHPS at that time. That girl would become my wife in 1996. We must have crossed paths dozens of times at that movie theater. I'm sure she thought we were all freaks. Well, we were. And proud of it.

The first time I laid eyes on Tony Brown, he was wearing a silver sparkle halter top and full Frank N. Furter makeup. His friend Frank was wearing a T-shirt that read "I Am Insane." Of course, we all hit it off immediately.

In the months to come we would meet Tony's friend Leon Hayes and their friends Candy Wiggins and Pamela Jean Wilhite.

Among the fond memories of hanging out with this group are the many parties over at another friend Melanie Barnett's apartment in Greer. Melanie was also a friend of our official *Star Trek* fan leader Becky Hoffman and a huge fan of Steve Martin, who at the time had not done a movie yet but was a popular standup comic. Melanie was a beauty and another kind soul.

Our small circle of friends had a lot of fun at times, and at others, well, it wasn't as much fun. One of the major problems was my falling in love with Pamela, a California beauty who played guitar and wrote songs and sang. We hit it off immediately, and somewhere along the line got closer than we should have and started a ritual of hiding from the rest of the group and French kissing and making out. Hey, no wonder I fell for her, huh? I'll never forget the first kiss. It was in the parking lot of the apartment complex where Melanie lived. It was dark and cold outside and Pam asked me to give her a hug. Then she said, "Are you a good kisser?" I was kind of taken aback. "Well, I don't really know," I said. She leaned in and kissed me, and then French kissed me again. She pulled back and smiled, "Very nice." I drove back home to Spartanburg with my heart pounding. On the way home it began to snow, and I felt like I had died and gone to heaven.

The only problem with my falling in love with Pamela Jean was that she was already betrothed to someone. Candy. Yep, they were a couple, and at the time I was too naive to see it. I believe when Candy caught on to our mutual attraction to each other she got very upset and things really began to crumble at the foundations. It was a strange situation to be in, for sure. But all's well that ends well, I suppose, and with time I have grown to recall only the happy memories, like helping Pam get a multitrack reel-to-reel recorder and listening to the demos she recorded on it. The girl had a lot of musical talent, and we could talk about music for hours on end. She was a good songwriter and had a great singing voice.

One thing I remember is Pam always talking about me getting an apartment closer to where she lived in Greenville. She said we could sit up all night and play records. It was a sweet idea for sure. Being a singer-songwriter, she wanted me to manage her career and be her "Brian Epstein."

She'd drive me around in her VW Beetle and we'd listen to tapes. Oddly enough, I can still recall her favorite songs—"Touch Me" by the Doors, "Eight Miles High" by the Byrds, and her favorite of all, "Life on Mars" by David Bowie. Oh, and one other thing. Gasoline was 45 cents per gallon back then. I always pumped her gas. That's as much as I want to say about that time of my life. This was one of those spiritual connections that I may never understand. I still get strange emotional feelings when I dwell on Pamela.

# 22

## THE SILVER TRAVIS BAND

I was working at Community Cash grocery store in the late 1970s when I first met my friend Tim Shook. Tim's a kind of short fellow with dark skin and a kind of Middle Eastern look about him. But don't judge a book by its cover. Tim is 100-percent redneck white boy.

We used to have some good times, me and Tim. Like the parties he'd sometimes have at his mobile home just off of Reidville Road Circle (which is no longer a circle) in Spartanburg. Tim would invite all his friends over, mix up PJ in the bath tub, and we'd all get plastered and listen to LPs on his stereo. Ah, to be young and fearless again.

Sometimes, when I'd be visiting Tim, his brother Mark would come around. Mark was a nice guy who worked on big rigs, big transfer trucks, for a living. I distinctly remember one Saturday in 1979 when I was over. Tim had purchased an off-brand copy of a Gibson Explorer guitar. He had aspirations of learning to play but never really had time to learn. Tim was always working at the Spartanburg General Hospital. That day, Tim was having fun getting me to play around on the guitar through his stereo (don't ask). Now, mind you, I really had not yet learned to play. I knew a few power chords and could noodle around on lead, but it was all just improvised. I wouldn't get serious about guitar until 1982. Still, Mark and Tim and I were rocking out to beat the band. Boys and their toys. I remember Tim had bought a new live Ted Nugent album, and we were rocking out on that and some Molly Hatchet. A fun day.

Later on Tim would marry his first wife Ann Williams, a very nice girl who worked with him at the hospital. I remember going over to their duplex in 1981 many times. MTV had just started up, and at the time the network was playing actual music videos 24/7/365. Before rap and reality took over the music channel.

There were so many cool videos, like those by Men at Work, Journey, and Pat Benatar, and there were even MTV concerts featuring Southern rockers like the Outlaws and the Marshall Tucker Band.

Many times Ann would cook countless tacos and we'd feast Mexicana while digging on the groovy videos of Scandal (Patty Smyth was a hottie), Journey, the Allman Brothers Band, and others. It was actually Tim who introduced me to a local band called the Silver Travis Band. I met the guys and we became fast friends.

The Silver Travis Band started out with the lineup of Mike Satterfield on drums, Joey Parrish on bass, Randall Calvert on lead guitar, Bill Johnson on guitar, and Steve Moore on vocals. The late Barry Moore, the singer's big brother, was their original vocalist before I joined.

Right after I began hanging around the Silver Travis camp—for a while they rehearsed rehearsed in the same Spring Street warehouse that was used by the early Marshall Tucker Band—they asked Steve Harvey, who was several years older, to join on guitar. The band began duplicating the three-guitar sound and double leads created by the Allman Brothers Band.

Shortly thereafter, Johnson departed, followed by Moore. The band auditioned singers and ended up with Rick Cash, the powerhouse vocalist who was baby brother to area favorite Mike Cash.

With this lineup, the Silver Travis Band went into Creative Arts Studio (later Evans Brothers) in Moore, then owned by members of the Tucker Band, and produced a 45 under the trained ear of friend and engineer Randy Merryman. The single was "Baby It's True," written by Harvey and Cash, with a B-side called "Web of Love," written by Harvey and yours truly. The record sold well at gigs and was available all around the Upstate.

When the band Slewfoot, which had inherited the gig following the rise to fame of the group Alabama, wanted a couple of weeks off from their steady job at the famed Bowery in Myrtle Beach during summer 1982, Silver Travis was given the opportunity to fill in. We all traveled to the Beach on the half-size school bus that Satterfield had, the band and me and my buddy Bobby Smith who also worked with us at Community Cash grocery stores. For me, it became quite the performance opportunity. Rick wanted time to talk to fans, and he would let me fill in, doing country songs that were requested. I sang "Take Me Home Country Roads" five times in one night, and each time the West Virginia college students tipped us $20. I remember doing Waylon Jennings' "Just to Satisfy You," "Family Tradition," by Hank Williams Jr., and similar outlaw stuff. Singing in front of those crowds was such a rush, I knew I would do it off and on for the rest of my life.

Now, the first night they told us we could have all the draft beer we wanted for free. Cool. But at the end of the evening and into the wee hours of the next morning, a pyramid of empty beer glasses was stacked onstage that was at least waist high. So on the second night, we were informed that the beers would cost a quarter each. On the third night it seems they went up to 50 cents, but they couldn't stop these young Southern rockers from drinking their beer. No sir.

When guitarist Randall Calvert quit the band in order to spend more time with his first wife, the band held another set of auditions, and Harvey's old friend Stuart Swanlund got the gig. Stuart brought in a fresh new rock and roll feel to the band, and the sound morphed from Southern rock to a more blues- and funk-based rock and roll. Swanlund, along with then-wife Mandy, cowrote many of the band's songs, and the group began to tighten up very nicely. Then, on a last-minute outing in the snow to Virginia, the tour bus broke down, the money went away, and the band crumbled.

Calvert went on to play in several bands, including the Regulators with C. P. Owens. Harvey, Cash, and Parrish formed a short-lived band called Broken Promise, which featured drummer Mark Burrell, a relative of MTB drummer Paul Riddle and a future Toy Caldwell Band member. Satterfield inherited the family heating and air conditioning business and semi-retired the drum sticks. Swanlund later joined the Artimus Pyle Band before settling in with Doug Gray and Jerry Eubanks in the Marshall Tucker Band lineup in 1985, where he remains today.

During the Silver Travis Band days, we spent a great deal of time at Creative Arts Studio. The Tucker Band was recording an album there, and we had all become friends with in-house engineer Randy Merryman, so we spent many a late night in the studio, which was housed in an old, old schoolhouse. Legend has it that some kids had been murdered in the school and that their ghosts were still roaming free in the structure. We had heard of strange occurrences that went on while the Marshall Tucker Band was in there recording, and we witnessed for ourselves some of the apparent poltergeist activity. It was kind of spooky at times, but we would put up with it for a chance to see one of the "Tucker boys," which we did, quite often.

Randy helped STB create some great demos and even a full on 45-rpm single in that studio. "Baby it's True" was played on local radio and the rock station in Myrtle Beach, and we all thought we were famous.

A few years back, I got the news that the Silver Travis Band was reuniting. Randall, Mike, Joey, and Rick brought in Terry Collins on B-3 and John Gillie on acoustic guitar and recorded a great CD. In years to come, I would work with the guys on many levels, including designing their album art, and bringing them in on our first all-star *GRITZ* Fest in Greenville with Bonnie Bramlett, Dru Lombar, Tommy Crain's band, and many others. Silver Travis continues to this day, sounding better than ever. In 2009 they released their best album yet, *Take the High Road*, to critical acclaim, but a serious auto accident involving drummer Mike Satterfield's son put the band on hold for a while. In July 2010, there was a CD release party at the Handlebar in Greenville. I opened the show, and we had a huge jam at the end with founding Marshall Tucker Band member Paul Riddle, longtime MTB bassist Tim Lawter, George McCorkle's son Justin, Toy Caldwell Band drummer Mark Burrell, and guitarist Donnie Duncan. Silver Travis ruled the roost that night.

In 2011 the band began work on a third album and continued to perform with their new keyboard player Brad Durden, opening for the likes of Marshall Tucker Band and .38 Special.

# 23

# THE JERSEY EXPERIENCE

It was 1980, and I decided I wanted to locate some music memorabilia for my collection. As a subscriber to *Goldmine Magazine*, a publication I would one day write for, I knew they had a huge readership and affordable rates, so I placed an ad. A couple of weeks passed, and I heard nothing. Then one day I went to the mailbox to find a really thick envelope with a New Jersey return address. Now, mind you, this was before eBay, before e-mail, before the Internet was in virtually everyone's home, so we communicated the old-school way, by writing letters.

The letter came from a girl named Holly Wilson who lived in Long Branch, New Jersey, just a hop and skip from Bruce Springsteen's home of Asbury Park. Holly's letters were second to those from only two other people in my life, Leon Hayes and Tony Brown's cousin Ann Marie Smith. Anne Marie sent great letters, sealed with wax seals like in olden times. This letter expounded on this girl's love for the band KISS, and even included a pro-quality cartoon of Gene Simmons and some sort of winged chick that she called Firebird. I would find out later that Firebird was Holly's alter ego and a character she had created and written about in fanzines. The drawing was done by her friend Leah Rosenthal, who would go on to become a professional cartoonist.

Over the next couple of months, Holly and I wrote each other a couple of times a week and spoke on the phone on the weekends. She sent me a photo of herself. She was quite cute, with big eyeglasses and fire-red hair. I returned a photo of myself, and we continued to write one another about rock and roll, science fiction, and life. Then somewhere along the line, a strange thing happened. We started flirting, in a sexual way, in the letters. You see where this is going, right? Well, as a twenty-three-year-old Southern boy, I started getting a bit horndog. She kept up the hot letters for another couple of weeks, and then one night on the phone she suggested I hop a flight to Jersey for a visit.

I was telling my buddy Weasel about the invite, just kind of laughing it off in a way. I knew I couldn't afford to fly up there at the time. Weasel jumped right in.

"I'll buy your ticket. Call it a birthday gift."

I was like, "Are you kidding?"

He said, "I'll get you a ticket. And I'll have the return ticket on standby. Once you get there and settle in, you can decide how long you want to stay."

Weasel comes through again.

I caught a plane at Greenville Spartanburg Jetport at 6 AM for a nonstop flight into LaGuardia in New York City. It was my first time on a plane and I was scared to death. All I remember is drinking a couple of cocktails and going out like a light.

I met Holly as planned at baggage claim. She was wearing this blue, quilted, full-length coat that looked mighty warm. It was early March and cold in New York. We were talking and talking as we made our way to a gift shop where we would hook up with her friend Leah, the cartoonist from Brooklyn. Leah was a sweetheart. Always kind. A great artist and writer who published a western-themed fanzine and idolized Clint Eastwood. One night, about a week later, I would have her and Holly in stitches as Leah called various friends on the phone and had me do my Eastwood impression. Wacky fun.

Holly and I went out to eat and then caught the train to Long Branch, a ritual that would be repeated quite often as my time on the Jersey Shore continued. When we got to the apartment, Holly disappeared into the bathroom while we talked. In about fifteen minutes she stepped out wearing red leg warmers and not a lot else. I had told her how hot I thought Kate Bush looked on her album cover wearing dancers' leg warmers. Well, I was blown away. She reached toward the sofa and pulled a handle, extending the sleeper sofa. At this point I will avoid the details. Let's just say that sweet girl really made me feel at home in New Jersey.

Holly had to get up early and catch the train to go to her job in New York City. Bless her heart, she didn't get but maybe two hours of sleep. Me, I was lucky. I got to sleep until noon. When I woke up, I took a nice walk around the neighborhood. Danny DeVito lived just two houses down the street, and Holly said she had seen him out there cutting his grass before.

That evening Holly came in at about six. I figured we'd go out to eat. I already got the message that she didn't cook much, so I figured we'd go somewhere in Long Branch. Wrong. I had no dinner that night, just desert. It was like a dream.

One day when she was off work, we went into the city. I met her boss lady who scored us third-row tickets to *Amadeus* on Broadway, which was amazing. After the play, we went to the stage door where we met my *Rocky Horror* hero Tim Curry (Amadeus), Sir Ian McKlellan (Salieri), and Jane Seymour, who kissed me on the cheek. I also received a hug from Sir Ian and one from Tim. I was so star struck.

Anyway, after we left Holly's place of employment, we went to the Village to haunt the record and book stores. I'd never seen a record store like Bleeker Bob's. It was great.

In the days that followed, I learned the Long Branch and Asbury Park area pretty well, seeking out Springsteen-related locations based on photos in Dave Marsh's *Born to Run* book. I also learned the trains real well and spent a great deal of time in New York. I grew to love the city. There was just so much going on. I loved all the theaters, the music stores, the clubs like CBGB's and Max's Kansas City, and especially the Village. In later visits to New York I would go to shows and see great bands like the Ramones, Television and the Talking Heads.

There are so many fond memories of my time in Jersey and New York. I especially remember attending a screening of Disney's *Fantasia* with Holly and friends. You haven't lived until you've made out while Mickey Mouse is on the big screen.

Our rock-and-rolling lust fest was short lived, and like so many other good things, it came to an end. But it was really fun while it lasted.

# 24

## GAMES WITH NAMES: MY LIFE WITH BETSY

It was the early 1980s, and I was sitting in front of the TV at my parents' mobile home in Spartanburg, chilling out on a lazy spring afternoon, when the phone rang. A female voice on the other end asked, "Do you know who this is?" I had no idea. None at all. She was, in fact, my friend Tony Pearson's second ex-wife, Betsy. She did not, however, let me know this during the conversation. It would be another day or two, and a handful of calls, before I discovered who she was. Betsy loved these games. Sometimes it drove me crazy.

"Okay, I give," I said. "Who are you?"

"My name is Domino," she said. She would later tell me that she had looked down at a nearby newspaper advertisement for Domino sugar and ran with it.

"I have heard a lot about you, and I want to meet you. I see where the Silver Travis Band is playing at a bar in Lyman. I want to come and meet you."

All I could think was that this had to be some sort of evil trick. This sexy voice on the other end of the line—one of my friends was gonna get it but good for this stunt.

"Okay," I said. "I'll bite. See you Friday night." I decided then and there that she wasn't really going to come to the gig. Guess I was wrong. She had an agenda.

Friday night came and I met the band at this new bar in Lyman. I was running lights. We had set the sound system earlier in the afternoon and it was good to go. The Silver Travis guys were really rocking out this evening, and I was doing my amateur light show, complete with lots of flashes of "lightning" during their show-stopper "Trail to Mexico." In retrospect, I was really overdoing it.

I felt someone tap me on the shoulder and turned to see this pretty, bleached-blonde woman smiling at me. She sat down, and I asked her to please fill me in on what the real story was. I wasn't the brightest candle on the birthday cake back then, but I had enough intuition to know something weird was going on.

"I'll give you a clue," she said. See, again, I didn't want to play the game, but my inner workings would not allow me to just blurt that out. "Listen, lady, either tell me what you want or take a hike!" That's what I wanted to say. But I didn't.

She leaned in and showed me a ring on her finger with a small diamond. She assumed I would recognize this as the ring from her engagement to Tony. Only thing is, I never paid any attention to rings and things like that. I was too busy rocking.

After about twenty minutes, she says "Mike, it's me, Betsy, Tony's ex-wife."

You could have knocked me over with a pinky finger. There was no Domino; just Betsy Cogdell Pearson.

After a few weeks of sweet-talking me on the phone, we went out on a date. Of course, it wasn't really a date. It was more a question-and-answer session about Tony, with whom she obviously remained obsessed. This would remain a pattern throughout the nearly ten years I spent around her. To this day I haven't got a clue what really went on during their marriage, or their second marriage, or even the third time they hooked up. Two words come to mind, kids: "fatal attraction."

The whole time I was with her, from our meeting on through my days at Spartanburg Methodist College—which I do credit her with, talking me into going back to school—to our countless road trips, and her leading me on and ripping my heart out time after time is like a bizarre dream now. Like I was under some sort of magic spell. All of my college buddies used to tell me to get as far away from her as possible. They could see it was a bad thing. My connection to her prevented any serious relationships from forming during college, at a time when I was attracted to a couple of beautiful girls.

What I remember most about Betsy during college was helping her do her homework. She majored in Retail Merchandising and Marketing, and I swear I remember doing so many of her homework assignments with her. Projects as well. On the other hand, she was pretty nice about running lines with me for the various plays I was in. We had some good times during those days, but there was also a whole shrimp-boatload of strangeness.

Rather than rehash detail by detail, I will sum it up to say that most of my fond memories are the many trips to Sunset Beach, NC, where she had a house. Escaping the reality. So what happened next? Well, I married her.

Yes, after feeling used and tossed aside like a dirty dishrag for over five years, going through countless episodes with her kids and generally having my heart handed to me on a platter, in 1987 I asked her to marry me. If you think that's something, get a load of this. She had been seeing Tony again and was now pregnant with his child. Only thing is, he was involved with someone else and had no interest in marrying her. Enter the valiant knight. I would give the child a last name. Like sands through the hourglass....

The child was born on February 2, 1988. Groundhog day. Tee Graham Smith. I had suggested Gram, after Gram Parsons. She of course changed it to add T. and claimed it was because of the famous singer T. Graham Brown. Actually, her T. was for Tony. I wasn't stupid. Oh, and she insisted on spelling Graham the traditional way rather than like Gram Parsons.

He was a beautiful baby and we bonded immediately after he was taken out of his mom by way of a C-section. I know I said before that the beach was the happiest part of my time with Betsy. In reality, Graham's arrival was very special, and during the three or so years Betsy and I remained married, I treated him like my very own child, giving him all the love I could give, singing him to sleep with "Crying" by Roy Orbison or "Simple Man" by Lynyrd Skynyrd. He was a sweet child.

When I think about my time with my first wife, I think about trips to the beach, working in the yard of the beach house under 95-degree heat; I remember her adopted parents Mr. and Mrs. Epps and being there for her when they died, one after the other, and being with her when she first made contact with her biological father and later with her biological mother.

In 2010 I would reconnect with her first two kids Kim and Chris Cogdell as well as with Tee Graham, thanks to Facebook. I was happy to hear from them and see that they had all grown up to be great adults.

We divorced in 1990, and the ties were broken. I would see her a few times after that, but not much. She and Tony and Graham came to visit me at the *EDGE* office in 1992. Pretty surreal. With she and I, it was a friendship gone bad. A friendship based on an initial lie that should have never become a romance. In fact, it never really was a romance. Just ten years of my life, wrapped in a veil of confusion. Sometimes happy, sometimes sad, oftentimes "Flirtin' with Disaster."

# 25

## MOLLY HATCHET

*"After so many years of playing in all the different clubs, I happened to meet Steve Holland at a local music store called Paula's Music in downtown Jax. He had just moved from Virginia Beach to Florida and I heard this voice behind me saying "That guitar really sucks." I turned around and asked who he was and he said, " I'm Steve Holland! Wanna start a band?" We started rehearsing that very afternoon and that band is what went on to become Molly Hatchet."*
—Dave Hlubek, interview with Buffalo, February, 2001

I remember living with my parents on Williams Street in Spartanburg. It was around 1979, I think, and that summer I spent a lot of time with my neighbor up the road Karen Scruggs, a rock and roll drummer. I was hanging out with her on the porch one afternoon as the Carolina sun began to set, listening to some good rock and roll on the radio, when the DJ announced a new song from a Florida band. The song was "Flirtin' with Disaster," and the band was Molly Hatchet. I remember looking over at Karen and shouting, "Crank it up!"

That was a pivotal Southern rock moment in my life. That song rattled the walls and I could feel it in my gut and in my balls, like a sonic bombast and nuclear explosion simultaneously hitting me.

It was a few weeks later that I ended up at Greenville Memorial Auditorium for a Hatchet show. I always had this ability to bullshit my way backstage. As an aspiring journalist, I claimed to be writing an article for the *Greenville News*, and the backstage curtain opened up. Danny Joe Brown was looking at me like a deer caught in the headlights, hunched over a road case, snorting a line of coke, a wicked smile on his face. I walked right up to him.

"Danny, I'm Michael Smith with the local paper."

"Well don't fucking write about this," he snapped."And close that damned curtain!"

"Don't worry, Danny, I won't," I said, calmly. Sheesh, Danny Joe Brown and many of the members of Molly Hatchet did drugs. What a surprise.

Over the next thirty minutes, I met all of the band members except for the drummer, Bruce Crump. I didn't know where he was. In fact, the band didn't know either.

"Where the fuck is Bruce?" yelled Danny Joe. "We go on in a few minutes!"

I really wanted to meet Dave Hlubek, whom I'd just seen on television just ripping on lead guitar. He looked like a badass biker, and as it turns out, he also acted like one. As I walked up to him, he was sitting in a straight-backed chair, nursing a bottle of some sort of adult beverage and reading a *Circus* magazine.

"Excuse me," I said. "I am with the *Greenville News*, and I just wanted to say hello."

Hlubek looked up over the magazine and without batting an eye said, "Fuck off, asshole." Then he returned to his article.

Flash forward some twenty-four years. I am sitting around backstage at a Southern Rock Allstars show, somewhere in Virginia. Dave is once again thumbing through a magazine, only this time, it is my magazine, *GRITZ*. We are all shooting the bull, and all of the sudden I feel compelled to comment on the strange parallel of my past experience and what was now happening.

"Hey Dave, remember the first time we met?" I asked, sarcastically.

"You mean last year, Michael?"

"No, the first time. It was 1980 in Greenville. We were backstage and I attempted to meet you and you told me to fuck off."

Dave's face went berry red. "Michael...he stuttered.... Michael...I am sorry...I never...I would have never...."

Jakson Spires cut him off, mid-sentence.

"You would have never treated Michael mean if you'd known he would one day own a Southern rock magazine and be writing a book."

Everyone laughed.

Back to 1980, Greenville Memorial Auditorium. The band had received their two-minute warning. Time to hit the stage.

"Where in the living hell is Bruce?!" Danny was fuming. The announcer was introducing them. "And now, from Jacksonville, Florida...."

"Bruce is already behind the drum kit," yelled Steve Holland.

I learned many years later that of all the band members, Bruce Crump was probably the most dependable. He'd been onstage preparing for the show, but because he didn't hit a single lick on the drum, nobody had noticed.

I walked back out onto the auditorium floor and bulldozed my way to the second or third row. There was a perky little blond girl standing in the dark, smoking a joint. She offered it to me, and I waved it on to the next guy. She asked if she could sit on my shoulders. Seems to be my lot in life, being used as a vantage point for chicks who want to see the stars. It happened many times, including a memorable KISS show where I held a girl on my shoulders in front of Ace Frehley for over an hour. What was I thinking? Anyway, the only difference was tonight my back was hurting. I had pulled a muscle lifting something at work. She stayed up there through for the first few songs, and I could feel the intense heat on the back of my neck. Suddenly I felt a dampness. Okay, she was really enjoying the band. I brought her down, and stood her in front of me. She was obviously into the music, and began rubbing her denim-clad butt against my crotch. Being a red-blooded, all-American male, I reacted, and before long we were kissing and groping to the music of Molly Hatchet. All I remember after that was taking some sort of a pill she handed me and waking up with her in a motel on White Horse Road at 7 AM. She got dressed, kissed me, thanked me for a fun time, and left. I never even knew her name. To me, she will always be "Little Molly."

I followed the career of Molly Hatchet after that, bought most of the albums, and read about them in the rock mags. I remember being at my friend Tim Shook's house one day. He'd just bought the new *Beatin' the Odds* LP, the first one with Jimmy Farrar as lead vocalist. Danny Joe had left and formed the Danny Joe Brown Band to cut a new record with a hotshot guitarist by the name of Bobby Ingram.

I loved Jimmy Farrar's vocals. Man, he was a powerhouse. Especially on Hatchet's version of the Mountain hit "Mississippi Queen." He was, and still is, one fine singer. These days he divides his time between the Southern Rock Allstars and a band called Gator Country, which collects many of the original members of Molly Hatchet. Them boys rock.

I started getting word through the grapevine that Bobby Ingram wanted to talk to me. This was around 2000, after Riff West had spearheaded a fundraiser called Jamming for Danny Joe down in Florida. Danny was accumulating massive medical bills as complications from diabetes, and his health was in a major decline. Jammin' for Danny Joe reunited most of the original members of Hatchet along with members of Blackfoot, the Southern Rock Allstars, and more for a once-in-a-lifetime event.

One day, I checked my e-mail and I had a nice letter from Bobby Ingram, who had effectively bought the Molly Hatchet name and was rocking all around the world with a whole new band of Southern metal players. A lineup that I would later find to be endlessly changing.

Bobby introduced himself, and we began corresponding. I met him in person for the first time on the tour bus in Greenwood, SC. (I had recently been doing a few shows with a Greenville band called True Blues, and we were opening the show.) Before long, we came up with the "Great Molly Hatchet Giveaway," also known as the "I Love Molly Hatchet Contest." *GRITZ* was getting well over one hundred thousand hits per month, and Bobby no doubt saw the marketing potential. With the contest, folks would write an essay entitled "Why I Love Molly Hatchet." The essays would be read and judged by Bobby and myself. The first-place winner and a guest would be flown out to Las Vegas for an all-star outdoor concert, and a beautiful dinner with the band and crew along with yours truly. He would also attend a private Hatchet show in the casino the night before the outdoor show. They would be treated like kings, picked up at the airport in a limousine, and receive a nice five-star room in the casino hotel.

The contest began on February 1, 2001, as *GRITZ* asked readers to write and tell us "Why I Love Molly Hatchet." Response was overwhelming and within days over 1,000 entries had been e-mailed. The final tally was nearly 3,000 entries.

Hours of reading by Bobby Ingram and myself narrowed the entries down to the top 500. Then came the top 100. Ultimately, it came down to

20. Every one of them was a winner, but in the end there was only one first and one second prize. Bobby was on the phone with me for an hour, and we finally made a decision.

A cat from Illinois would win the trip to spend a weekend with Molly Hatchet. Another guy from Virginia would win a new Peavy Predator guitar autographed by the band. Hatchet flew me out to Vegas from Greenville, SC, and the winners were flown in from Chicago. We all converged on Vegas on June 1st, where Hatchet's road manager Bob Abrams met us with a limousine.

It seems Abrams had been holding a sign at the airport labeled "*GRITZ.net*" when he was approached by Night Ranger's Brad Gillis, who thought Abrams was his limo driver. Inevitably, he was, as Gillis rode to the Sunset Station Hotel and Casino with us.

On the way in, Abrams briefed us on the "battle plan," giving us our laminates. It must be noted here, Bob Abrams was very good at what he did. I observed his cool confidence, taking care of Bobby and the rest of the band and the business end of the show.

Bob informed us that Hatchet was playing a pre-jam show at club in the hotel, and that we could check our bags at the desk and just go into the show, which of course we did. The boys had been playing for about half an hour when we got there. Our winners, Larry and Suzanne, went backstage and I just walked down to the front of the stage and stood. Bobby saw me and smiled, reached out and shook hands. Phil was grinning at me and saying "Hi" while the band rocked through "Gator Country." This show was for a few hundred in a small club, so the volume was sliced way down—it was a comfortable volume for these old rock and roll ears. The guys played all the old Hatchet hits and a couple of great tunes from their latest album—"Angel in Dixie" and "Why Won't You Take Me Home." Our contest winners seemed to be enjoying themselves, but then again, so was I.

After the show, we went back to speak to the boys and I finally got to meet the voice on the other end of the line, Stephanie Ingram, Bobby's wife, a very kind girl. (Sadly, a few short years later she died at her home in Florida.)

Following the usual autograph session, Molly Hatchet treated us all to an unbelievable banquet at Capri's Restaurant in the hotel casino. We feasted on appetizers of fried calamari, artichoke dip, and stuffed Provolone cheese as well as a whopper of a house salad, all sorts of fresh baked breads, and a choice of one of three great entrees. (I chose the fillet mignon.) A good time was had by all, and I had an hour or so to pick the brain of Phil McCormack. We talked about everything from his old band the Road Ducks, to the Marshall Tucker Band, music in general, and had a few laughs while Phil put a serious hurtin' on the appetizers.

Sometime very late on Friday night, we all parted ways for some sleep. The rooms (at least mine) were awesome at the Sunset Station. I felt like I was in the presidential suite.

Saturday, we all rode over together to the venue, where we hung out on the bus and in the dressing room until time for Hatchet to play. Excitement reigned supreme, and when Molly Hatchet kicked off its part of the show, the place went wild. Phil and Bobby brought me and the contest winners on stage and introduced us to the audience, which was another "bonus" our winners hadn't counted on.

For the rest of the day our winners were treated to all-areas access and enjoyed the music of Billy Squier, Night Ranger, Styx, Bad Company, and Journey. It was a classic rock feast for the senses. Another very cool thing that happened in Vegas was that I got to meet one of my online buddies. Kirk Munchoff and his wife Misty met us at the show and came backstage. Kirk headed up the Edgar Winter fan website and we had been supporting one another for a few years. It was great meeting him and his lovely little lady. Good people, the Munchoffs.

I would fly out Sunday at noon. It had been as much fun for me as it had been for Larry and Suzanne, and as I said goodbye to Bobby Ingram, we were making plans to do it again in 2002.

The Second Annual Molly Hatchet Contest didn't happen until 2003. This time, it didn't come off nearly as well as the first one. Rather than bore you with the details, I will just say that it was the combination of a lame road manager, a lot of confusion, and a happy couple that almost—repeat, almost—got married onstage at a Molly Hatchet concert. Other than making friends with Sean and Angel Stapleton, it's one of those memories I'd just as soon forget. Next.

A couple of years later our buddy Dave Hlubek rejoined Molly Hatchet, adding an original founding band member back into the mix and kicking things up a notch. I was really happy for Dave, seeing him back on the big stage and getting his kudos, and the twin guitars of Dave and Bobby gave Hatchet more of that old familiar Florida swamp sound.

In October 2009, a seven-year-old girl named Somer Thompson was abducted while walking home from school in the same community where Bobby lives. Somer's little body was found some days later in a Georgia landfill. The tragedy deeply affected Bobby and the band, who staged a benefit for the family. Then they helped establish the Somer Thompson Foundation to help other parents in similar situations. The whole ordeal caused Molly Hatchet to shelve the songs they had been working on for their new album and start from scratch on a concept album dedicated to Somer. The record, called *Justice*, was released in 2010 and features a beautiful song for Somer called "Fly on Wings of Angels." Molly Hatchet had turned another page in the band's long history. A very important page.

# 26

## SPARTANBURG METHODIST COLLEGE AND USCS

Like I said earlier, it was indeed my first wife Betsy who talked me into going to college nearly seven years after high school. She had just started at Spartanburg Methodist College and told me about the grants a person could get. Next thing I knew, I was enrolled. I wouldn't trade those years for anything.

So there I was, entering college with a group of students some seven years younger than me. I immediately made friends with roommate Robert Lenehan, as well as Jody Weisner, Sander Morrison, and a handful of other artistic types. The age thing would not be an issue, other than when one of my friends whispered to me, "You are gonna get laid big time, man. The girls all want a daddy." Well, I wasn't sure what to make of that statement, but I was willing to learn.

One of my first accomplishments upon arrival at SMC was to seek out the theatre department. I had long wished for a chance to try my hand at acting, and I had signed up for drama classes at the junior college. During my first week I met the Drama Department head, Kent Newberry, a man I would grow to admire as a teacher and a friend.

Of all the plays I went on to act in while attending SMC, the one that really stands out in my mind is *Tartuffe* by Moliere. I was cast in the role of Orgon, a character I would embrace with every fiber of my being. It was a great experience, but I was very happy when Newberry elected to do the modern translation of the script as opposed to the original, which was written in rhyming verse.

Besides acting, I helped build sets, secure costumes, do makeup, help with props...a little bit of everything. In fact, it was a whole lot of everything. But it was worth it. I ended up receiving an engraved trophy and plaque for Most Valuable Player from my fellow blossoming thespians.

During my tenure at SMC, I played Mr. White in "The Monkey's Paw," multiple characters in two productions of *Spoon River Anthology*, a singing guard in *Once Upon a Mattress*, Russian ballet instructor Boris Kolenkhov in *You Can't Take It with You*, and others. And then there was our self-produced show.

Clark Nicholson, myself, and Dennis Haimbaugh decided to ask if we could stage our own production of *True West* by Sam Shepherd. Dennis would direct and Clark and I would appear as Austin and Lee. It took a lot of work to convince the Dean to allow us to present a play with so much adult content and profanity at a Methodist College, but she finally gave in.

We worked our asses off on that show, and the three performances will live forever in my memories. Especially opening night.

That was the night my sister and parents were in the audience. I'll never forget catching a glance at my family while I was on a Lee tirade, cursing to beat the band, pouring beer over my head, and generally acting a fool. They looked mortified. My dad later explained to my mom that it wasn't me, it was just a character. I don't think she bought it.

At one point, Lee was just going nuts onstage. I grabbed a heavy wooden chair to sling it across the stage and caught a splintered piece of wood in my left hand, ripping it open. Blood started pouring out. I immediately grabbed the tablecloth, pulling it from the table, spilling the things from the table onto the floor. I wrapped the cloth around my hand, and in shock improvised something like, "See what you caused, Austin? See what you fucking caused?" We only took about three minutes to get it back on track with the script. Not so on our second night.

There is a scene where Austin is beginning to act more like Lee and vice-versa. Austin ends up breaking into neighbor's houses and stealing their toasters. At one point, he is putting sliced bread into something like ten toasters, which we had plugged into electrical outlets on set. Don't read ahead here. Yep, they caught fire. Big time. Clark and I were scrambling, putting out fires and unplugging toasters. It was sheer panic. I am not sure my memory matches· reality, but I truly recall that we improvised script for at least ten minutes before we calmed down and found our way back to the story line. Sam Shepard would have had our heads on a paper plate.

I credit Clark with turning me on to the greatness of Sam Shepard. After reading several of his plays I became a hardcore fan. When it came time for me to do a scene for a big grade during acting class, I chose Shepard's *Fool for Love*. It was a scene between one of Shepard's cowboy characters, Eddie, and his girlfriend May, played by my friend Stephanie Saizon, on whom I had a bit of a crush at the time. (Although she was seeing someone else, plus buddy Dennis Haimbaugh made no secret of the fact that he too had a crush on her.) I didn't mind the rehearsals at all for this scene, which culminates with a long, passionate kiss. Of course it is followed by May driving her knee into Eddie's groin and sending him buckling over to the floor in pain. Needless to say, Stephanie and I worked much harder on the illusion of my balls being busted than the kiss, which seemed to come quite naturally for both of us. Not only was sweet Stephanie absolutely beautiful, but the girl could flat out kiss. No acting there.

There were so many pretty girls at SMC. My eyes were wandering all the time. Between April Haimbaugh, the kid-sister of my friend Dennis, to the sexy Trudy Cora Parrot. Babes for days.

It seems like SMC was more of a two-year party than anything else. The first two semesters I lived in Hammond Hall. The dorm was a hub of activity, from alcohol to marijuana to girls sneaking in to party with us. We played music a lot. I remember carrying boxes of LPs up three flights of stairs at the beginning of the school year. What was I thinking? Those things are heavy. But we were digging on everything from Elvis Costello's *Imperial Bedroom* to Bob Dylan's *Infidels* to Lynyrd Skynyrd's *Second Helping*, Johnny Cash *Live at Folsom Prison*, Bruce Springsteen *Born in the USA*, and old gold like Leon Russell's *Asylum Choir*, Ted Nugent, KISS, Molly Hatchet, Firesign Theatre, James Brown—a little bit of everything.

Another semester the dorms were kind of crowded, so they moved some of us into apartments about a mile down the road. At this point all of the "troublemakers" wound up together in one apartment. It was me, Clark, Sander Morrison, and Allen Heavrin. We weren't really trouble makers. We were just artists.

We did have some pretty fun parties in the apartment, and the goings-on would make a great teen movie. One thing I remember is the area where a washer and dryer was supposed to be, behind the double folding doors. We started putting empty beer cans in there, and a few weeks into the semester you couldn't even open the doors it was so full. It was then that someone, I forget who, in their infinite wisdom started feeding aluminum beer cans into the garbage disposal in the sink. Not a great idea. Not a pretty sound either.

Looking back, I guess we did exactly what kids always do in college. We learned. We learned more outside the classes than we did in them, but we did learn a lot.

Flash forward to 2010. During my year of eye issues and blindness, college buddy Jody Weisner came to the rescue in a big way. We started hanging out again and working on a project he had created. Jody took me to the eye doctor many times, as did Tim Shook, Jaryd Walley, Jay Taylor, and a guy from our SMC days that I never knew during college, Jeff "Burley" Bannister.

Back at SMC, Burley worked on security. He was a military type, and after school he ended up serving in Desert Storm. He also ended up married to his SMC sweetheart, one of our star athletes, Miss Olga, a real sweetheart. When Burley resurfaced in my life, I learned he had been made alumni president and that he was working hard with the new college dean to bring SMC up several notches. Burley was like a gift from God. I was at a point where I had no income. He came in and offered to pay my bills and even buy me some new clothes. I will never forget his kindness, or the many lunches he treated me to. Lots of sushi. Yeah, baby.

After graduating SMC, I went on to the Spartanburg campus of the University of South Carolina, where I, like many others, was hit between the eyes with a big reality stick. If SMC had been a "glorified high school," then USCS was like not knowing how to swim and being tossed into the deep end.

I did enjoy my classes at USCS, especially art and my various theatre history and acting classes with Jimm Cox. I ended up with a degree in Theatrical Arts and a minor in Journalism. Both sheepskins are stuck in a drawer someplace, but the life experiences from those college days taught me volumes. Oh, and Spartanburg Methodist provided an introduction to a friend named Greg who would kick my rock and roll star dream up fifty notches.

# 27

# A COALITION IS FORMED:
# THE BIRTH OF THE BUFFALO HUT

I met David Haddox while attending Spartanburg Methodist College in 1984. It was during that two-year stretch that fellow student Greg Yeary and I decided to form a band. Greg had gotten hold of Dave at Alexander Music House, where he taught drums, before moving his practice to Smith Music. Haddox had taught drums for years, and one of his finest students had been a fifteen-year-old Paul T. Riddle, who would go on to fame as drummer for Marshall Tucker Band. Along with Haddox and bassist Joey Parrish, we formed a band.

Our first gig was held at the Pacolet Amphitheater and featured the band going by two different names. The country version was called Desperado, and the rock and roll version was Standard Deviation. We would later find that Desperado was taken, and a few months later the band became the Buffalo Hut Coalition, a name used off and on for over eleven years.

Haddox had tons of performing experience as well as studio work under his belt, including the Soul Survivors and a stint drumming for Jerry Lee Lewis, and we all felt it an honor to work with the guy. And work we did. For several years, and with an array of bass players, we played all types of clubs, bars, shows—David even booked us a few parties and a bar mitzva. Too much fun. It wasn't until years later that I fully realized the scope of this man's accomplishments.

The core of the Buffalo Hut was Pacolet guitarist Greg Yeary, my old Silver Travis buddy, Joey Parrish, me, and Haddox. Over the years, Lake Bowen resident Dennis Longshore sat in for Haddox on many a gig when David was required to be in two places at once. In between the time Joey began as bass player, and the time he came back into the Hut, the band featured a diverse lineup of bassists including the late Ernest Greene of Jonesville, Lee Ridings of Fingerville, C. P. Owens, and Allen Heavrin, an old college buddy who was later lead guitarist for a band called the Ex-Presidents with Matthew Knights and later Barney Barnwell's Woodstick band.

One of the most memorable moments from the BHC years came in fall 1987. While working at a record store, I met Marshall Tucker Band guitarist George McCorkle. I knew he was an old friend of our drummer, so I invited him to come out and jam at a tiny bar we were playing on a regular basis. The place, in Cowpens, was called the Breakaway Den.

When show time came, I was quite pleasantly surprised that George showed up. I handed over my brand new pink paisley Telecaster, a reissue of the one designed by James Burton, and switched from guitar player to vocalist for a forty-five-minute set of blues including "Stormy Monday" and "Kansas City." George smoked like he was playing at Madison Square Garden again, with a tiny audience of about twenty people, many of whom knew nothing of the man's musical legacy. He didn't care. He was jamming with his life-long friend, Dave Haddox, and any musician worth his salt knows there ain't nothing like it.

Talking to George on a break, he was telling me how it felt when he had ended up jamming onstage with his hero Carlos Santana for the first time. The music was rocking along nicely, and Santana turned to George and said, "Take a lead." It was the same way I felt jamming with George.

Over a period of three to four years, the BHC played anywhere and everywhere, from rock shows to country gigs and everything in between. We developed a pretty cool stage show, bringing girls up out of the audience during "Willie and the Hand Jive." While Dave did a drum solo, Greg and I would invite folks on stage to dance the hand jive. We also did Bruce Springsteen's "Pink Cadillac," complete with my kazoo solo. During the song, Greg would tease a number of other tunes, including Bob Seger's "Her Strut." We did a cow punk version of "Folsom Prison Blues" that included a section from Aerosmith's "Walk This Way." The band was great fun while it lasted, but in 1988 it all ended.

In 1992, the reformed Buffalo Hut—myself, Joey Parrish, Dave Haddox, and Steve Harvey—got the opportunity to back up *Days of Our Lives* soap star Stephen Nichols, who had made quite a name for himself as "Patch." The benefit blues show was scheduled to be held at

Greenville Braves Stadium, but rain forced the people in charge to find an indoor venue quickly, and the whole thing moved inside.

The day before, I had accompanied Nichols, his fan club president, and another lady to dinner and then down to band member Steve Harvey's house for a rush rehearsal. It was amazing to watch the effect "Patch" had on Steve's mom and sister, who stayed for the whole rehearsal. It was very apparent that soap stars can really have a hypnotic effect on their fans.

The Buffalo Hut Coalition played quite a variety of songs over the years, from Marshall Tucker Band's "Can't You See" to Charlie Daniels' "Still in Saigon" to Los Lobos "Will the Wolf Survive" (I am still amazed how Dave played all those multiple drum parts on his small drum kit with only two hands) and a medley that included "Wild Thing" by the Troggs, "Hey You Get Off of My Cloud" by the Rolling Stones, and "Hang On Sloopy" by the McCoys. But no matter where we played, it seems, there was always at least one request for the enigmatic David Allan Coe's "You Never Even Called Me by My Name."

# 28

## DAVID ALLAN COE

*"The highlights [of my career so far] were being on the Grand Ole Opry with Bill Anderson as his guest. That was very important. And being on tour with Kid Rock, that was an important thing. Willie Nelson's Farm Aids and Picnics were special in my life, and then the movies. Meeting my friend Kris Kristofferson, who is of course one of my best friends. Between him and Johnny Cash and Waylon and writing the liner notes for Johnny Cash's album, that was a big deal in my life as well as singing a duet with Johnny Cash."*
—David Allan Coe, interview with Buffalo, August, 2004

The first time I ever heard David Allan Coe, I was working at WBBR radio in Travelers Rest, SC. I was going through the seemingly endless bins of LPs, pulling music for my radio show, when I came across Coe's Rides Again LP. I decided to play the first track on the album, a song called "Willie, Waylon and Me." I was hooked. I liked Coe's songwriting and singing, not to mention the whole mysterious outlaw image.

In the months to come I would seek out other Coe albums and find myself drawn to the softer side of this country rocker, songs like "Mona Lisa Lost Her Smile," "Jody Like a Melody," "Tanya Montana," and "Would You Lay with Me in a Field of Stone."

At one point during the early 1980s, I worked at a radio station that had Coe in the studio for an interview. They instructed me to tell Coe that, due to FCC regulations, we would appreciate it if he could avoid cursing on the air. He told us there would be no problem. Of course, the minute I opened up the microphone he let fly with a string of expletives and just smiled. Just Coe being Coe. It would be over twenty years before I would be in the same room with the Mysterious Rhinestone Cowboy again.

July 26, 2006. It was not your ordinary, average day. No, not by a long shot.

I had been in contact with Miss Kim, David Allan Coe's wife, for a long while, and Jill and I had wanted to see their show for months, so it was indeed a pleasure to not only see their show, but also perform as the opening act. How cool is that?

Turns out Miss Kim was driving the big pickup truck down from Ohio with her mother Judith and David on board. The bus with the band and crew came earlier in the day, and Kim and David got into Greenville in the late afternoon. I met them at Home Depot to led them over to my house, but David needed to go by the club first to check in with his road manager. Then I led them over to the hotel, where we left David to shower and rest a while.

I then led the ladies back to my house, where Miss Kim and Jill and Judith immediately hit it off and had a blast talking astrology and girl talk. By then, it was time for me to run back to the club for a sound check.

We set up our equipment and got a sound check, and in an hour I was headed back home to dress for the gig. When I got home, Jill, Kim, David, and Judith were eating dinner. I had David Allan Coe at my home, with only minutes to chat before I had to rush back to the Handlebar for the gig.

We did a brief interview about his new CD, *Rebel Meets Rebel*, recorded with Pantera prior to the death of guitarist Dimebag Darrell. Then we were treated to a promotional DVD for a new reality TV show called *The Coe Show*, a kind of "Outlaw Country Osbournes." He also let us see the music video from the album for "Nothin' to Lose," a real "wild thang." Gambling, girls, trains, and heavy-metal country. Now *there*, my friend, is a party waiting to happen.

It was time to rush back to the club. Coe and I jumped into my CR-V and left the girls. David wanted to see and hear my set, which obviously made me happy. We chatted on the way over about *GRITZ* and about music. When we got to the Handlebar I whipped in front of his tour bus, and we met his road manager Bruce and went in the backstage door to David's dressing room. I introduced him to Jay Taylor and John Ervin from my band, and soon it was time to play.

The show was great fun, and when I finished and came off stage Coe was standing there to meet me. He had watched our whole show, and he said some cool things about my music. Then it was time for the main attraction. I made my way down front, where I had a seat between the stage and the barricade. I got up every so often to take a photo, then returned to my seat, enjoying every minute of the Coe show. Halfway through his set, Miss Kim came charging out onstage to rock things up alongside David. I found out later that Kim and her mom and Jill had gotten there just minutes before time for Kim to sing. Ah, the excitement of show biz.

When they finished their set, the band kept on playing while Coe and Kimberly hit the back door and took off amidst a downpour of hail and rain. I went inside, packed up my gear, and came out to the bus, where I finally met Coe's son Tyler, to whom I introduced my daughter Hannah and her friend Elise.

I was on the way to Taco Bell for a late-night burrito when my cell rang. It was Kim calling. She and David were on the way to Asheville and on to Ohio. I told her how much fun we had all had, and how Jill and I looked forward to seeing them again.

We sat up talking until 4 AM. As I fell asleep, I thought back to the days I had as a country DJ back in the 1970s, playing all of David's music, and my years as a singer, singing Coe songs into the wee hours of the morning at some stale-smelling honkytonk in front of twenty drunks. Now he had been a guest in my home. Funny how things end up sometimes. It was an experience for sure.

# 29

# RADIO, RADIO

Another vocation I dove into off and on for a number of years was radio broadcasting. It all started back in high school with the Junior Achievement Radio Club and the Byrnes Broadcasting Association. I still remember the very first record I ever introduced on the air. It was at WORD Radio in Spartanburg, the Junior Achievement hour under the direction of then-morning air personality Steve McCoy, and the song was "Island Girl" by Elton John. As it happens. I also recall the second 45 I cued up and played. It was "Lyin' Eyes" by the Eagles. I thought my heart was going to come out of my throat. Nerves.

My friend Tony Pearson and I worked really hard during our early high school years to get our radio licenses and made several trips to the FCC building in Atlanta to take tests. Now I understand you can get a license by simply writing and requesting one. Sheesh.

The first station I worked at was WBBR, a 1000-watt AM station in Traveler's Rest, SC. Tony was working there and helped me get the gig. I played country records part of the time and gospel music in the late afternoons and on Sundays. It was an experience, keeping all of the programming going, threading the reel-to-reel tape machines, recording commercial spots, and cuing up records. I got into trouble many times for sneaking Southern rock records into the playlist. I'd play "Ramblin' Man" and halfway into the record the boss, Mr. Kirby, would call me up and give me a talking-to. Still, I couldn't resist attempting to broaden the audience's musical horizons.

When I played the gospel sets, I was always playing records by a young newcomer by the name of Amy Grant. One time I was offered a gig as emcee for a concert she was performing with Terry Talbot (formerly of the Southern rock band Mason Proffit) at Furman University in Greenville, where she was also a student. The night of the show I broke out in huge welts all over my back and shoulders. Big, red, itchy things that I later discovered were caused by nerves and by holding in my emotions. My dad had gotten into another of our many fights with me, and I was upset. Well, I was talking to Amy Grant after the show and somehow ended up telling her about it. She was very sweet, and I'll never forget. She placed a hand on my shoulder and said she would pray for me. Mere moments later, the welts were gone. I never again doubted the power of prayer. Twenty-five years later I met her husband Vince Gill in a diner in Nashville and told him the story. He just smiled and said, "Yeah, she's very special."

Jumping back, my first ever radio experience came at the hands of Danny Dyer, a blind DJ who worked at Top Gun 1530, WASC, a country AM station in Spartanburg. I called him on the phone a lot, and when I expressed an interest in the radio profession, he invited me over to spend some time. I was sixteen years old, and Danny made me love radio. Danny ruled the studio. He let me "cue up" my first record, and then he gave it to me to keep. I still have it. "Ashes of Love" by Dickey Lee. Danny never once let being blind even slow him down, and to this day he remains one of my true life heroes.

In years to come, I would work at many other radio stations including WSJW in Woodruff, SC; WSPA-FM in Spartanburg; WTYN in Tryon, NC; and WHKP in Hendersonville, NC. When I wasn't working in radio, I was working at a newspaper. I couldn't put my finger on exactly what it was I wanted to do with all of these experiences, but in retrospect it becomes very clear. I wanted to write and entertain. I dropped out of radio for many years, but in 2010, I returned via the Internet with "The Buffalo Show," interviewing guests like Bekka Bramlett, Henry Paul, and Billy Crain from the Outlaws, Bobby Ingram from Molly Hatchet, and many others, as well as taking calls and playing records. It was like riding a bike. I just jumped back on and hit the ground running.

# 30

# DANCING ON THE EDGE

In 1991, I was working at a newspaper in Columbus, North Carolina, that was printed in Landrum, South Carolina. Bored with the mundane day-in, day-out news, I had started, along with some friends, a tabloid newspaper called *UTOPIA*. It was 90 percent environmental-type stuff and 10 percent music. Those 10 percent were my favorites.

We only printed three monthly issues, launching the first on Earth Day 1990, but those three months were filled with a renewed sense of freedom and creative fire. Then, while performing in a play called *When We Were Married* at the Tryon Little Theatre, fate stepped in. I met James Irwin.

James, a fellow actor in the community theatre, took me aside one evening to tell me how much he liked *UTOPIA* and that he had been harboring his own dream of publishing an independent newspaper. Not one on ecology but an entertainment magazine. He caught my ear, big time.

James came over to the upstairs apartment I shared with Stephen Long, my coconspirator at *UTOPIA*, and watched Dave Letterman with us a couple of nights following rehearsals. It was then that he approached me about the dream. I was thrilled.

The next day, he invited me over to his apartment, where I met his roommate David Morris, a sprightly young man with a decidedly business-oriented head. The same evening, I was introduced to Charlie Bergman, the man who had also been invited to join in as one-third of the founders. It was Charlie who came up with the name and the logo for what became *EDGE Magazine*. And while he and I clashed on many issues, there were countless times when his creative genius was proudly displayed for all to see.

So, after several meetings, the three of us became James S. Irwin, Publisher; Michael B. Smith, Executive Editor; and Charles Bergman, Graphic Designer. Soon after, we "hired" David Morris as business manager. We decided to use Greenville, SC, as our home base, and I set the wheels in motion to move to Greenville, as did James. Meanwhile, we had teamed up with a group of like-minded folk in Greenville, who also joined our staff. David and Julie Moss were the ring leaders of that group. I remember David Moss buying our first Mac computer, agreeing to just let us pay him back. I have such happy memories of all those folks, Julie's sister Mickie Ansel and her brother JohnWickliffe, Hunter Hodge, just a whole group of wild and crazy guys—like us.

We looked at several possible office locations, settling on a space on South Main Street, right in the overwhelming shadow of the Greenville News building. Our space was owned by the neighbor, a realtor named Roy Gullick. Mr. Gullick was a great guy with tons of war stories from his time in World War II. When we first moved in, the space was being used for storage and had been for many, many years. It was quite dirty as well. Mr. G. gave us the first three months rent free just for cleaning it up. What a great guy.

There were a few old and heavy metal desks in there, and he just gave them to us. I remember painting mine purple. In fact, it didn't take long for us to get the whole office looking like a rock and roll dream.

Our first issue came out on May 1, 1991. It was happily hand-distributed at Greenville's River Place Festival. Everyone was taken aback by this free newspaper, and we started getting lots of great compliments right away.

During the first weeks of our new venture, we acquired staff staples like Bethany Williams, Phillip Knighten, and others. In early July, we hired sales representative Jill Greene, who would go on to make great strides in sales, not to mention great strides in stealing my heart. In the not-too-distant future she would become my beautiful bride.

*EDGE* was really catching on. Jill, along with Millicent Howell, an African American Woman with a capital "W," were selling the paper to advertisers like hot cakes. James and I were writing our fingers to the bone, Charlie was doing his thing, and David was handling the business end. It was pretty great.

Together, we created a paper full of interviews with local and national celebs like George Harrison (one of the biggest thrills of my life was talking to the "quiet Beatle"), Gene Simmons, Lewis Grizzard, Jerry

Jeff Walker, and many others. We employed the old "walk fast and carry a brief case" tactic, presenting our publication as larger than life. We never lied, we just sounded confident, and the name *EDGE* sounded familiar to folks in the entertainment industry. I once even received a phone call from Sir Elton John, thanking me for a glowing review I had written. It was pretty darn exciting. We traveled on press junkets to Disney World, Chimney Rock, Carowinds, and everywhere you can imagine and wrote about it all. We borrowed an idea from David Letterman, James's favorite, and created our "Reader's Lists." We had a "Free Space" for poets and artists to display their heartfelt creations. We put our efforts behind local events, cosponsoring Freedom Weekend Aloft, Reggae Starsplash, River Place Festival, and our own events—Weedom Freakend Aloof, Banned Together, and others—giving profits to AIDS and other charities.

We held meetings that ran deep with wine and bullshit and had lots of laughs and tears. We pushed the envelope, bucked the system, gave the finger to *The Greenville News*, and stood our ground.

In 1993, I pulled out of the company due to personal reasons, but James carried on. At least until his untimely death in 1994. By then, the wheels had already been set into motion for a merger with the *Creative Loafing* group based in Atlanta. Merger or not, things would never be the same without James.

Watching from a distance, I saw *EDGE Magazine* fall into the hands of the *Loaf* and watched as it became a mere shadow of its former self. Each week, there was less *EDGE* and more *Loafing*, until the indie giant swallowed the former *EDGE Magazine* whole. That was in 1995.

A few short years later, Charlie died, and in 2003, David Morris passed away, leaving only myself from the original *EDGE* guys. Hard to believe.

When I think of all the staff members that came and went during my three years at *EDGE*, I have to smile. That's where I met David Windhorst, a guy that remains a true friend to this very day. David was and is a great writer, not only of articles but also of stories, songs, screenplays, and more. He was also one of the most athletic individuals I ever met. David was always biking, running, swimming—he was what you call a triathlete, and he even competed in the Iron Man event a few times. If you've never read about the Iron Man, Google it.

David was also a movie critic, and a damned good one, until he hurt his back badly in a bike wreck. From then on he was unable to sit comfortably in a movie theater for two hours.

Another friend was Phillip Knighten. Phillip was great fun. I remember him most for introducing me to some really interesting music I may never have heard had it not been for him. Things like Ice T and Perry Ferrell's band Jane's Addiction. I'll never forget the time that Phillip, James, and I went to the local watering hole, the Casablanca Lounge, to "research" our cover story called "Cold Beer." We were tasting all the different brews and comparing them, and after an hour or so we were all lit. At one point Phillip walked by with a beer in each hand, and from then on he was dubbed Phillip "Two Beers" Knighten. Ah, the great memories.

The Casablanca was our hangout, and we all became friends with Cliff and Arthur, the bartenders, as well as all the other folks who worked and hung out there. Including me and my sweetheart, Jill.

# BLUE EYES CRYING IN THE RAIN

When I sat down to write a chapter about my second wife Jill, a million and one stories popped into my mind, all at once. Should I begin by telling the story of how we first met? Well, I already told that one. Should I begin with the wedding and the magical experiences that surrounded that event? Should I start out by telling the story of how I fell for her at first sight the very first time she walked into my office? Then I thought about Jill. What would she suggest? No doubt, she would pull out one of her favorite sayings. "Go with the flow." So I shall.

I never will forget our first date. I suppose it was a date. Truth be known, it was more like friends going out together. She didn't know I had already begun to fall in love with her. If she had, it might have scared her so badly, we might never have gone to the show.

And what a show it was. Johnny Winter. A more rockin' bluesman you'll never see. I had seen Johnny on his 1975 tour, and Jill had seen him around the same time. One of the many parallels in our separate yet cosmically fated lives.

We were both working at *EDGE Magazine* at the time. Like I said earlier, the first time she came through the door, I was blown away by her looks, her attitude, and the sweetest Southern-belle drawl you've ever heard. I had never seen a more beautiful woman in all my life. I told my business partner James that I was "in love." He laughed and said, "She really is a knockout." I gave him the classic "Wait a minute, this is going to be my girl" look, but I wasn't really worried since he was a hundred percent gay. Still, she was hot enough to make a gay man rethink his libido. I told James that I was going to marry her. Funny thing is, he looked at me as if he believed it, too.

So we went together from Greenville to Clemson to hear Johnny play his heart out. We had to park pretty far away, and it was raining. I remember catching a glimpse of Jill's blue eyes, and for a moment it looked as if she were crying. But it was only rain drops. My heart jumped into overdrive. I could never remember seeing a woman so breathtakingly beautiful.

That Johnny Winter concert was in January. It was the 28th, to be exact. The next year, we would see Johnny in Atlanta on January 27th, for our first-year dating anniversary. The next year, on January 28th, Johnny was back in Clemson, and so were we. During the first couple of years we dated, we saw concerts by some of the best—Eric Clapton, Elton John, B. B. King. Little Feat, Dr. John, Los Lobos…on and on.

There are so many memories from our years together. One of the best was a trip we made to stay in Charleston in a bed and breakfast. It was a wonderful weekend. One of Jill's friends was starring in a play down there based on the life of country star Patsy Cline. We went to the show one night and, when we came in the back door, noticed that most of the seats were already filled. We had no idea that they were using some audience members onstage, as a part of the show. They lead us straight down to the front and seated us on stage left. It was nothing to me, since half of my life had been spent onstage, but Jill seemed a little apprehensive. During one of the scenes, they got me up and into an impromptu square dance, a performance I hadn't counted on but took on anyway. I must admit it was fun.

That night, I went outside and got into the Jacuzzi, just enjoying the warm jets of water pulsating all over my body. Pretty soon, Jill came out and joined me in the hot tub and it was like some sort of dream. She said that I looked like Poseidon. I took it as a compliment.

Jill and I had so much fun together over the years, traveling, going to concerts and movies, doing things with her (our) kids Ben and Hannah. The experiences were some of the best ones of my life. Many of them much too personal to publish. So I shall refrain. But there sure was a lot of love.

Of course, like all good things, it had to end. Jill and I started moving in different directions a few years ago, and by 2011, we had both decided to break up. Twenty years together had come to an end, but I would not trade my years as her boyfriend and husband for all the gold in California.

Baby Buffalo—Michael B. Smith, 1957.

Papa Sorrells, my grandpa and his soda-swilling pooch.

Mama and Papa Sorrells holding a baby Buffalo.

Above, my Grandma and Grandpa Smith of San Jose, California. Below, my parents wedding—Mom and Dad (in middle) flanked by Uncle Jack and Aunt Jo.

Above, mom with her happy kids, Michael and Patsy. Below, my dad, Junior Lee Smith when he was an Air Force mechanic.

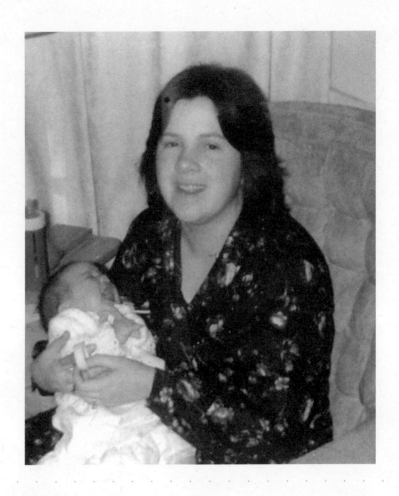

My sister Patsy with her pride and joy, baby Kelly Michelle Winter.

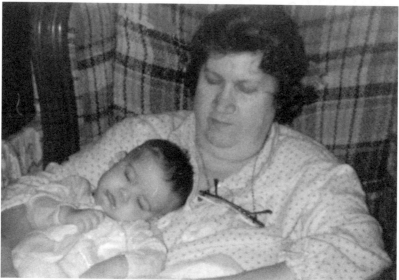

Above, my sister Patsy and my niece Kelly Michelle. Below, my niece Kelly Michelle Winter naps with her Grandmother Smith, my sweet Mom.

Clowning around with Patsy after her 50th birthday party at my home in Greenville, South Carolina.

Uncle Sonny, my mom's brother, was my childhood hero.

Uncle John, my Dad's youngest brother, was always the coolest.

My great stepson Benjamin Greene on his wedding day.

**Hannah pregnant with Zoe** (photo by Krissy Baldridge).

My grandchildren Zoe and Baby Leila.

I played Lee with Clark Nicholson as Austin in Sam Shepard's *True West* at Spartanburg Methodist College (photo by Dennis Haimbaugh).

The Buffalo Hut Coalition, my longest-lived band, consisted of (left to right) Greg Yeary, David Haddox, me, and Ernie Greene.

Above, my first exposure to the Marshall Tucker Band (other than early Toy Factory gigs) at the Thunderbird Drive-In in Spartanburg, 1972. Below, Doug Gray and Tim Lawter of Marshall Tucker Band in the late 1990s.

The Godfather of Southern Rock, Charlie Daniels.

Charlie Daniels, Charlie Hayward, and Tommy Crain at Angelus the night after Kerry Creasy passed away. Everyone signed Kerry's hat, which Tommy is wearing.

Having a laugh with another real musical hero of mine, Charlie Daniels, in Spartanburg, South Carolina.

Dickey Betts and me on his tour bus in Charlotte, North Carolina
(photo by Scott Greene).

A Capricorn drummers summit, backstage in Charlotte. (L to R) Allman Brother Jaimoe, Marshall Tucker's Paul T. Riddle, and Brother Butch Trucks.

Dickey Betts rocks the Handlebar in Greenville, South Carolina in 2010.

Above, my friends, Bonnie and Bekka Bramlett, and me (photo by Roxanne Lark).
Below, Molly Hatchet's Dave Hlubek and I jam during one of our countless
Southern Rock Allstars shows. (photo by Scott Greene).

The Southern Rock Allstars, Jakson Spires, Charles Hart, Jay Johnson, and Dave Hlubek look over the first issue of *Gritz* Magazine.

Clowning around on stage with the mighty Hulk Hogan (photo by Scott Greene).

A white trash reunion—Edgar Winter and Jerry LaCroix reunited
in Port Arthur, Texas for a special Millennium Concert, January 1, 2000.

Phil Walden, Bonnie Bramlett, and me at Songfest in Muscle Shoals.

Singing at one of Dick Cooper's parties in Muscle Shoals (photo by Dick Cooper).

Dru Lombar and Eddie Stone in Lake City, Florida

Above, Stan Robertson and Tommy Talton of Cowboy, Jimmy Hall of Wet Willie, and me at Proctor's High Lonesome Saloon in Rome, Georgia (photo by Sandy Robertson). Below, Donnie and Dennis at the annual Winters Brothers Southern Summer Jam in Tennessee.

Above, real brothers of the road, Danny Toler and Tommy Crain (photo by Rick Broyles). Below, with hero and friend, Billy Bob Thornton (photo by Mike Shipp).

My dear friend Tommy Crain's stage rig.

In the studio with my friend the late George McCorkle, who was given the name K.G. early on for "Kool George" (photo by Bruce Wall).

Donna Hall, Tommy Talton, and Bonnie Bramlett smile for the camera
at Gritzfest II.

Allstars Jack Hall and Tommy Crain at soundcheck.

Jimmy Hall and Bonnie Bramlett at Gritzfest II.

Above, Phil Stokes, Bob Burns, and I at a benefit my friends put together after my ten-month blindness (photo by Roxanne Lark). Below, Skynyrd drummer Artimus Pyle and me with a signed guitar for auction at the Buffalo Benefit (photo by Tim Shook).

Another brother to me, the late Ray Brand of the Crawlers.

Blackfoot guitar-slinger Charlie Hargrett and me in Angel City, Georgia
(photo by Scott Greene).

Molly Hatchet burns it up at the annual Angelus benefit in Tampa.

My travelin' mate, Scott Greene, with Tommy Crain at the Angelus event.

Angel City Bike Rally. Jamming with the best, The Southern Rock Allstars (photo by Scott Greene).

One of my favorite bands and some of my best friends, Silver Travis, 2011.

Above, on the Molly Hatchet tour bus en route to Vegas, playing Russ Maxwell's Les Paul (photo by Russ Maxwell). Below, on the set of *Jane Mansfield's Car*, June 24, 2011, with Chuck Leavell, Billy Bob Thornton, and Rose Lane Leavell (photo by Tim Shook).

Above, me and The Outlaws at the 3rd and Lindsley benefit, November, 2011 (photo by Roxanne Lark). Below, Hanging out with members of The Boxmasters on the movie set in Cedartown, Georgia. Michael "Bubba" Bruce, Billy Bob, and J. D. Andrew (photo by Tim Shook).

With my buddy, the late Robert Nix of The Atlanta Rhythm Section at a show in Huntsville, Alabama (photo by Tim Shook).

With my buddy Bekka Bramlett at the 3rd On 3rd benefit staged by Rick Broyles (photo by Roxanne Lark).

Eddie Stone, Donnie Winters, Buffalo, and Rob Walker at the Hearts
of the South benefit at Grant's Lounge in Macon, Georgia, March 24, 2012
(photo by Tim Shook).

Alan Walden, me, and Bob Burns at the benefit at Grant's Lounge in Macon, Georgia, March 23, 2012 (photo by Mary Tomenski).

With the living legend herself, Mama Louise Hudson at H & H Restaurant in downtown Macon, Georgia (photo by Roxanne Lark).

# THE BIG CHILL

The full moon cast its golden reflection across the sparkling waters of Lake Lure as I looked out our third-floor window, just enjoying the cool air whipping its way through our room at the Lake Lure Inn. I felt a real sense of peace for the first time in several hours, and when I laid down to go to sleep, all I could feel was numbness. That's it, just numbness.

It was 1994, and the night before Jill and I were slated to leave town for the weekend on a much deserved and highly anticipated mini-vacation, I had received the tragic news that my former business partner and longtime friend James Irwin had died in the Laurens Hospital after a two-week bout with pneumonia and spinal meningitis. My friend was dead at the age of thirty. I felt so much anger, sadness, and confusion it would be impossible to put into mere words. Needless to say, my whole vacation was spent talking about James and reliving the fun times we had shared during our three-year friendship.

James and I, along with our mutual friend and fellow thespian Donna Orzanno Christopher, wanted to start an acting troupe together. We would tour and do small, two- or three-character shows. We even went so far as to name our company the Act III Players and had some wild publicity photos done. However, *EDGE Magazine* soon began to take up all of our time.

Like I wrote earlier, we had set sail on an adventure that would bring about laughter, tears, freedoms, censorship, happy times, and sad times. James and I, along with the rest of the staff, worked our butts off for two years and over fifty issues before I left the company. He and I would work late hours almost daily, trying to make the paper the best it could be—and we'd drive down to Laurens every two weeks to paste up, get it printed, rent and load a U-Haul, and bring it all back home. God only knows how many times we did that, or how many times Mr. and Mrs. Irwin fed us sandwiches and Cokes. It really was fun.

We joked and talked about how one day he and I would own Jags and be living in condos. We really loved to dream. I believe those dreams meant everything to James, I really do.

When I broke away in 1994 to start *The Color Green*, it was a business decision. I wanted to cater to a little older crowd and delve into the arts and history end a bit more, leaving the younger crowd's music and film and stuff for *EDGE*. James and I talked about it. So we parted ways, but we never parted friendship.

As I found myself looking out over the moon-drenched waters of Lake Lure, under crystal-clear skies, I could see that unique and wonderful smile of his and remember all of the good times I was fortunate enough to have shared with James: the spring press trip to Disney World; the countless movies; the Braves games; his understated correcting of my numerous spelling mistakes; laughing at the wit of our favorite, David Letterman; all of the staff parties; cooking hot dogs on the balcony on South Main; his love of books and movies; being scared stiff riding with him in his tiny Honda to Charlotte in a torrential downpour to see the Edie Brickell show; lunches at Annie's Natural Café and overdosing him on the Asian House; all the concerts, the festivals, and the fun.

James was too young to die. He had so much more to offer. But all we can do is be thankful for the times we had together and never, ever forget him. I know I won't.

# 33

## KIDS WITH KIDS

I have nothing but happy memories of helping to raise Benjamin and Hannah Greene. In my heart they have always been just as much my children as their mother's and their father Joe's. They grew up with two dads, and I believe they learned a lot from both of us as well as their mom.

When I first came into their lives, Hannah was only three years old and Benjamin was seven, so I have been around for the biggest part of both of their lives and have loved every minute. There were so many great times. Countless trips to the beach and to the mountains, lots of Ben's basketball, baseball, and football games and Hannah's many dance recitals and chorus performances. Both of the kids always struck me as having unusually large amounts of skill and talent. I enjoyed every second of every church league basketball game and high school football game, and there were many times I was literally moved to tears watching Hannah Jane dance her recitals. Of course, she could have easily been my own blood. The child was a ham, just like me. She kept all of us in stitches with her improvised home fashion shows and other antics, oftentimes accompanied by her partner in crime, cousin Kensey Frady.

One of my fondest memories is of the countless shows and concerts I performed with Jill, Ben, and Hannah front and center cheering me on. That meant more to me than 5,000 screaming fans.

In 2008, Ben and Hannah would both be married. "Time flies" is not just a cliché; it is the truth. Ben married Austin Heard, Hannah married James C. Maxey, and, on September 30, 2008, Hannah gave birth to a little miracle named Zoe. That very night I wrote a song about her. It has always been my way of expressing my heart. I had written "Hannah's Song" when she was only four years old, and suddenly I found myself writing one for her daughter called "The Baby Song."

J. C. and Hannah were living in Honolulu, Hawaii, on the Navy base, but Hannah came home a few times just long enough for us to spoil the baby a bit. Then on December 15, 2010, Hannah gave us a second grandchild, the equally beautiful Leila. Suddenly it dawned on me that I had two grandchildren. Seems like only yesterday it was me, Jill, and tiny Ben and Hannah shooting basketball in the back yard and taking our baby Jack Russell Taz for walks in the neighborhood. Taz left us in 2010 at the age of eighteen. Another chapter in our lives came to a close, but like all of the chapters, it was filled with love and joy and a whole lot of fun. Tessa, another Jack Russell the kids and I had given Jill for Mother's Day 1998, has also been a wonderful pet and continues to thrive.

# THE COLOR GREEN

After *EDGE* I thought I'd never ever get involved in another publication. I was wrong. I guess it's true what they say about ink in the blood. Before I knew it I was looking for a printing company, selling ads and doing all of the same stuff I swore I'd never do again.

Jill was right there by my side for the whole ride, and we teamed up with our friend Bob Jones, one of the most creative guys I have ever known. Bob had spent many years in advertising and was responsible for the timeless Oscar Meyer "My bologna has a first name" TV commercial. Bob came up with the name *The Color Green*, and Jill came up with the slogan, "Because Life Is Not Always Black and White."

There were some good times with *The Color Green*. We set up shop in the newly opened Little Stores of West End, housed in a very old and haunted building. We were downstairs starting out in a small corner office that was actually intended to be a glorified closet or storage area. Over two years we moved up the hall to a much larger space before landing all the way on the other end in a very nice two-room suite.

As for the ghost. I used to be in the office, the first one, working late at night in an empty building. I would hear steps upstairs and what sounded like a man dragging a bum leg across the floor. I remember calling Jill on the phone to tell her about it and walking upstairs to investigate but finding nothing. Those ghosts are hard to see.

Much like *EDGE*, the *Color Green* years were filled with ups and downs. I eventually got to the point where I wanted out. I put the paper up for sale and ended up selling to my old friend from *EDGE*, David Windhorst.

There are a plethora of great memories surrounding the magazine, including many great live shows I covered for the publication. One that stands out in my mind is the time I saw the Gregg Allman Band at Cowboy's. Now *that* was a show.

# THE ALLMAN BROTHERS BAND

*"Duane and I were musical brothers. We would sit up late at night and get us a bottle of ripple you know, and talk about how the thing that breaks up every band is jealousy, and fighting over women. So we had the women thing figured out. Nobody messes with anybody else's girl. But we talked all the time about how easy it was for he and I to get jealous of each other. It was just a human nature thing. It was just something we dealt with straight ahead and talked about it in private. I'd say "Sometimes when you play, I either get jealous or it makes me want to play harder." But Duane was just so assured and straight ahead. When he wanted to get something done, he would just go straight ahead, and nothing would stop him. And that's what he offered to the band. That confidence and the "We can do it!" Not a cheerleader, but keeping everyone's morale up. And of course his playing was incredible. Laughs. We know about his playing! But when Duane got his mind set, he was straight ahead. And he would inspire people around him."*
—Dickey Betts, interview with Buffalo, June, 2000

The Allman Brothers have always been my favorite band. The Allmans, the Marshall Tucker Band, and the Beatles. I have told the story many times about hearing *At Fillmore East* for the first time while on vacation at the beach, and later borrowing a copy from a friend at school. That record remains my all-time favorite album. Well, tied with *Layla and Other Love Songs*, that is. I have gone through countless copies on vinyl, 8-track, cassette, and CD.

The first time I heard "Ramblin' Man" was on the radio on the way home from work at a temp job. I loved the song, and even today when I hear it, I crank the volume up to ten. That whole *Brothers and Sisters* record rocked my world. I loved "Pony Boy," and I remember sitting in my tiny bedroom when we lived in a mobile home learning the lead to

"Jessica" note for note, picking the stylus up from the LP, rehearsing a lick, and playing it again. I must have woodshedded for a solid weekend learning that twin lead.

I was not lucky enough to ever see the Brothers play live with Duane. My first Allman Brothers concert was in the early 1980s, when I went with members of the Silver Travis Band to see the lineup that included Dan Toler on guitar and the only official "Allman Sister," Bonnie Bramlett. The Dixie Dreggs opened the show.

There is one "missing" show I attended sometime in the 1980s at Greenville Memorial Auditorium. They played in Greenville and I went with some friends. In the parking lot, one of my friends pulled out some airplane blotter acid, which I had taken a few times in the past, and we all did a hit. For the next few hours the Allman Brothers provided the soundtrack to my own personal living, breathing nightmare. My first bad trip. And my last.

Around 1990, I saw the Brothers in Greenville again with another friend, Stephen Long, who had cofounded our *UTOPIA* newspaper with me. This time the band included Warren Haynes, Allen Woody, and Johnny Neel. Blues Traveler opened. The show was so amazing that Stephen and I decided to drive to Charlotte the next night and do it all over again. Another great set. It was identical to Greenville other than trading "Dreams" for "Ramblin' Man."

I attended several more shows during the coming years, including one of the last to include Dickey Betts up in Asheville, NC. All good.

In the early twenty-first century, Scott Greene and I attended a Great Southern show in Charlotte. At this time, Dickey had "Dangerous Dan" Toler in the band. We were invited on the bus, where we spoke with Dan for a while before Dickey and his wife Donna and their Jack Russell terrier came on. Dickey came out and spent some quality time talking to us before hitting the stage with a blistering-hot set.

I had the opportunity to see Dickey perform several times at the annual Angelus event in Florida. One night he did an acoustic set with Bruce Brown and Tommy Crain, along with Bonnie Bramlett. Dickey and Bonnie had a ball singing some Everly Brothers songs and a stripped-down version of "Ramblin' Man." That same weekend Dickey joined the

Charlie Daniels Band onstage at the Angelus country concert for some real, honest, Southern-fried jamming.

In 2007, a pair of benefit concerts were held to help out Cowboy founder Scott Boyer, who was amassing medical bills related to his arterial disease. The first one was held in Muscle Shoals, and the second in Birmingham, Alabama. The second show featured a special guest, one Gregory Lenoir Allman. Just before Gregg's set, his personal assistant Chank Middleton hooked me up and I finally got a few minutes with Gregg. I had interviewed him by phone and briefly met him backstage a couple of times, but this was different. This was a totally straight, absolutely together brother Gregg who treated me like an equal as he boldly signed the cover of my *Fillmore* album in silver Sharpie. My opinion of Gregg skyrocketed in ten minutes. Thanks, Chank.

In March 2009, I did something I had never ever done before. I reviewed a concert from my office. Actually, fifteen of them, all during the Allman's 40th Anniversary Beacon run. The band had played the Beacon Theatre in New York every year for the past twenty years, but this year was to be the biggest and best fifteen-night run ever, with a lineup of guest stars that included everyone from Eric Clapton to Johnny Winter, Sheryl Crowe, Bobby and Phil from the Grateful Dead, and so many more. Of course my favorites were Bonnie and Bekka Bramlett, Tommy Talton and Scott Boyer from Cowboy, Jimmy Hall, Paul T. Riddle, and Chuck Leavell. The "Can't You See" jam with Paul T. on drums, Jimmy Hall on harp, and Kid Rock singing was stellar.

This was all possible because of an invention Butch Trucks of the ABB came up with called Moogis. The shows would be broadcast live with multiple cameras and top-quality sound and High-Def video image. Every night, I hooked my Mac up to the speakers and just rocked. I would sit up until 2 AM nightly to post my reviews on *GRITZ*. It was great fun and reawakened my love for Les Brers.

When I first started *GRITZ*, or *Hot Grits* as we were calling it then, the first phone interview I ever did was with Rook Goldflies, who played bass with the Brothers during the early 1980s. Later I would interview Gregg Allman and Butch Trucks for a 30th Anniversary cover story in *Goldmine Magazine*. The future would afford me opportunities to meet all the Brothers and hold many, many interviews with Dickey Betts, Dan Toler, Les Dudek, Warren Haynes, Allen Woody, and Derek Trucks.

In 2011, I would do the same deal for Universal Music Tribe, having missed out on the 2010 run due to my blindness. But the 2011 run was another great experience, and again the special guests were popping up every night, from Dr. John to Donald Fagen to Steve Earle.

In October 2009, Dickey Betts and Great Southern burned up the stage of the Handlebar in Greenville. Betts had a capacity crowd on their feet and dancing from start to finish. Greenville's own True Blues opened the show with an ultra-tight set of blues rock originals and cover tunes.

Betts greeted everyone at the Handlebar and then strapped on his Les Paul goldtop. The band kicked things off with the Grammy-nominated instrumental "High Falls," with Betts, his son Duane, and Andy Aledort hittin' the note on an amazing triple-lead bombast. Nearly fifteen minutes later, the band struck the familiar opening notes to "Statesboro Blues" and we were off on another ten-minute ride filled with smoking slide guitar, with keyboard man Mike Kach sounding at times a lot like Dickey's former partner in crime, Gregg Allman.

Set one continued with "There Ain't Nothin' You Can Do," and then Dickey's son Duane Betts stepped up to the mike to sing "Paradise."

Next came the perennial "Franklin's Tower" tease, so we all knew a true Betts classic was looming nearby. "Blue Sky" did not disappoint. I never get tired of that song, even after all these years.

Before you could say "Eat a Peach," Dickey took off on "One Way Out," with the jam-packed Handlebar audience up on their feet dancing. The ten-minute jam was followed by an absolutely stellar thirteen-minute-plus "Jessica," with Betts again taking us into the stratosphere.

After a short break, the band returned with "Good Times," a song yet to appear on a Betts album but a really good one that he wrote about Jerry Garcia. I had just turned to the guy beside me and said, "I sure hope he plays 'Back Where it All Begins,'" and the minute I got the words out of my mouth, they kicked into it. Man oh man, was it ever a ride! Fifteen minutes of guitar pyro. That Andy Aledort can really rip it up! And let's not overlook the bass playing of Pedro Arevalo, who is just amazing and fun to watch onstage.

Next, Mike sang some more Gregg on "You Don't Love Me," playing a very tasty piano solo inside the groove. Then it was "In Memory of Elizabeth Reed," thirty minutes of it, including a brilliant "drums" section from Frankie Lombardi and James Varnado and a thumping bass solo from Pedro. Things had reached a boiling point, and the crowd was levitating.

Dickey closed it all out with "Nobody Left to Run With," but the Greenville crowd wasn't about to let him leave just yet, clapping and screaming for his return.

For his encore, Dickey pulled out his greatest hit ever, the 1973 Allman Brothers Band tune "Ramblin' Man." Eight minutes later, it was all over. Dazed children of the sixties and seventies began making their way out of the club, huge smiles plastered across their faces. The temperature outside was cool, and oddly enough the fall air smelled like peaches.

Over the years I amassed a huge collection of live Allman Brothers, Dickey Betts, and Gov't Mule show recordings, cassettes, and CDs by trading with other fans. I became obsessed. I am sure there are dozens of shows I have never even found the time to listen to. But one thing is for sure: there can always be some Allman Brothers Band music found on my stereo or iPod. I don't see that changing anytime soon.

# 36

# A WEDDING IN THE CLOUDS

It was March 31, 1996, and I was driving from Greenville to Caesar's Head to a spot called "Pretty Place," where Jill McLane Greene would soon become my wedded wife. I had butterflies in my gut but was happy as a clam. I had just gotten my hair cut and was decked out in my "Sunday go to meetin'" clothes. I had recently developed this intense headache above my left eye that remained with me for years. At one point the doctor said it was nasal polyps, but it wasn't. Then someone said it had something to do with the way my jaw bone worked after having several teeth taken out a few months prior to the wedding. But hey, I wasn't going to let a little pain stop me.

We all came together under a dark sky and drizzling rain at Pretty Place, a chapel that sits on the edge a cliff near Caesar's Head. It is a place of majestic beauty, rain or not. In fact, Jill and I really loved the way the clouds surrounded the chapel, which had no wall behind the altar, only sky and cloud. I kept thinking about the Cloud City in *Star Wars*. She took it as a blessing.

On the way up the mountain, I saw something step out of the woods and right into my path. I hit the brakes. Right in front of me was this magnificent deer with huge antlers, standing in the road and looking me right in the eye, not 10 feet away. I'm sure it was only there for a few seconds, but it seemed like time stood still. People will always interpret these things in their own way, but the Cherokee part of me took it as nothing less than a blessing on my marriage.

The chapel was filled with our closest friends, most of whom were friends with both Jill and me. Our friend Gail performed the ceremony, which included vows Jill and I had written. Both of our kids, Ben and Hannah, were part of the proceedings. In years to come, I grew to love the kids so intensely that I hated to call myself "step" father, choosing instead to be their "other dad." After all, they still had their dad as well,

Joe, with whom I ended up being good friends. But me and the kids had our own special bond too and still do.

The music for the wedding was provided by my friend and Buffalo Hut Coalition band mate David Haddox, his wife Ingeborg, and Paula Powers. They played and sang the songs I had selected, Kris Kristofferson's "Moment of Forever," Bob Marley's "Three Little Birds," and my own composition, "New Eyes."

The wedding was quite pretty and special, and afterward we drove back to Greenville to Annie's Natural Cafe, where our friend Tim Tyler hosted the reception, complete with a carrot wedding cake. Yes, carrot cake. Jill and I have never been conventional. In fact, her wedding ring was not a diamond but a watermelon tourmaline. Her choice. Jill is not your average girl. There's something different about her that drew me in from the very first time I saw her walk into my office.

The plan was to honeymoon at Lake Lure Inn in North Carolina, but on the way to paradise Jill's tooth began to hurt so badly that we turned around and came back to Greenville. It would be okay, we'd have lots of honeymoons in the future. Between her tooth and my headache, coming home was the right thing to do. I remember us doing virtually nothing for several days but resting. The husband-and-wife fun would come soon enough, in abundance.

# 37

# INTO THE STUDIO

Honestly, my first-ever recording studio experience had come back in the early 1980s, when the Silver Travis Band was recording at Creative Arts Studio. We had just enjoyed a two-week run at the Bowery in Myrtle Beach, where I had stood in on lead vocals for a few songs. When they got into the studio to cut a booking demo, the guys suggested I sing Waylon Jennings's "Just to Satisfy You." It was my first studio experience and really exciting.

In 1991, I cut my first album. A cassette-only EP of five of my songs, done in duet with my friend Donna Orzonno. The songs were recorded in one session at a studio in downtown Greenville called Café Pleasurematic. It was on the second floor just above Café and then Some. The set included "Fairytales," "Fire on the Water," "I'm Leavin'," "Love Me One More Night," and "Hannah's Song," a song I wrote about my love for my stepdaughter Hannah back when she was only four years old.

That same year, the new version of Buffalo Hut Coalition (Dave Haddox, me, Joey Parrish, and Steve "Guitar" Harvey) cut my song "She's Got a Hold on Me." The song was included on yet another cassette-only release from X-Records called *The Hoe Cake Hour*.

In 1996, I went into the studio to record my first full-length CD, *Happy to Be Here*. The album was recorded over a period of five weeks and featured the talents of old friends Dave Haddox and his wife Ingeborg, Joey Parrish, David Windhorst, and new friends Chris Cordell, Paula Powers, and Toy Caldwell Band drummer Mark Burrell. The songs, all written by me, ran from the autobiographical "Stone Houses" to the gospel duet with Dave Windhorst, "Higher Ground," to the rockabilly of "The Snake" and included a new version of "She's Got a Hold On Me" as well as a retooling of "Hannah's Song."

The title for the CD came from one of my favorite books by Garrison Keilor. For the cover I asked Hilda Morrow, editor of *The Inman Times* newspaper to allow me to use her SCPA award-winning photo of Ernest Chapman, the elderly gentleman who would sit in his front yard in a straight-backed chair and look into a mirror balanced on another chair while shaving every morning. The photo said *Happy to Be Here* better than any other I could imagine.

My first national CD review was written by Russell Hall of *Goldmine Magazine*, who said some mighty nice things about *Happy*. The album eventually sold out of all 2,000 copies.

# 38

## ANGELS AND SAINTS SURROUND ME

In June 1998, Jill and I had run into a friend of ours downtown while we were out to lunch. Gail, whom I spoke of earlier as performing our wedding ceremony, had been a friend and teacher over the years, and we had both taken classes from her in meditation and healing.

On that day, Gail commented that she'd like to do some "body work" on me. She could sense that I was dragging around far too much weight and guilt. In the weeks that followed, I visited her office several times to let her perform jin shin and reiki on me. I didn't understand what she was doing, but I always trusted Gail, and she always made me feel better.

On the night of June 28, I noticed a sore spot on my right buttock, close to my anus. I put some infection ointment on it, and thought it was nothing more than a small boil that would rise to the top and burst. Boy, was I wrong.

June 29 found me with an extremely sore butt, and I called and asked Gail if I could come over for a treatment. Of course she said yes, and I felt somewhat better after the one-hour session. That night, the boil seemed to be getting larger, and over the next few days, it began to mutate.

Gail came over one day and performed a house call. A lot of the events surrounding the days and nights between June 30 and July 5 have been forever lost in my mind. I remember Jill calling the doctor's office on July 3, only to find that they were all closed for the long holiday weekend. And I recall July 4 as the date the infection moved into the peritoneum and then into my scrotum. I remember the intense pain of that July 4th and hearing fireworks going off while I laid in bed in agony. We didn't know what to do. We just kept thinking it would be okay. Then my scrotum swelled. Filled with poison, it enlarged to five times its normal size, and there were black legions covering it, which were oozing out some black liquid that smelled like death. It was *The X-Files* made real.

The morning of July 5, Jill called the doctor and they recommended she take me to the emergency room at St. Francis Women's Hospital. The person she spoke with said that I would be seen a lot quicker there than at the other hospital. With Hannah Jane and Jill's friend Ann in tow, I managed to squeeze myself into Jill's car for the ride to the hospital. At this point, I didn't say anything, but I felt death all around me. I was absolutely sure that I was going to die.

In the ER, I was taken back almost immediately. The memories here seem to blur too. It was around 10 o'clock in the morning. There was a nurse, a guy named Steve, that kept talking to me, calming me down while they took my blood pressure, checked my blood, and asked me a million questions. I remember being told that I couldn't have anything to eat or drink. Well, I didn't want anything to eat but I was devastatingly thirsty. They said no water, no ice, nothing.

The hours ticked away as I waited for the doctor to arrive. He finally made it there at around 4 in the afternoon. He asked me if I knew I was diabetic. I said no. He said that my blood sugar level was at 800. Wow. Then he told me what I had was something called necrotizing fasciitis, better known as flesh-eating bacteria, and we were going to have to go into emergency surgery. He said I had a massive infection, and it had to be cut out. He also warned me that I could lose my testicles. Then he asked the nurse if the operating room was available. She told him that there was an amputation being done in there. I felt sick. Then he told her to make sure and let him know the minute they were finished, and that time was of the essence.

About an hour later, Dr. Tommy Bridges returned, telling me were going down to surgery. I asked to see my wife and he said that she and Ann had gone to get something to eat. They had missed lunch and were hungry.

It took Steve four times trying before he could get an IV into my arm. I don't know why, but it's always been like that. They'll think they have the needle in a vein, but it turns out that it isn't in. Then they'll pull it out and start again. I went into this with a dreaded fear of needles.

Now, I still don't like them, but after all the pokes I received over the next month and a half, at least I no longer have a phobia about them.

Everyone was hovering over me now, attaching cardio machines and every possible monitoring device to my body. I felt like Boris Karloff in *Frankenstein*.

I would find out later that Dr. Bridges had spoken with my wife Jill during the hour-long wait prior to surgery. He had warned her that I would be lucky to live through the ordeal. He told her that I was "morbidly obese" and that I was in critical condition. I tipped the scales at 440 pounds. Thing is, I had actually been a good deal heavier than that back when I got married to Jill.

As they wheeled my bed into the OR, I saw Jill and Ann at the end of the hallway, returning to the waiting room. I waved at Jill and felt a sense of peace having seen her.

The last thing I remember was having my IV hooked up to some sort of anesthesia. The doctor patted me on the arm, and I looked up to see the anesthesiologist turning a little wheel under the IV bag. I was out like a light.

Surgery lasted for over four hours. I remember dreaming that I had died—at least I think it was a dream. I felt as though I was floating in a bright light. I later discovered that they had indeed lost me for about thirty seconds during surgery. When I awoke I was in the intensive care unit. Jill was there. I had made it through the initial surgery but the most trying time was yet to come.

Dr. Bridges spoke with Jill again outside the door of my room. She was a basket case, crying and scared. He told her that I could still die, and that was why I was in the ICU.

I don't remember a whole lot about the day I spent in ICU. I can remember waking up and thinking, wow, this isn't so bad. I was feeling no pain and hadn't been clear enough to realize that the reason I was pain free was because of all the medicine they had given me. In days to come I would learn to appreciate that time in ICU, as the pain from my surgery became unbearable.

When I was taken to my room, the real challenge was issued. At first, the doctor had the nurses give me shots of morphine to kill the pain, but the drug was making me sick to my stomach, and I eventually threw up on myself and had to be changed.

The day in ICU and the four days in my room prior to being moved to the other hospital tend to blur together in my memory, but I do remember Jill being there and one day she brought Ben and Hannah up to see me. I was as white as my bed sheets and totally disoriented, which I believe scared the children. Jill said later that maybe I shouldn't have had any visitors that soon, but having never experienced anything remotely like this in our lives, we were both playing it by ear.

By now they had hooked my IV up to a morphine pump and told me to push the button whenever the pain became hard to bear. It would release a measured dose of the drug into my blood stream. Thankfully the thing had a safety feature whereby it wouldn't let the user introduce the morphine more than once every hour or so. One day, one of my nurses checked the counter on the unit and told me that I had pushed the button several hundred times during one night. Like I said, thank God for the safety feature.

I remember that at one point I felt I was beginning to like the feeling of the morphine a little too much; as they plugged a hypodermic needle into my IV and it went into my arm, I could feel the heroin derivative running up my arm, across my shoulder, and hitting my head hard, locking my jaw. Months later I would jokingly say that I felt like Gregg Allman on a Saturday night in Macon, Georgia, during the early 1970s.

The one nurse I remember most from the Women's Hospital was a sweet, strong, African American woman named Rose. Rose took very good care of me. On that first day, in the afternoon, I felt my first urge to use the bathroom. It was Rose who helped me out of bed and onto the bedside toilet. She had to muster up all of her strength to pull my large body, which was as weak as a newborn kitten, up from the bed and onto the toilet. I remember the pain being intense; I never thought in my wildest dreams that I'd ever endure such excruciating pain. Unable to clean myself, it was Rose that took on those duties as well, never once complaining.

During surgery they had put a Foley catheter into me, but every time I urinated it was burning like fire. Some sort of residue was blocking the flow, and they took me off of the catheter on day two.

Every time they brought food into my room, as soon as the dietician would lift the cover from the plate, the smell made me ill. I just couldn't eat a bite. For several days, I was living off the fluid that flowed into my arm from a suspended IV bag.

The first day in the room, my friend Doug Gray of the Marshall Tucker Band came by to visit and brought me an *X-Files* book. I was so spaced on morphine and everything else that was going on in my body that I remember his visit almost as a dream. I remember holding Doug's hand and being able to see far beyond the calm exterior he was displaying. He was really worried about me. I remember seeing a tear forming in his eye. It bonded our friendship like Super Glue.

One day, three friends that played in my little rock and roll band came by to visit. Again, I was out of it. Michael Merck, Jay Taylor, and Freddie Wooten stood at the foot of my bed. Freddie acted as spokesman for the trio. I could sense the fear coming from all three of them. After all, it can't be easy seeing a friend so close to death. Freddie tried to lighten the mood by drawing a really cute cartoon of me in the hospital bed. I would tell them all later just how much it meant to me that they came by to visit.

Jill was by my side a lot of the time, but she had to do her best to stay grounded and go home to care for the children and the dogs. She would pull herself together in front of me and then go out into the hall and talk to Dr. Bridges and cry her eyes out. I'm sure she was going through one of the hardest times of her life as well.

On my fourth day in the hospital, my doctor came in to tell me that they were transferring me to their bigger hospital, which had a whirlpool. He was going to have me go downstairs every day and get into this device, which resembled an oversized bath tub, that would blast hot water between my legs and clean the open wound to promote faster healing.

Later that afternoon, two guys came to get me. They lowered the side rail on my bed and pushed their stretcher up against it. Then I painfully slid myself off of the bed and onto the stretcher. The guys took me out of the room and into the elevator. Soon, we were outside the hospital. What I remember most was the intense heat. It was one of the hottest summers in years, and I had not been outside the hospital for five days. While the guys were hoisting me up into the ambulance I heard one of them quietly whisper to the other, "God, this guy's heavy!" You can imagine how that made me feel.

Inside the ambulance, it was hot. The ride across town to St. Francis Hospital was a rough one. Every little bump we hit felt like we'd hit a deer or something, and the pain would shoot through my body like electricity.

Arriving at the hospital, the porters took me to my room and got me all situated. I remember placing family photos on a table near the bed, as well as photos of our "best kids," the Jack Russell terriers Taz and Tessa. Tessa had been a Mother's Day gift from me and the kids to Jill just weeks earlier. I bought her with the paycheck for my first *Goldmine Magazine* cover story on the Marshall Tucker Band.

It took a couple of weeks before I was ready to eat food. I was living off of the IV fluids and just going along one day at a time. One day some guys came in and started installing all of these bars around my bed with a triangular bar on a chain suspended above the bed. It was there for me to use to exercise and pull myself up. Obviously, my muscles had begun to atrophy.

While all of the angels in St. Francis treated me like a king, two of them will forever remain in my memories. Teresa and Joyce from physical therapy. They both worked with me on a daily basis, cleaning my wound with this gun-like device that sprayed warm water into the wound and then sucked it back out with a vacuum. Now bear in mind this is on my testicles. Yeah, that's what I'm talkin' about.

One day Joyce announced that they were going to take me in a wheelchair down to the whirlpool. After some major heaving and pulling, they got me up and into the chair, down to physical therapy, and into the whirlpool. They had draped a sheet along the bottom of the steel pool where it would run under me and could be used to help pull me out of the pool if I became weak.

Now, the feeling of that water after a couple of weeks in bed was a beautiful thing indeed. I'll never forget just how good it felt. Fifteen minutes passed far too quickly, and I asked Joyce for a second round. Reluctantly, she turned the timer on for fifteen minutes more of pure bliss. Now, the second round was a mistake. I had no idea how the water would relax my already nonexistent muscles. I simply had no power at all. I couldn't pull myself up to save my life. It was time to call in the big guns. There was this really cool black guy named Jim that worked in physical therapy. He wore prescription glasses that were tinted, so it looked like he was cooling it with shades indoors. He also wore a gold chain around his neck and a diamond earring.

Big Jim joined Joyce and Teresa and another person to pull the sheet and lift me unceremoniously from the now-drained whirlpool. They were pulling and saying things like "pull up, Mr. Smith," but I was weak as a kitten. Joyce was patting me on the arm and telling me it was okay. I felt so helpless, you know? Big Jim looked me in the eye and said, "Ain't nothin' but a thang, man. Happens all the time." It made me feel a lot better at the time.

For the first couple of weeks, I didn't want visitors outside the family. I asked them to turn the ringer off on the phone. I didn't want to see anybody. When you're in that kind of shape, you just want to be left alone. After two weeks, I was feeling somewhat better, had received a room full of flowers and cards, and began seeing visitors. My cousin Jack Buchanan, a minister at the time, came by and prayed with me. I always loved Jack. He was my kind of minister. A Christian, but with an open mind, you know.

My sister Patsy came to visit a few times, as did friends like Joey Parrish, Bill Hudson, Larry Whitfield, and Jim Brown, who brought me a cassette Walkman and some live tapes of the Grateful Dead, the Allman Brothers Band, and other great live music.

A few things, random memories I have to this day, include the day I discovered that if I didn't want to eat the regular cardboard hospital food, all I had to do was call the cafeteria and make a request. That's how I got on the salad jag. I would get a bed of lettuce with a scoop of chicken salad, a scoop of tuna salad, and a scoop of cottage cheese, adorned by fresh fruit. It was like a little bit of heaven in that prison that was the hospital.

Changing the dressing on the spot where I had the surgery is something I'd rather forget. At that point I had never experienced that kind of pain. Still, it had to be done at least twice a day.

While lying in the hospital bed, I noticed that the big toe on my right foot was extremely numb. Little did I realize that this was the beginnings of diabetic neuropathy, which would plague me for years to come, sometimes as numbness, oftentimes as pains like thousands of pins sticking in my feet. Learning that I was type-2 diabetic was a shock, but even more of a shock was learning to draw up my own insulin and give myself shots twice a day. At first I swore I'd never be able to do it. After a few years, it was nothing but a thang.

The whole time I was in the hospital I refused to wear a gown. I was putting the buff back in Buffalo! The only thing between me and the Lord was a sheet. For some reason, the thought of clothing just wigged me out. Maybe it was the meds I was on.

When it came time to start walking again, I felt like a baby trying to take his first steps. It took a couple of weeks before I was off the walker and on my own. During the forty-eight-plus days in the hospital, I lost 80 pounds. Hospitals will do that.

Another thing I recall is that while I was in the hospital I couldn't watch anything on TV that was violent in the least or showed blood. The ads for the movie *Saving Private Ryan* made me cringe, as did the one for *Something about Mary*, where Ben Stiller gets his privates caught in his pants zipper. That anti-blood/anti-violence ban stuck with me for well over a year.

One night Gayle and Jill had a meeting with a bunch of their new age friends and sent all of these healing guides to my room. Believe it or not, I felt it. In fact, I slept better that night than I had in weeks. Never underestimate the power of healing guides—or women.

It was the hottest summer in years, and everyone on the floor was talking about it. In a way, I guess I was lucky to be chilling in an air-conditioned room. Albeit with an exposed scrotum. One night an amazing storm came through. The lightning was like a fireworks show as I lay staring out my window. It was beautiful. I put on the headphones and Walkman Jim Brown had brought me and turned on a live concert tape of Gov't Mule. Soon I would be home and safe in my own bed. Back home with my wife and kids. Back home with my sweet puppies Taz and Tessa. I could hardly wait.

# 39

## RIDIN' THE MULE

*"One thing I feel about the Mule is that we are there for each other. I'd do anything for them anytime. Sometimes you have to thank your maker that you're in this position, playing great music with good friends. You don't want to ever take for granted that God almighty has put you on the same plane with guys who are dedicated to making good music."*
—The late Allen Woody, interview with Buffalo,
        January, 2000

The first Gov't Mule show Jill and I ever went to was at the Peace Center in Greenville. It was December 30, 1998, just months after my near-death hospital experience, and in one of Southern rock's most surreal moments, Warren Haynes, Allen Woody, and Matt Abts were playing at the decidedly snobbish Peace Center in Greenville. It was a venue that usually hosted things like Broadway road shows, adult contemporary artists, and the like. It was obvious by the looks on the faces of the employees that they had never been kicked by the Mule. It blew their minds when various tapers began setting up their rigs to record the show.

Still, the Mule delivered the goods. It was my first time seeing them live, but it was Jill's first exposure to their music at all. Of course, by the end of the set she was a fan and Gov't Mule had become our official "date band."

Backstage we met the guys in the band, and Warren was warm and funny. I gave him a tape of Blues Traveler's new, at the time, Christmas song, which I had promised him during a recent phone interview. While we were speaking with Warren, I spied this tall, lumbering, Chewbacca-looking shadow coming down the hallway. It was Allen Woody, who was equally kind and introduced us to Mule drummer Matt Abts. The guys had forged a couple of fans for life just by being approachable. Oh, and by being one kick-ass rock and roll band.

In years to come Jill and I would see many Mule shows in Georgia including the historic Sco-Mule show at Georgia Theatre in Athens, which featured John Schofield and opener Chris Whitley. The now-historic show lasted into the wee hours of the morning. I remember us walking back to Holiday Inn Express and closing all the window shades. We would not be rising and shining any time soon.

Another memorable Mule performance was in Spartanburg, SC, where the band played outside for the Spring Fling. It was a kicking show, and Paul T. Riddle along with future Marshall Tucker guitarist Rick Willis joined the band onstage to play "Can't You See."

On August 26, 2000 we heard that Woody had died in a New York hotel room, and we were devastated. Jill and I stayed home all weekend and cried. It was like we had lost a friend. No matter how great the Mule would become in later years, it could never be the same. Woody was gone, and I just had to accept it and move on.

As the years passed, Warren and Matt kept the band going as a four-man outfit and it was still great, but there would never be another Mule like Woody's. Great, yes, but different.

# 40

# HOT *GRITZ* ANYONE?

After the 1998 hospital ordeal, I found myself in quite a pickle. I couldn't sit because of the surgery, so I laid in bed a lot. During these days I came up with an idea. There was quite a buzz happening on the web, especially around Southern rock bands like Lynyrd Skynyrd and Marshall Tucker. In fact, after I created my first website in 1996, I also created one of the first Marshall Tucker Band fan pages online. Some friends created a MTB chat room that got together to talk MTB once a week. I think it was on Monday night. It was during the same hour that the weekly *ER* episode was running on TV.

I saw the massive interest in Tucker and other Southern rock bands blossom right before my eyes. While lying around after my surgery, I decided to post a Southern rock news page on my Geocities site. All just for fun. I called it *Hot Grits*.

Just a week or two into my project, an online friend called me up to offer her services as webmaster for *Hot Grits*. We were up and running.

As my body healed, I began writing for the newsletter as it quickly became a full-on webzine. As I said earlier, my first interview for *Grits* was with former Allman Brothers bassist Rook Goldflies. From there it snowballed, and I was soon interviewing Charlie Daniels, Gregg Allman, Jimmy Hall, Edgar Winter, and more.

That first year was exciting, but it was only the beginning. Right as we were moving into year two I split from my business partner and *Grits* went through a major overhaul. Upon a suggestion from singer-songwriter Marshall Chapman, I dropped "Hot" and added a "Z." *GRITZ* was born.

Another friend, Bob Timmers, the founder of the Rockabilly Hall of Fame, volunteered to be my webmaster. Bob saved the ship. Things really started to cook.

We were gaining a huge worldwide audience, doing interviews with Dickey Betts, Johnny Winter, Peter Frampton—countless others. We started doing lots of concert reviews, CD reviews, and more.

I hit on my first controversy in 2000 when I interviewed Lynyrd Skynyrd drummer Artimus Pyle for the first time. Artimus, as anyone who knows him is aware, is always outspoken, and I had caught him during a time when he was upset and speaking his mind. The interview caused an uproar. Fans loved it, some hated it, but we got the people talking for sure. Some of the "powers that be" contacted me and asked that I edit the interview to omit a few personal comments they thought bordered on slander. Whether I did the right thing or not I am still unsure, but the next day, there were six fewer paragraphs in the piece.

*GRITZ* was really growing, and I saw an opportunity in summer 2001 to live a dream I had harbored since I was a teen: own my own full-color rock and roll magazine. Once again, it was decision time. The webzine was doing very well, but I really thought I could create a Southern version of *Rolling Stone*.

With the help of an investor, we launched *GRITZ* magazine in June. The cover featured Dickey Betts, complete with a casual conversation with Betts about his career. There was also my interview with Jefferson Airplane/Hot Tuna guitarist Jorma Kaukonen, part one of my interview with legendary producer Tom Dowd, and a conversation with Mayberry's own "Goober," George Lindsey.

Through a never-ending series of ups and downs, we managed to publish eleven quarterly issues of the print magazine before the price of paper forced us to return to our roots on the Internet. Truth be told, there was a growing trend of paperless magazines at the time, and we managed to slide comfortably right back into the spot we were in before.

Through my many years with *GRITZ*, I was introduced to countless Southern rockers, many of whom were my heroes during the seventies and many of whom I now call friends. Life can really be interesting sometimes.

In late 2006, I got an offer I couldn't refuse. Staff writer and friend James Calemine introduced me to a music business veteran out of Florida who merged with *GRITZ*, and my creation became part of an even bigger collective called Swampland. It was the start of a whole new era for *GRITZ*.

I would maintain the *GRITZ* section of the web site while James would man his own section called Mystery and Manners. The boss later added a couple of other sections, including Southern Pro Football.

While my association with *GRITZ* ended in 2010, it had been a great ride for me, affording me the opportunity to meet, interview, and become friends with everyone from Billy Bob Thornton to Paul Hornsby, from Tommy Talton to the great Bonnie Bramlett.

# 41

# BONNIE BRAMLETT

*"Oh, I love Bonnie. That's the singing-est son of a bitch. [Laughing] She taught me how to sing. I'd be a great singer if I had a voice, you know? [Laughs.] 'Cause I can really sing, I just don't have a voice! But what little I have I got from her. She told me, "You can't try to control it. You just got to open up and let it go!"*
—Dickey Betts, interview with Buffalo, November, 2000

I remember reading about Delaney and Bonnie a lot back in high school, during those days when I was constantly engrossed in a rock and roll magazine. It seemed to me this husband-and-wife duo had worked with every really good musician out there, from Duane Allman to Eric Clapton, George Harrison, Joe Cocker, Rita Coolidge, Bobby Whitlock— even Gram Parsons. I was a huge fan.

Flash forward to the early 2000s. I met Bonnie for the first time at Charlie Daniels's Angelus Benefit in Clearwater, Florida. She was wearing a tie-dye T-shirt and she and one of her girlfriends came over to the press tent and sat and talked to my wife and me like she had known us forever. Jill had done a phone interview with her, but this was our first face-to-face meeting. Every year I see Bonnie at Angelus, and she never ceases to amaze me.

Speaking of being amazed. When I was getting ready to record my *Southern Lights* CD down in Huntsville, Alabama, I called Bonnie and asked if there was any way she would honor me by singing on it. The lady didn't hesitate. She was happy to do it. That night I sat up until the wee hours of the morning writing "I Don't Want to Say Goodbye," a duet just for the two of us. I just couldn't let Southern Rock Soul Sister Number One do strictly backing vocals. She's too damned good!

She drove down to Huntsville from Nashville herself in the sweltering heat. When she got to the studio she walked in and said, "Can any one of you gentlemen get a bottle of water for a lady?" Lord, every man in their was tripping over the other guy to get her water. Bonnie is the Queen.

She nailed the vocal on the duet within half an hour, and then added vocals to "Into the Light" and Johnny Wyker's "Hooker's Boogie."

Bonnie would return to Huntsville to headline my release party for *Southern Lights*, and a couple of years later she would headline GRITZfest in Greenville, SC, at the Handlebar. The benefit was for Greenville's Safe Schools program and I lined up a bunch of my friends, including Tommy Crain and the Crosstown Allstars, Donnie Winters, Tony Heatherly, Mark Burrell, Mark McAfee, Mark Emerick, the Silver Travis Band, Denny Walley, and Dru Lombar from Grinderswitch.

In 2006, Bonnie returned to the silver screen alongside Kevin Costner in *The Guardian*, and in 2007 she recorded a great new album called *Beautiful*. A perfect title for a truly beautiful lady. Both inside and out. Then, in February 2010, Bonnie once again offered her talent for GRITZfest II, a benefit to aid the earthquake in Haiti organized by myself and Sonny Edwards in Huntsville, Alabama. The event again featured Tommy Crain & the Crosstown Allstars, along with Tommy Talton, Jimmy and Donna Hall, Shawna P, and Karen Blackmon Caldwell. I had been a real fan of Karen when she fronted the Artimus Pyle Band back in 1982.

Later on I was fortunate to meet Delaney and Bonnie's daughter Bekka, a spittin' image of her mama and one of this writer's favorite singers in the whole wide world. We became friends and now both Bonnie and Bekka are among my very favorite people. I only wish Delaney had not passed away. I did the last ever interview with him and man oh man, was he a cool guy. I could have talked to him about music forever. He invited me to call back any day, any time, and I would have, had the Lord not taken him home.

Bonnie Bramlett is one of a kind. One of the greatest voices in music, and especially in the history of good ol' Southern rock. I love you, Bonnie.

# 42

# LAYIN' IT DOWN IN LINCOLN

I got to know Bobby Lowell after being given his phone number when my editor at *GOLDMINE* magazine asked me to write about the death of Boxcar Willie. Lowell had been the head honcho at Roto Records in Lincoln, Nebraska, which had recorded Boxcar's first record. It didn't take long before the 1950s rockabilly star Lowell took up with the Carolina writer-musician, and before you could say "Um Baby, Baby," I had been invited to attend a Rockin' Weekend in Lincoln and had my Greyhound bus tickets in hand. This was 1999.

Don't even say it. I didn't realize that the bus would prove to be hell on earth. We drove all over hell and half of the USA to get to Lincoln, stopping off in Atlanta, Nashville, Bowling Green, and Chicago, among other ports of call. Thank God for Captain Dean Taylor, who sent me back home at the end of the fabulous weekend on an airplane. Three airplanes, actually.

Meeting Bobby Lowell was great. I learned all about his musical legacy and his affinity for yard sales (which would inspire me to later write a song called "Yard Sale Man") and the Mo Java Coffee Shop and the M & N Sandwich Shop. Our times together were great fun, and before it was all over I had received a pair of his personal Tony Lama boots, previously owned by none other than Carl Perkins and worthy of the Hall of Fame, and had recorded a duet of "Blue Suede Shoes" with Bobby in the Jam Palace Studios with Cowboy Bob at the board. Also on hand for the weekend was my friend Bob Timmers, curator of the Rockabilly Hall of Fame, along with his friend Dave Hermsen, who is a great compliment on bass guitar to Timmers on lead. And there was Bill Barker, a friend of Timmers, and a printer. (And part-time amateur stand-up comic.) The "three amigos" had come over from Wisconsin, and I was treated to a few cool stories about the Green Bay Packers. Cheese, it was great!

The Saturday afternoon block party at the Rock and Roll Runza featured the Nebraska Rock and Roll Hall of Fame Concert and Induction Ceremony. The music was smoking, as I joined Lowell, Dean and Joanne Taylor, Freddie Lowell, Zeke, and some of the other Tribesmen Motorcycle Club guys for a great afternoon of music.

I want to note here that meeting Zeke was a true pleasure. He is the national president of the Tribesmen motorcycle club and a heck of a nice guy, just like the other bikers present. Performers and inductees included the Fabulous Flippers, the Fay Hoagan Experiment (featuring Cowboy Bob, who runs Jam Palace Studios), and the Smoke Ring, with their killer Tower of Power style horn section. Individual inductees included Janice K., Pat Glenn, Joe Gray, Jim Akin, and Jim Cidlik.

I recall Bobby telling me that there was one major player who still needed to be inducted into the Hall of Fame. Dave Robel. Bobby told me one day "Dave has played with me, and played with most every major band in town at one time or another. He's been on numerous 45s, LPs, and CDs. He's toured Europe. He's played Greenwich Village. He's played with the Nebraska Rock and Roll Hall of Fame All Star Band, but he still hasn't been inducted. I don't understand that." Robel had recently played drums on a wild new CD by the group Shithook, a favorite of rock writer and former Brownsville Station member the late Cub Koda. Of course, Robel has since been inducted.

Another musician I had the pleasure of meeting was Jim Jacobi. The original Lincoln Punk Rocker. We met over a sandwich at Norm's. Jim Jacobi fronted the band called Crap Detectors from 1978–1998. The band was started in Lincoln, Nebraska, and debuted with the release of their LP *Victims of the Media*.

Saturday night's Zoo Bar concert featured Bill Kirchen and Too Much Fun, along with Ronnie Dawson and the Mezcal Brothers. The Rockabilly Weekend was an experience I will never forget. The music was great, the people were wonderful, and Lincoln was a great town to visit.

A few months later I got the news of Bobby's cancer. The doctors weren't giving him long to live, and his friends decided to throw him a big party. Bob Timmers told me to drive over to Burns, Tennessee, and ride with him to Lincoln. Now that was an experience.

The party was great, and we had another all-star jam session. Bobby was weak but still smiling. We had a great time, and I mentioned to Pinky Semrad and Sean Benjamin that I'd like to record a CD in Lincoln with Bobby singing with me. Those plans were changed forever in October 2000 when Bobby's son called to tell me his dad had passed. I was brokenhearted.

The plans to record moved forward and the album became a tribute to Bobby. *Midwest Carolina Blues* was recorded live in the studio with Sean Benjamin on guitar and piano, Bob Timmers on guitar, Dave Robel on drums, Pinky Semrad on bass, Jim Cidlik on keyboards, Jim Jenkins on sax, and Toni Baustian on vocals. We called our little band the Rockabilly Hall of Fame Blues Band, and the CD came out on Bob's Rockabilly Hall of Fame label.

The record included Sean singing a Lowell song called "It's Been So Long" and Toni singing a Bob Timmer's composition called "Rockabilly Blue." Timmers suggested a cover of the instrumental "Red Eye," written by Gene Vincent & the Blue Caps guitarist Johnny Meeks. I did the old blues song "Jelly, Jelly" and Toni and I did a medley of "Stormy Monday Blues" and "Redhouse." There was a rocking take on Steve Young's "Lonesome, Onry and Mean" and my own "She's Got a Hold on Me." We all joined together in a gospel tune by Edgar Winter and Jerry LaCroix called "Fly Away."

The night before the recording session, I made the mistake of rocking out and singing with all the guys at Zoo Bar. Come recording time, my voice was just plain gone. We recorded everything except the lead vocals, which I would later record at Wes Nance's studio in Asheboro, NC.

Bobby didn't live to see the finished CD, but he was really excited that we were all coming together to record it. He would have loved the Lowellpalooza show we would later stage at Zoo Bar as a combination CD release party and tribute. Of course, he was there in spirit. I could feel him there, and in my third eye I saw that big, happy grin of his and felt a rush of cold air run up my back.

# 43

# TURN OF THE CENTURY IN TEXAS:
# EDGAR WINTER, JERRY LACROIX, AND JANIS JOPLIN

*"We were one of the first white bands to play the Apollo theatre when we recorded Roadwork and I will never forget being introduced at the Apollo as Edgar Winter's White Trash Band. It was really something. Gladys Knight and the Pips were headlining that night and there were mixed reactions when we walked out onto that stage. There were some people who actually had heard some of the songs on the radio and thought we were black, some wanting their money back, but I explained to them to give the music a chance and then if not satisfied you can have your money back."*
—Edgar Winter, interview with Buffalo, July, 1999

During the seventies, I became a die-hard fan of both Edgar and Johnny Winter and their "extended family"—that is, Rick Derringer, Dan Hartman, Chuck Ruff, Ronnie Montrose, and of course Jerry LaCroix. When we heard that there was to be a special White Trash reunion concert at the turn of the century, we knew we just had to be there.

New Year's eve 1999–2000 is one I will never forget. It was a week filled with fear—the fears of Y2K. Remember that? Fears that all of our computers would crash when the clocks moved past the midnight hour on December 31st, sending financial institutions crumbling and airplanes plummeting out of control. Not since the paranoia surrounding the H-bomb during the 1950s had so much fear run rampant in the homeland.

Still, Jill and I boarded a plane bound for the small Gulf Coast town of Port Arthur, Texas, for a rocking New Year's concert reuniting Beamont's pride, Edgar Winter, joined by his former Edgar Winter's White Trash partner Jerry LaCroix.

When we arrived in Port Arthur, we read in the local paper that the massive concert had been rescheduled for the evening of the first because Edgar had been invited to play in an all-star band at the Washington Memorial for President Bill Clinton.

As fate would have it, that schedule change landed me onstage with Jerry LaCroix at fifteen minutes into the new millennium.

Earlier in the day I had sat down for a one-on-one interview with LaCroix over a few beers. Jerry recounted his days with White Trash as well as the pair of albums he released as Rare Earth's lead singer and his single outing with Blood, Sweat, and Tears. One of the finest vocalists in classic rock, LaCroix smiled and spoke honestly, his solid white hair and beard offset by the red, white, and blue band on his hat.

During the jam session in the lounge that night, the music stopped every time we saw Edgar appear on the big-screen TV broadcasting live from Washington. Local musicians jammed with members of the band that would open the show the next evening, and Jerry sang his heart out on White Trash tunes like "Keep Playing that Rock and Roll" and "Free Ride." I ended up singing backup with Jerry's brother Julian.

But it was during a rendition of "The Sky's Crying" that LaCroix came down into the audience and took me by the hand, leading me to the stage, where to my surprise the guitar player took off his Strat and handed it to me. Jerry got behind the keyboard, and we launched into "Redhouse." I sang with all I could muster and played my best. All the while, my mind was flashing back to high school. Back to White Trash. I was onstage with Jerry LaCroix, and he was smiling at me like a brother. At the end of the song I pointed at Jerry and for some reason spoke into the mic—"People keep asking me—Where's your brother?"

Jerry laughed.

That was one of the lines Edgar had spoken during his introduction of brother Johnny Winter on the album *Roadwork*, one of the best live albums ever recorded and one of my all-time favorite records. Back in high school, I can remember bringing a jam box to school and playing *Roadwork* for everyone on 8-track, rocking the school bus until the six D-size batteries in my player died on me, usually halfway through "Tobacco Road." I know that I singlehandedly turned at least forty kids on to the heavy rock and blues of Edgar Winter's White Trash. I had everybody singing "Save the Planet" and "Turn on Your Love Light."

Of course, that was in 1972, and by 1973 Edgar Winter would be fronting a new band called the Edgar Winter Group—made up of guitarist Rick Derringer, bassist Dan Hartman, and drummer Chuck Ruff, who in 1998 would become an e-mail buddy of mine, creating another of those "rock-n-roll dreams come true" moments.

While we were in Port Arthur, some really good people took us around to see Janis Joplin's birth home and the place she went to school. We visited the Museum of the Gulf Coast, which houses her psychedelic-painted Porsche, as well as displays of Edgar and Johnny Winter, Jerry LaCroix, Coach Jimmy Johnson, and lots of regional history. Jill and I ended up buying way too many Janis Joplin books, posters, and postcards. Absolute fun.

January 1, 2000 brought the Edgar Winter concert. We went over to the Port Arthur Civic Center for sound check and then back to the hotel to rest up for the show.

The concert was awesome. Seeing Edgar and his wife Monique and meeting his manager Jake Hooker was very nice. I spoke to guitarist Mitch Perry for quite some time outside. He is a nut. Funny and very friendly. I also got to meet Edgar's drummer, Rick Latham, who it turns out is also from Greenville, SC. But then again, so is Jason Patterson, who drums for Chris Duarte. We met Chris, too, and he was every bit the gentleman. A great time was had by all.

The next morning we headed back home with a pocketful of memories and the sound of White Trash stirring through our heads.

Speaking to Chuck Ruff by phone in 1999, I found myself reliving the shows I had seen in the mid-seventies, recalling a special concert memory from October 1973 at Greenville Memorial Auditorium here in South Carolina. The show featured the Edgar Winter Group and openers Foghat. I recall Lonesome Dave and Foghat putting on a great set, playing hits like "Slow Ride" and "Fool for the City."

The Edgar Winter Group blew me away that night. Edgar appeared in multicolored feather pants with that Univox portable piano strapped around his neck playing all the hits from his current LP *They Only Come Out at Night*, including "Free Ride" and the Top 40 instrumental "Frankenstein." Chuck was beating the soup out of the drums, Dan danced all around the stage playing bass and singing, and Jerry Weems filling in for the absent Derringer played stinging guitar. The show was one I'll never forget.

# 44

## THE TAPE IS ROLLING

I have really enjoyed doing the hundreds of interviews I have conducted over the years. Some I've enjoyed more than others, but all have been good. Of course there were a few that made me a little nervous at first, like George Harrison, Delaney Bramlett, and Gregg Allman to name a few. Mostly because I had elevated them to such a lofty status in my mind over the years. Like I have said so many times, the reason I started writing about music in the first place is because I am such a fan.

When the time came for the first interview I had scheduled with Buddy Miles, I called him up and he was soaking in a bubble bath. He asked if it would be okay to reschedule, and of course I obliged. While on the phone we started up a conversation and just talked about music for an hour until, as he said, his "pecker shriveled up." I just laughed. I caught back up a week later with the tape rolling. The interview went great and Buddy gave me stories about Jimi Hendrix and Janis Joplin that I had never before heard. After we hung up, I excitedly replayed the tape to transcribe the interview. There was only one voice on the tape—mine. In the immortal word of Charlie Brown, "Rats!"

The very same thing happened ten years later with Delaney Bramlett. A great interview, but when played back nothing but my voice. Both times it was machine malfunction that caused my ulcer to flare up. Oddly enough, I would not get my Buddy Miles interview until 2006, some five years after my ill-fated first attempt, and a short two years later Buddy passed away. As for Delaney, he kindly did the whole interview again. It was to be his last media interview before his passing.

When I first spoke with KISS bassist Gene Simmons in 1991, I was still pretty new to the interview game and a bit nervous. I said something, I forget what, early on in the interview, to which Simmons asked, "What's the matter, Michael?"

"It's just that I'm a little nervous," I replied.

"Why?"

"Well, I am a longtime fan, and you're Gene Simmons."

"So?" He said. "You're Michael B. Smith, the magazine editor, and I'm not nervous."

The king of all egos put me at ease and I learned a real lesson that day. I don't believe I was ever star struck again. Well, not *too* badly anyway.

I interviewed the one-and-only Dr. John back in 1992. Now, the singer has a unique speaking voice, and a real drawl, so it's a bit hard to understand him on the phone even on a good day. On this day, I made the mistake of conducting the interview too close to the computer, and some sort of electronic interference caused a loud buzz on the tape. The only words I could decipher when I played it back were "Professor Longhair" and "Nu Awlins." Please refer back to the aforementioned Charlie Brown quote.

When I interviewed Danny Joe Brown for *GRITZ*, he was very kind. Diabetes and complications had beaten down the Molly Hatchet singer, and sadly, just two years later, he would be dead. One of the rules the doctor had given Danny was "No drinking," so when he began slurring his words, he stopped and said, "Michael, please don't put it in the interview that I am drunk. That wouldn't look good. But hell, I am tired of all the pain and I needed a drink." Been there, done that. I fully understand where he was coming from.

I always loved the "in person" interviews the best. Like sitting with Jerry LaCroix down in Port Arthur, Texas, having a beer and chatting, or hanging out with Scott Boyer at his home in Killen, Alabama, with Dave Peck and talking while his hyperactive puppy chewed on everything in sight, my shoe included. Or the series of interviews I had with members of the Marshall Tucker Band, past and present, in their homes and on the road, and Charlie Daniels in his office in the big log cabin in Lebanon, Tennessee, drinking coffee and staring at all the cool Southern rock history that adorns his walls.

And then there was my third ever interview with one of my favorite entertainers and people, the former Carolina turned Nashville girl, Marshall Chapman, who took us all "Somewhere South of Macon" in 1976 and continues to be one of Music City's brightest songwriters.

Chapman and I met up near Vanderbilt College at one of her favorite restaurants. It was a historic soda shop called Vandyland, and Marshall was more than a little bummed out that it was scheduled to be demolished in the name of "progress." We had a great lunch and a great interview, and I got to meet half a dozen people who dearly love her. I enjoyed my day and my interview more than any I could think of at the time.

# 45

# MARSHALL CHAPMAN

*"The best musical memories of growing up in South Carolina were seeing all the great black acts that came through...Ray Charles, Jackie Wilson, James Brown, the Shirrelles, Maurice Williams & the Zodiacs, little Stevie Wonder. Also, my first night at summer camp—Camp Pinnacle near Hendersonville, NC—this girl named Debbie Dial got up and sang a song while playing a ukulele. All the girls screamed like she was Elvis. I must have made a mental note right then, because it wasn't long before I was learning to play the ukulele."*
—Marshall Chapman, interview with Buffalo, June, 2004

The first time I heard the name Marshall Chapman was when I sighted an article in *The Spartanburg Herald* back in the early seventies. After reading that piece in the paper about Marshall, I decided to drive over to Westgate Mall, walked into the Record Bar, and promptly purchased her debut Epic album, *Me I'm Feelin' Free*. Now, I swear on a stack of Bibles, I got to the car, turned on the radio, and Billy Mack was playing "Somewhere South of Macon." It was great. At that moment I became a fan of the self-proclaimed "tall girl," this singer-songwriter who grew up in Spartanburg, the daughter of nearby Inman Mill owners, a wealthy textile family.

I always included Marshall in my conversations with friends about Southern rock, although she leaned more toward the country music side. But let's face it, the girl could always rock. Long before Chrissie Hynde there was Marshall, slinging a mean Telecaster and rocking out on her original songs. Songs like "Betty's Bein' Bad," a tune that Sawyer Brown took to the top of the country charts. Over the years I have had the opportunity to interview Marshall several times, but none of those conversations was more fun than our 2005 face-to-face meeting at Vandyland in Nashville. It was just a lot of fun talking about her latest album and her memoir *Goodbye Little Rock and Roller,* one of my favorite rock and roll books.

During the seventies I must have seen Marshall play live twenty times, including her set opening for the Marshall Tucker Band at their 1977 Homecoming in Spartanburg. Marshall is a great talent and a good ol' girl for sure.

# 46

## MY THIRD TRIP TO LINCOLN, VIA NASHVILLE

If I thought the first trip to Lincoln, Nebraska, was "Michael B's Big Adventure," I had no idea of the adventure that lay in store for me in January 2001.

The plan was simple. (*Yeah, right.*) By some mode of transportation I'd get to Nashville from Greenville, SC, where I'd hook up with band mate/friend Bob Timmers, who would put my Carolina butt into his car and drive to Lincoln, Nebraska, for our CD release party, which would also serve as a tribute to our late friend Bobby Lowell, a well-loved rockabilly and blues singer who passed away on September 30, 2000.

Well.... At first I bought Amtrak tickets to Nashville but promptly returned those after discovering that the sales "person" had failed to inform me that the train would carry me to Atlanta where I would board a Greyhound bus to Nashville. *Nope. I don't think so. Not again.* When all the feathers shook out and the dust settled, Jill and I decided that I would take the family car to Nashville—Burns, actually—where I would hook up with Bob and roll on, big mama.

For a week before the trip I watched the Weather Channel. Ice and snow was everywhere, but I was determined to make it, and with more than just a little blessing from up above, I did.

I left out pretty early on Thursday morning for the six-hour drive to Music City, which became a nine-hour trip after an unending traffic jam in Knoxville and rain/sleet and dark-of-night all through Nashville and into the greater twin cities of Dickson and Burns. The trip was uneventful for the most part, other than the hour-and-fifteen-minute traffic jam in Knoxville, where I stared at an "I Love Jesus" billboard until I thought I actually saw the Lord.

When I got to Burns Station Sound Studio (also the home of the Rockabilly Hall of Fame) on College Street, I happily parked the Honda and went in to greet Bob. We spent a little time catching up and talking about *GRITZ*. Bob is not only the curator/creator of the Rockabilly Hall of Fame, but at that time he was also the *GRITZ* webmaster, a thankless job for which I am eternally indebted to him.

At the present time the Rockabilly Hall of Fame exists primarily on the Internet, so Bob's office consists mostly of computer equipment, although there are rockabilly CDs and T-shirts for sale. The decor is pure country and rockabilly, thanks mostly to Gordon Stinson, who owns Burns Station and has recorded countless country albums in that fine facility. You've heard the old adage "if these walls could talk?" Well, these walls can, in a way. Signatures adorn the walls, scribed by the likes of Johnny Cash, Loretta Lynn, various NASCAR drivers, Web Wilder, Ramona Jones (Grandpa's wife), Ronnie Stoneman, and Gordon's old friend and client Johnny Paycheck. The studio is great.

Bob and I took in the local Chinese buffet and I went back to the studio to spend the night on the sofa while Bob returned to the bed and breakfast where he currently lives. My night was peaceful, although I felt the ghosts of country music past all around me. Not a scary thing—more of a nice, warm feeling with a strong Southern accent.

The next morning we awoke to snow and drove into Dickson, where I showered at the B&B and prepared for the long journey to Nebraska.

My memory of the entire day is kind of a blur now, but I can decipher a few gray-faded memories. Bob's windshield wipers were falling apart at the seams, so we pulled into an auto parts joint and Bob purchase some new ones and grabbed a jug of wiper fluid on the way out the door.

For the next fifteen hours, Bob burned up the highways and byways of this great land of ours. We traveled northwest into Kentucky, Missouri, and finally Nebraska. The most excitement came in the form of one St. Louis, Missouri, as Bob did his impression of Richard Petty and/or Luke Skywalker, racing through the dips, turns, and obstacles with the professionalism of a true Jedi NASCAR driver. There were trucks and cars merging from the right, from the left, from overhead....

Bob's car now has chubby finger impressions dug into the dash, but other than that, no problem. It was pretty nifty seeing the archway in St. Louis at 150 mph, too.

We arrived safe and sound in Lincoln after driving the last 100 or so miles through fog so thick we could see nothing but a little of the white line. Oh, and a tip of the Stetson to MapQuest.com. Their directions were perfect and took us right to Dave Robel's front door. Just one problem. Dave wasn't there, and it was butt-freezing cold in Lincoln.

Now, if this chronicle were a soap opera, and it ain't, even though it contains all of the earmarks of *Days of Our Lives*, at this point we would plaster a big "To be continued" across the screen.

Bob and I had the brilliant idea that perhaps Dave was at Zoo Bar waiting for us, so we rode into town and asked around at the Zoo, but they had not seen him. We checked a couple of other places and then returned to Dave's place. After sitting in the car with the motor running for about thirty minutes, Dave came wandering out of the house. Seems he had fallen asleep with the TV on and couldn't hear us knocking, screaming, and convulsing outside.

Inside the Robel mansion, life got back on track quickly. Warmth and a shot of brandy brought me back down to terra firma. We spent the time between 11 PM and 3 AM chatting and watching a bizarre video and listening to *Al Kooper's Bus Tape*. Pretty strange, but it was just right for the "stoned from traveling" mood I was in. At 3 AM, the big man retired to the Billy Bacon Suite for a long winter's nap while Timmers made the sofa his new domain.

Saturday was rehearsal day, but prior to the get together, Bob and I drove out to the market to visit what has become one of my favorite used book stores. Leaving in the rain, Bob backed into a concrete post, putting what he called "a ding" in his bumper. Back at Dave's I saw that it looked more like it had been pummeled with a sledgehammer. Must grow them dings BIG in Wisconsin, eh Bob?

The rehearsal party was great. Toni Baustian and her man Thomas brought a pic-a-nic basket and we had finger foods before and during rehearsals. Later, Dave broke out the George Foreman grill for burgers-deluxe.

Everyone was at the rehearsal. Sean Benjamin, Dave and his lady Tammy, Pinky Semrad, Bob Timmers, Toni and Thomas, and Jim Jenkins, who went above and beyond the call by driving a bunch of icy miles to be at rehearsals. Great musicians, great friends. And I thought for a minute, I'd never have met any of these folks had it not been for Bobby Lowell. Man.

That night we stayed in and watched the Weather Channel as they called for "the storm of the century" to hit Lincoln overnight. One thing I have learned over my years is that weather forecasters are not always right. Thank God, this was one of the times they were wrong.

Sunday morning, Dave took me and Bob out to breakfast at a really neat diner furnished in gasoline pumps and signage from days gone by. After that, we went out to the cemetery to visit the gravesite of our friend Bobby Lowell. I said goodbye to Bobby and dropped one of my guitar picks on his snow-covered grave.

We loaded into the Zoo Bar at about 3 PM, and the show got under way at 4 PM. Great fun was had by all, and all of the bands did a killer job. Shithook, J. Harrison B. & the Bumbles, the New Atomic Robert Band, the Mezcal Brothers, and Michael Buffalo Smith & the Rockabilly Hall of Fame Blues Band rocked on and on, and every band made dedications to the man of the hour, Bobby Lowell. Bobby would have loved that.

There were lots of hugs that day. Lots of genuine affection between friends, including the members of the Tribesmen Motorcycle Club, of which Bobby was a member. It was so great seeing Zeke, Brad, and all the others again.

The next morning, Bob and I said our goodbyes to our friends David and Tammy and hit the road. We were blessed with clear, often even sunny skies during the duration of the trip. Somewhere in Missouri we stopped back by this really great nostalgia store we had run across on the way up and bought a bunch of cool stuff. A mere fourteen hours later, we were back in Burns, Tennessee, safe and sound. Well, safe at least.

I hit the sofa and awoke the next morning to the smell of coffee brewing and the sound of Gordon Stinson mixing some tracks in the studio. I introduced myself and talked for a while with Gordon before Bob came in. Then, before you could say "Um Baby, Baby," it was time to begin my seven-hour return trip, plowing through Nashville like a bat out of hell (I learned well from Timmers!).

Somewhere near Knoxville, out in the country, I saw a box turtle crossing the road. I pulled over, put the turtle on my front seat, and drove to the next exit, a nice, country road with a beautiful tract of land to the right dipping down into a small river. I took the shelled one out and released him towards the water. One less road kill on I-40. I felt good inside.

By late afternoon I was home once again, filled with indestructible memories that will stay with me forever, happy to see my family but already missing my friends and fellow musicians. But hey, I know we'll get together again. We are like brothers and sisters now. No, scratch that. We are more than brothers and sisters. We are fellow rockabilly musicians.

# NINE-ELEVEN

I was having a bowl of Life cereal in the den, getting a slow start on my day. Jill was in Hannah's bedroom watching John Edwards (the psychic who talks to dead people) on TV when I heard her call me into the room. She said that the news had broken in during her program and reported a terrible accident. Apparently a passenger airplane had somehow lost control and ran right into one of the World Trade Center towers in New York City.

While I was watching TV with Jill, trying to figure out what had happened, the second plane hit the second tower. It was obvious. We were under attack. None of our lives would ever be the same.

We sat and watched CNN the entire day. Numb and not believing. In retrospect, it may have been a bad idea to sit glued to the TV for those two days. It burned those horrific images into my mind forever. Images I, like everyone else, will carry with me always. The biggest tragedy of our lifetime brought us all together as flag-flying Americans like never before. I'd never seen so many flags as I saw in the wake of the attack. When I played an American Cancer Society benefit at the BMW plant in Greer, SC, with True Blues and the Southern Rock Allstars just three days later, the somber mood was offset by the multitude of American flags and the sheer American spirit. SRA's Jay Johnson sported an American flag shirt that summed up how we were all feeling. We were all still upset about 9/11, but we were all very proud to be Americans.

In years to come I would see our country hit by both natural and man-made disasters like Hurricane Katrina in 2005 and the 2010 BP oil spill, all terrible. But for the life of me, the images and feelings of September 11, 2001 are the ones I will never be able to shake. Ever.

## "SHOUT BAMALAMA!" MY ALABAMA CONNECTION

One Sunday I sat in front of the TV flipping channels and soon came to the realization that, as Bruce Springsteen once sang, I had "52 Channels with Nothing On." I got into the video shelf, and since Jill and I had just watched the Eddie Hinton and John D. Wyker video the night before, I decided to look through tapes of some of my performances with various and sundry bands. I came across the tape from Songwriter's night at the Fizz in Muscle Shoals. It includes the first time I came down to play and the second time nine months later. Well, guys, I was grinning from ear to ear from beginning to end.

We were taking my son Ben down to visit at Ol' Miss, where he was considering enrolling. (He later chose College of Charleston instead). Mitch Lopate, a friend and writer for *GRITZ*, had turned me on to the music of Ray Brand and the Crawlers, and we had spoken at length about the enigma wrapped in a pearl necklace known as John D. Wyker, a man no less legendary than Mickey Mantle, Divine, or Hunter S. Thompson. We decided to make a real trip out of it and I forget exactly how I ended up being booked at the Fizz. I know promoter Debbie Dixon was involved. She has always been helpful and supportive.

The first night, I was scared shitless. Hosts Jerry McGee and Mickey Butkus made me feel right at home, and I got up there and played all by my lonesome. Now, this ain't really that big a deal usually, but Travis Wammack had just left the stage. Man oh man, "Scratchy" Wammack. What a talent! He did a killer version of "Dreams to Remember" with Mickey and Jerry. Wowzer. Travis did several other songs as well. It was cool, man.

Right before show time I had run into Rick Moore in the lobby of the hotel. I had no idea he was playing that night. See, I had become "phone pals" with Rick and he was an advertiser in *GRITZ* and we sold his CDs in our online store. I came up to Rick in the lobby and said, "Is this really you?" We had a few laughs. He and his great band Mr. Lucky would close the show with that amazing Sammy Stafford on lead guitar. Sammy has this long ZZ Top beard and the boy can squaaaaal....

At the end of my solo set, I asked the band to join me for my twelve-bar blues version of "Folsom Prison Blues" and a take on "Can't You See" that turned into quite a little jam.

Earlier in the day, Jay Johnson had kindly led me and the family on a tour of the Shoals studios, top to bottom. The Jackson Highway studio blew my mind. To think of all the big acts that recorded in that small building. Not the least of which were the Rolling Stones.

Jay took us to FAME Studios, where Rodney Hall (son of FAME founder Rick Hall) was the coolest and let us see where brother Duane Allman played. I stood there for a while trying to absorb some of Skydog's mojo. Jay then took us out to Muscle Shoals Sound on the river. Man, what it must have been like to record there in the day. We also visited the Alabama Music Hall of Fame, which was a blast.

About nine months later, I was invited by Mickey and Jerry back to the Fizz and was really pleased to see all kinds of music legends in one room. Jimmy Johnson was there, as was Bobby Whitlock, CoCo Carmel, Spooner Oldham, Kelvin Holly...wow.

I was joined on my set by the late great Ray Brand, and we played the song "Into the Light," which had been written only two weeks prior. We brought Thad Usry up and Stephen Foster for "Mad Dog," another tune I had just written that we would end up recording on the *Southern Lights* record. I felt blessed to be jamming with such musical talents as these, to be sure.

Foster did an incredible solo set that had everybody, especially my wife, mesmerized. Then we set up for a jam. Now, it blew my mind; I'll say that at the outset. Here I was singing "Stormy Monday Blues" with Foster on the organ, Ray Brand, Thad, Spooner Oldham on piano, Bobby Whitlock on a Strat, Coco Carmel singing backup, and Jerry McGee on guitar. Aussie country rocker Keith Glass came up to the stage, and many of us backed him up on a great set. Then we all did an extended version of "The Weight" to close it out. Oh, I forgot to mention, when Mickey and Jerry were opening up the show Whitlock stepped up to the plate with his Strat and knocked it out of the park, singing "Roll Over Beethoven." Awesome? You bet your sweet bippie!

The memories of these two shows are like diamonds in my mind. In the future I would return to the Shoals, Decatur, and Huntsville many times; open for Steppenwolf and Marshall Tucker at the Trail of Tears concert with Wyker and the Crawlers; record two fun albums with the Crawlers, Foster, Bonnie Bramlett, Pete "Guitar" Carr, George McCorkle, JoJo Billingsley, Danny Hall, Larry Perkins, and more; play two CD parties for *Southern Lights*, one for *Something Heavy*, several Christmas Charities gigs, and, sadly, the Ray of Light Ray Brand Memorial Show. All of this, and I had never even visited the area prior to summer 1999.

And all this was because of my friend Mitch Lopate, who called me one day and said, "Mike. Wait 'til you hear this guy Ray Brand. I'm telling you, Mike, you need to play with him." I sure do miss Ray. Every day. But I feel blessed by the good Lord for having known him, as well as for all my friends on the Mighty Field of Vision. I will have friends in 'Bama for the rest of my life. Thanks, Mitch.

# 49

## SOUTHERN LIGHTS

It was summer 2002. Here I thought I was almost finished chronicling the events of my life in the form of an autobiography. I thought, well, I am still a young man. Maybe one day I'll write a second book to cover any exciting things that may happen between the time this particular volume is published and the next one, hopefully at age seventy-five or so. Little did I know that the month of July would bring not one, but two life-altering events my way: the recording of an album with some of my all-time musical heroes and the closest visit to death's door that I hope to make until many, many years from now.

Down in Huntsville, Alabama, a band I had become friends with just a year earlier called the Crawlers made me an offer. I could use their studio to record my next album, absolutely free. Not only that, but they would play on it. How cool. By the time the album was ready to be recorded during one magical week in the heat of summer 2002, I had enlisted the Crawlers, Stephen Foster, and several other Alabama talents. On top of this, Tommy Crain, who had spent fifteen years as lead guitarist in the Charlie Daniels Band, offered to play. Tommy showed up in a big truck with the cargo bed filled with instruments—guitars, pedal steel, a Dobro—wow. As previously stated, Miss Bonnie Bramlett added to the project her beautiful, soulful voice. She sang her tail off, as always. Only, this time, it was on my album. How cool is that?!

Also adding to the mix was John D. Wyker, songwriter of "Baby Ruth" and half of the leadership of the early-seventies band Sailcat, who hit the charts back in 1972 with "Motorcycle Mama." I remember having that 45 in high school, complete with the picture sleeve, same as the album cover, with art by *MAD Magazine*'s Jack Davis. Wyker brought in a song he had written as a tribute to the late John Lee Hooker called "Hooker's Boogie." John joined me in singing lead, with Bonnie adding some soulful flavor. Later on, Pete Carr would add to the record his magic guitar and immaculate tone. Pete was in the group Hour Glass with Gregg and Duane Allman and later became a much-sought-after session guitarist, playing familiar licks on records by Bob Seger, Rod Stewart, Simon & Garfunkel, and many more.

I was so proud of that CD, and so happy that all of these great talents were willing to play with me. In months and years to come, I would have the opportunity to play several gigs with the Crawlers, as well as to jam with Bonnie, Tommy, Pete, Wyker, and everyone else. Good people, each and every one.

# 50

## RETURN OF THE ANGELS

July 2002—just four years after my near-death experiences with bacterial infection, I was hit again. Blindsided, baby. I never even saw it coming. Sure, I had not lost all the weight I needed to have lost over the four years since what should have been an awakening. In fact, to a certain extent I had grown complacent. And that, my friends, is never a good thing. Always keep one eye open.

I had just completed the most thrilling musical experience of my entire life, recording with heroes and friends an album that I was really, honestly proud of. And now.... Now the angels were coming for me again. I got sick while I was down in Huntsville staying with Thad Usry, and by the time I got home I was on my way back to see Dr. Bridges. He looked at me and said, "Are you ready to go back into the hospital?" Oh no, not again.

The necrotizing fasciitis had returned. I went straight to surgery for another extensive tissue resecting. It would be another thirty-two-day stay at St. Francis.

I don't remember a lot about this visit except that I had just published the first print issue of GRITZ, and I had nearly finalized the tracks from my upcoming CD. I remember listening to it over and over, especially my duet with Bonnie Bramlett, just to take my mind off of the pain.

This time, the doctors used something new to help heal the would after the surgery. It was called a wound vac, and it used suction to promote healing much faster. Changing the dressing took time and a lot of gritting of teeth, but once the job was done, the machine worked very well.

The year before this all struck, I had traveled out to Washington state for the Whitehorse Mountain Music Festival, which was held in the mountains not very far from Seattle. It had been a great trip hanging out with friends I had met on the Internet, Bill and Karen Majkut, great people. Bill plays bass guitar and at the time he was in a fine rock and blues band called Smokin' Gun. He would later play Leon Wilkeson's bass lines in a really great Lynyrd Skynyrd tribute band called Whiskey Creek. Well, sir, the next year I was invited to play the festival in a lineup that included Leslie West, Elvin Bishop, and more. Smokin' Gun would back me up. As fate would have it, that was when my second bout with flesh-eating bacteria hit. Sadly, I could not make the trip, but luckily I had some other new friends in Washington who were more than happy to take my place. Don Swensen, Billy Moss, and their excellent Southern rock band Rebel Storm filled the gap. And by all accounts they knocked one out of the park.

A lot of friends dropped by to see me in the hospital as I fought through the pain, the night sweats, the rehabilitation and crawled back toward the land of the living. Without the friends and family, I really don't think I would have survived. Blessed again.

My first night home from the hospital, I bled out. Some of the medicine I was on combined with the ALEVE headache medicine, and my stomach bled. I sat up on the side of the bed and fell backward. I couldn't even sit up. My wife called the home healthcare nurse on call, and she came out to find me as white as a bed sheet. She called an ambulance, and at 5 AM I was on my way back to the hospital. The medic was putting a needle that looked like a tenpenny nail into my wrist to give me blood. It was surreal.

At the hospital I was told that my hemoglobin had been 3 when they picked me up. Not too good. But after three more days I was stable and returned home with my wound vac. A few months later I would be good as new.

# 51

## SOMETHING HEAVY

In 2004, I returned to Mill Kids Studios in Huntsville, Alabama, to record my next album. I must say here and now, none of this would have ever happened without Billy Teichmiller, who owns the studio, and Ray Brand. The two of them produced the album, and their willingness to work with me was just as big a blessing now as it was the first time.

The sessions were great fun. Some of the highlights I recall include the day George McCorkle came down from Nashville to play lead guitar on several tracks. George just came in and aced it as always, playing on "Rocket City Express," "Everyday Grind," "Hangin' Judge," and others. JoJo Billingsley of Lynyrd Skynyrd fame joined local favorite Jan Elkins to add backing vocals to "Hard Drivin' Man," a song written by Johnny Wyker and Tommy Talton, as well as "Chapel of Ease," a gospel tune I wrote while visiting the ruins of an old church in Beaufort, SC. The girls sang on several other songs as well, sounding great.

I'll never forget drinking Jack Daniels whiskey to help my voice while trying to hit the high notes on Eddie Hinton's "Something Heavy," all the while being coached verse by verse by Ray Brand. And that night we all sat in awe watching Danny Hall chart out the Meat Loaf/Jim Steinman classic "Two Out of Three Ain't Bad," writing the charts as the CD played. The guy is a genius.

One night we had a bunch of visitors from the Mighty Field of Vision in the studio, and we decided to put them on the album. There was a repeating line in my song "Redneckin'" where we had the whole room shout out the word "Redneckin." It was too much fun.

Once again Pete Carr kindly added some of his guitar magic to the mix, and by the time it was all said and done, *Something Heavy* had turned into a pretty decent record. I just felt lucky to play with such great talents once again.

We would later have a two-night CD release party back at the Space and Rocket Center Marriott, bringing George, JoJo, Pete, and everyone else out to raise money for the Arch Angel Foundation, a helping organization founded by my friend Tim Shook. The organization never got off the ground, but in 2011, Tim and I would combine our efforts to launch a 501c3 called Hearts of the South. But, speaking of Arch Angel, one band that was always willing to pitch in to help others was the Southern Rock Allstars.

# 52

# THE SOUTHERN ROCK ALLSTARS AND BLACKFOOT

*"We all kind of grew up together in Florida and we were in different bands. Blackfoot and Skynyrd, the Classics IV, Johnny Van Zant, .38 Special, the Allman Brothers, Grinderswitch—all of us grew up together within a 3-mile radius in Jacksonville. But we were in two bands that were playing a lot of the same places and we just formed Blackfoot like that in September of 1969."*
—Jakson Spires, interview with Buffalo, March, 2001

Of all the bands I have had the privilege of knowing and working with, none hold a more special place in my heart than the Southern Rock Allstars. When I first met them the band consisted of Jakson Spires from Blackfoot, Dave Hlubek from Molly Hatchet, Jay Johnson from the Rossington Band, and Charles Hart Jr. from Radio Tokyo. Later they would swap out members, including Mike Estes from Lynyrd Skynyrd, Jimmy Farrar from Molly Hatchet, Ace Allen from the Marshall Tucker Band, and Duane Roland from Molly Hatchet, adding Scott Mabry on guitar.

It seems like I became friends with these guys from the outset. They were just that kind of people, all of them, but none more than Jakson Spires. I remember the first night I met Jak was at a benefit for Danny Joe Brown staged by Bruce Brookshire of Doc Holliday in Warner Robbins, Georgia. Jak was just so friendly. Everyone loved him, and I was no exception.

Through the years I had so many great times with the SRA, playing numerous shows, oftentimes with my friends from Norfolk, Virginia, the Rhythm Pigs, featuring my pal Timmy Fodrey on drums. Of course there were also a lot of shows I attended, usually with Scott Greene, where I didn't play. We would just go to enjoy the SRA. But nine times out of ten I'd end up jamming on a couple of songs.

In 2005, one of my Southern rock dreams was coming true. Three out of the four original members of Blackfoot were reuniting for a tour. Greg T. Walker, Charlie Hargrett, and Jakson Spires. Rick Medlocke was a member of Lynyrd Skynyrd at the time, so the guys brought in an old friend, Bobby Barth of Axe. It was really exciting.

Then the unthinkable happened. Jakson Spires suffered a brain aneurysm at his home in Fort Pierce, Florida, and went into a coma. A few days later on, March 16, 2005, he was dead.

Jak's death hit me really hard. He had a way of making each of us feel like we were his very best friend. I have said it before and I will always maintain that I feel extremely lucky to have called Jak my friend during the short five years I knew him.

Jakson was truly one of a kind. A Cherokee warrior with a heart bigger than most anyone I have ever known. He truly cared about all of his friends and kept up with every one of them. As for me, he called at least once a week just to chat. He'd ask about the family, all by name. He even knew the dogs' names.

Jak was a giver of gifts. Just days after the tragedy of September 11, 2001, my band opened for the Southern Rock Allstars at a biker benefit for the American Cancer Society. When we first arrived, Jak made a beeline to me and hugged me and kissed my cheek. He was not a man afraid to express his love. He gave me several gifts that day, including some "Buffalo" tea bags he had gotten out west and a spearhead he said was over a thousand years old that had been blessed by a Navajo shaman. That artifact meant the world to me. He told me to wear it around my neck when I perform for protection and blessings. And I did just that, from that night onward until it was stolen from a dressing room at a gig in 2011.

Jak was also the funniest man on earth. I was so fortunate to hang out with him so many times when he was in Southern Rock Allstars. He was always pulling stunts and jokes. He and Jay Johnson, Charles Hart, and Jimmy Farrar were always playing tricks on Dave Hlubek, who seemed to take it all in stride. Jak had a habit of pulling up the leg on his shorts to expose his privates to many of us, just for shock value or a laugh. He was also pretty quick to show you a Cherokee moon, if you catch my drift.

Every gig with the SRA was a barrel of fun. Most of the time it was Scott and me, and we just had one laugh after another, all wrapped around some of the best Southern rock ever played. I was fortunate to open countless shows for them, usually along with the Rhythm Pigs of Virginia, and we would always jam somewhere during the show. I would get up and play guitar on "Can't You See," "Sweet Home Alabama," "Call Me the Breeze," "Train Train" or "Rock and Roll All Night."

Standing on a small stage in Virginia one evening, I ended up directly in front of the drum kit during "Train Train." It felt like a jet was taking off. I was praying Jak wouldn't break a stick. I began to picture a shard from a heavy Ludwig drumstick flying straight into my jugular.

Jak was really excited about the Blackfoot reunion. We spoke about it many times, and I was completely stoked when I got word that my band would be opening for Blackfoot in Florida. The sad part was, by the time the gig got here, Jak had died. The show turned into a memorial. I was asked to say some words just before Blackfoot took the stage, which I was honored to do. Then the Blackfoot members' wives each came onstage to give a rose to their husband. Very sweet.

I drove to Orlando for a memorial service. I spoke briefly with Sherry Spires, who was still in shock. Sherry had been Jak's girlfriend many moons prior, and they had just recently reunited. I know for a fact he was crazy about Sherry. He told me several times. He called her his "Indian Princess."

When Jak died, a void was created in my life that was unlike any other I had ever known. It's a void that will always remain with me. I had lost a brother.

# 53

# RAY OF LIGHT

In 2005, I lost another true friend. Ray Brand of the Crawlers passed away from cancer. Before I knew it, I was headed back to the Rocket City to take part in a memorial concert and benefit August 27–28 for my fallen brother.

Arriving at the Space and Rocket Center Marriott, I only had a few minutes to check in and join Sonny Edwards of Railroad Bazaar and George McCorkle (founding member of the Marshall Tucker Band) on a short jaunt over to the music store. Thanks to the efforts of Sonny Edwards, the folks at Railroad Bazaar had teamed up with the kind folks at Sammick guitars to sign George on as an endorser for their guitars, and that afternoon they were to present him with a beautiful Greg Bennett signature Sammick. I was there in the role of journalist, to take pictures.

Later that evening, a crowd began to gather at Otter's, the bar inside the Marriott, where we would be performing a "songwriters in the round" as a prequel to Sunday's show. Joining yours truly and my buddy Sonny Edwards would be George McCorkle, Larry Byrom (Steppenwolf), Amanda Quarles, and others, all friends of Ray's. We took turns singing our original songs and jamming. It was great fun. The set ended up with McCorkle performing his most famous song, "Fire on the Mountain."

After a break it was time for a set from some of Ray's old band mates from Buckeye and Slaughter Road. It was fabulous. Sonny Edwards joined back in for an awesome version of Little Feat's "Willin'." I made my way back up to the stage for a rousing take on "Will the Circle Be Unbroken," and we closed it all out with "Can't You See."

Sunday at the 721 Club was nothing short of spiritual. I met so many of Ray's friends and family that I had not met before, and the huge nightclub was wall to wall with people there to remember Ray, everyone from doctors to Saints Motorcycle Club members. It was awesome. Dick

Cooper was acting stage manager, and Thad Usry of the Crawlers joined Ray Brand Jr. to emcee the event, which lasted from 2 PM until 2 AM.

Excellent performances were delivered by the Southern Boys Band (George's nephew's band) with George McCorkle; Muscle Shoals Southern rockers, Messenger; the always fabulous acoustic blues singer Amanda Quarles; Scott Boyer (Cowboy); Larry Byrom and friends; Microwave Dave and the Nukes; Tommy Crain and the Crosstown Allstars; and many others. I was thrilled to perform my songs backed by Billy Teichmiller and Owen Brown from the Crawlers, Larry Perkins on keys, Sonny Edwards on guitar, Tommy Crain on guitar, and JoJo Billingsley and Rodeo Jan Elkin on vocals. We closed our set with "Can't You See," bringing Lee Dunlap from Tommy's band up to the mike for lead vocals. He dominated, sounding like Marshall Tucker meets James Brown. Lord, have mercy!

Later in the evening it was star time, with Lee Roy Parnell jamming with Jack Pearson (Allman Brothers), Tommy Crain, and a mighty set from the Crawlers. The spirit of Ray Brand was all around, and you could feel it.

In the end, several thousand dollars were raised to pay Ray's medical bills and to help his family. It was a wonderful celebration of a wonderful human being. A guy I wrote songs with, a guy I was honored to perform with, a guy I was always proud to call my friend. We love you, brother Ray. We'll keep the music going and your memory will never fade. As for me, I'll just "keep on smilin' in the rain, laughing through the pain" and holding your spirit forever in my heart.

# 54

# JIMMY HALL AND WET WILLIE

*"I wouldn't take any amount of money for the time in which I was born, and the time in which I grew up. I wouldn't take anything for the situation I was in. Doing what we did—rocking in the seventies—it was the best of all worlds. It was like being indestructible. I was in a rock band, we had records, and we were on the road playing with everyone we'd ever idolized. How can you beat that?"*
—Jimmy Hall, interview with Buffalo, April, 1998

Wet Willie was one of those great bands I found out about because of Capricorn Records and saw for the first time on the previously mentioned *Don Kirshner's Rock Concert: Saturday Night in Macon, Georgia,* back in 1973. The energy coming off of that R&B band kicked my ass. Jimmy Hall did everything but levitate off of the stage. "Keep On Smilin" was burning up the airwaves, and in my book Wet Willie could do no wrong. I always wanted to see them in concert but would not experience the band live until 2006 at the Iron Angels Bike Rally in Unadilla, Georgia, when most of the original members, including Jimmy Hall, his brother Jack on bass, and sister Donna on vocals, delivered a blistering set on an exciting bill that also featured Blackfoot and the Southern Rock Allstars.

In fall 2006, I made my way over to Rome but I didn't see the new Pope. Might have been because the Rome I was visiting was Rome, Georgia, and I was accepting the invitation from Chris Hicks (Marshall Tucker Band) to be among a chosen few to witness the rehearsal of a new project he was taking on with Jimmy Hall (Wet Willie). It was a really cool project that included the two of them being backed up by an excellent band called the Mobile Homeboys.

The interesting thing was that the rehearsal was to take place at this really cool little bar-club called the High Lonesome Saloon. It's a great little place that can handle maybe a hundred souls packed in good—that is, if there aren't too many plus-size rednecks crowding the bar. The place is great. The owner Mike Proctor has it decorated with an autographed Lynyrd Skynyrd guitar, a Charlie Daniels fiddle, and lots of autographed pictures, posters, and such from the world of Southern rock. Makes this ol' boy feel right at home, indeed.

Now, the High Lonesome is in a top-secret location. Kinda like the Bat Cave. It is so secret, in fact, that I was asked to put on a blindfold before I drove in.

It's a private place, and Mike's customers are his closest friends from the area. He throws concerts a few times a year, but they aren't advertised outside the group of regulars. I mean, his place would be overrun. So it remains, like Bruce Wayne's Bat Cave, a deep, dark secret.

Mike and them were mighty good to the Buffalo. Everyone was so nice, and they served up some hot dinner, cafeteria style, for everyone. Good eatin', good conversation, and adult beverages. Could it get any better? Oh, hell yeah! The music!

Soon, Jimmy Hall came in. He had just returned from a whirlwind tour of England and Japan with Jeff Beck, and man did he look tired out. But Jimmy's a trooper. After a plateful of Southern cuisine including an ear of fresh corn, Jimmy was ready to join Chris and the band in getting down to rehearsal.

Boy howdy, did they ever rock. I felt like top dog sitting front and center, my feet propped up, drinking a bottle of ice-cold water and digging the music. The guys were rehearsing for a show in two days that would find them opening for Lynyrd Skynyrd right there in Rome.

They ran through a set of killer songs, including the duet they did together on the latest Marshall Tucker Band album, "King of the Delta Blues," a heavy rocker about the legendary Robert Johnson. Chris sang one from his upcoming solo album called "Georgia Moon," an absolutely beautiful tune written by veteran producer Paul Hornsby. When they kicked into Wet Willie's "Street Corner Serenade," I could barely contain my inner redneck. I wanted to jump up in the chair and scream "yaaaaaahooooo!" Instead, I sat there with a big, silly grin, drinking my H$_2$O and taking it all in. Jimmy moved from harp to sax to vocals and back again throughout the show-slash-rehearsal, just ripping it up.

They played a bunch of Chris's songs and a bunch of Jimmy's, including the Wet Willie/Little Milton tune "Grits Ain't Groceries," "Rendezvous with the Blues," "Love Will," and a rocking Hicks tune called "Southern Comfort." Oh yeah, and there was that little ol' song "Keep On Smilin'." Awesome, yes indeed.

A great time was had by all, especially the ol' Buffalo. Wish I could have witnessed the boys open for Skynyrd, but hey, there's something downright cool about being one of only a handful to see this private rehearsal. I felt blessed. It was super bad.

On February 26, 2010, Jimmy Hall agreed to come out and play for us at *GRITZ*fest II in Alabama, along with Bonnie Bramlett, Tommy Talton, Tommy Crain, and more. One of the highlights of the magical evening was Jimmy's set, backed by Tommy Crain and the Crosstown Allstars with his brother Jack Hall on bass, along with sister Donna Hall on vocals. Three members of Wet Willie. So good. "Keep On Smilin'" was great, and "Swing Low, Sweet Chariot" took us all to church.

I have every one of Wet Willie's albums, as well as Jimmy's solo works. I still get to rocking when I hear "Street Corner Serenade" or "Keep On Smilin'" on the radio. You'd be hard pressed to find a better singer than Jimmy Hall anywhere, and Wet Willie remains one of my all-time favorite groups.

# 55

## PLAYIN' IN THE BAND

Back when I was a teenager, I used to dream of playing in a band. The only real problem was, I didn't know how to play an instrument. While I played "at" the guitar, I didn't really learn how to play until I was about twenty-three.

At the time I was in junior college, and while I knew some chords, I didn't really put it all together until I met Greg Yeary and started playing a lot. Like I say, I had learned a bit from Doug Hooper back in the seventies and Stuart Swanlund in the early eighties, but the real trial by fire was when Greg and I teamed up. The first real band I played in was the Buffalo Hut Coalition.

In the years that followed, I would play with Carey Upton in his band the Rockland Tramps and form a country group called Frontline. During the early nineties, I would reform a version of the Buffalo Hut for a bit, and toward the end of the century would play in several bands with friends Fred Wooten, Michael Merck, Jay Taylor, and Joey Parrish, among others.

Around 1992, I ventured out solo. I'll never forget how scared I was when I played my first solo acoustic show at Annie's All Natural Cafe in downtown Greenville. I played a lot of originals and covered songs by Garth Brooks, Elton John, James Taylor, and such. After I made it through that first night, there was no stopping me.

In the years that followed, I played all around Greenville, including a regular gig at the Blue Ridge Brewing Company, where I played many times solo, as well as in duet with Michael Merck, David Windhorst, or Travis Brown, the son of my friend and fellow traveler Jim Brown.

Lugging my own PA system to the venues, I would work my butt off to get it all set up, then play all night, and then tear it down and load it up, take it home, and unload at 4 in the morning. Sometimes friends would help me load up, but most nights it was me, the handtrucks, and a tired back. But hey, anything for my art, right?

There are too many stories to tell from these late-night fiascos, but some of the highlights included hosting "Michael B's Acoustic Jam and Open Mic Night" at a Greenville coffee shop and driving an hour each weekend to Hendersonville, NC, to perform solo at Hannah Flannigan's Irish Pub, where I once played a forty-five-minute improvised medley that began with "Bo Diddley" and went into "Willie and the Hand Jive" then "I Want Candy" then "Scarlet Begonias" then "Hey Bo Diddley" then "Wild Thing" and ended up by going back into "Bo Diddley." The crowd loved it. I learned quickly that the more I could improvise, the better it would go over.

The gigs slowed down with my health issues flaring in 2008, but I still played at every Winters Brothers Southern Jam and every December at the Angelus Benefits in Tampa, Florida. Of course, music runs through my veins, and I have no doubt there are many more gigs in store for me, when the time is right.

# DENNY AND ME

During the print phase of *GRITZ*, I was introduced to a man who would quickly become a friend and spiritual brother, Denny Walley. I met Denny through a friend of my wife named Jeff. I wasn't aware of Denny's musical legacy but soon learned about his tenure as guitarist for both Frank Zappa and Captain Beefheart. Denny can be heard on such gems as *Shut Up and Play Your Guitar*, *Joe's Garage*, and the Zappa/Beefheart collaboration *Bongo Fury*. A few years back he reunited with past members of the Magic Band to record and perform in a tour that rocked Europe and thrilled fans, among them Matt Groenig (*The Simpsons* creator), a huge Beefheart fan.

Jill and I became fast friends with Denny. We'd have him over to the house whenever he came to town or just go out for coffee. I loved talking music with him. Still do. Of course the biggest thrills were the nights he and I would set up guitars in my den and just improvise jams. "Air sculptures" he called it. The music was pretty cool, moving between sounds reminiscent of Zappa to Delta blues to Southern rock to jazz. It was a very spiritual thing that I really enjoyed with Denny.

Of all the folks I have been fortunate enough to meet on this musical journey, Denny stands out as one of the finest. A great talent and an even better human being. The great thing is, his son Jaryd is cut from the very same cloth. The special cloth not found in the remnants section. The kind of cloth you can wrap yourself up in and it just makes you feel good.

## HALF A CENTURY OLD AND STILL ROCKIN'

Who would have ever guessed I'd be spending so much time in Macon, Georgia, during 2007. Certainly not me. But my first trip of the year to that famous home of Southern rock would be to attend a benefit for the Big House, which was being converted into the official museum of the Allman Brothers Band. Oh, and to play the after-party at 550 Blues.

The day started out at the H&H Restaurant, where I was to meet Chris Hicks for lunch. Unfortunately, Chris was being pulled five different directions that day and couldn't make it. However, John Charles Griffin, a local promoter who was working on the Big House benefit, dropped by for a while, and we had a good time talking about all that was getting ready to happen later in the day.

I fully enjoyed my meal at H&H. The legendary (and absolutely sweet) Mama Louise Hudson and staff hooked me up with some Southern fried chicken, collard greens, black-eyed peas, and corn bread and, of course, some good iced tea. Anybody reading this that has yet to enjoy a meal with Mama Louise, do yourself a favor and drop in. If you are an Allman fan (isn't everybody?), the walls of the restaurant are covered in Allman photos and memorabilia, including a platinum album award for *At Fillmore East*.

When John headed out, I followed suit and made my way back over to the park to pay another visit to the Otis Redding statue and take a brisk walk along the trail. It was another beautiful day and I found myself singing "Blue Sky" as I made my way through the park.

Around 4 PM I made my way over to 550 Blues to set up for the night's gig and sound check. My band came rolling in from Greenville right on time, and Josh the club owner introduced me to the sound man, Carlton, a great guy and, as I would later discover, a heck of a sound man.

After sound check it was time to head over to the Armory for the Big House Foundation benefit. I followed Josh and his wife Lee over to the Armory Ballroom and we were off and running. The first person I met was the longtime writer for *GRITZ*, James Calemine. It was indeed a pleasure to finally put a face with the voice on the phone after seven years!

Chris Hicks brought the house down with some of his original songs, including one he did with Marshall Tucker called "Ride of Your Life." He also performed "Georgia Moon," an incredible tune from his upcoming solo album, backed on piano by the phenomenal Paul Hornsby.

The Randall Bramblett Band soon took the stage, and the former Sea Level sax man and his group boggled our collective mind, playing a set that was absolutely amazing. This band simply smokes.

I met so many old friends and new ones at the event. It was good to see Alan Walden and his wife Tosha again, and Alan introduced me to members of Otis Redding's family, his daughter Karla and her husband Tim Andrews, along with Carolyn Killen, which was indeed a pleasure. Phil Walden's son Phillip was there and I had a chance to see and speak with him once again as well as former Allman Brothers accountant Willie Perkins, author of *No Saints, No Saviors*, a great book about being on the road with the Brothers.

It was nice to see Col. Bruce Hampton (RET) again, one of my very favorite spirits in the whole world. I met Gregg Allman's personal assistant Chank Middleton, who was a lot of fun. He later came out to my gig at 550 and we had a blast. I also had a chance to speak to Lisa Love, our old friend from the Georgia Music Hall of Fame, and editor of *Georgia Music Magazine*. Speaking of magazines, it was great to finally meet *Hittin' the Note* editor John Lynskey as well.

I had to cut out early to return to 550 Blues and begin my set. I was really happy to see so many folks from the benefit show up for the gig, including Paul Hornsby, Judi Petty (wife of the late Joe Dan) , Chank, John Griffin, Pam Lockhart, and Melvina from the Georgia Music Hall of Fame, and many others. Judi was very kind and said some really sweet things about me and my music, and we talked for a bit about Grinderswitch, Joe Dan. and Dru Lombar.

The show was great fun, and as always we had a few special guests jamming. Tony Tyler, the nineteen-year-old hot-shot guitar player,

211

turned it up to "eleven" during our second set and sounded great. John Griffin joined us a couple of times to blow harp and sing, and Mike Hines, guitarist for the Randall Bramblett Band, sat in and smoked on my Burns Steer for a while. A good time was had by all, but at 2 AM we had to end the party.

The whole weekend in Macon was excellent, and even though Gregg Allman wasn't there (the rumor mill at work. We had heard online and from several people that Gregg would be at the event), we had a true "Allman style" weekend.

# 58

# ON THE ROAD AGAIN

As I said earlier, during summer 2007 I had been down to Macon, Georgia, several times, and every time I visited I felt the spirit of Duane Allman washing over me like a spiritual cleansing. One time I felt it stronger than ever as I watched from the front row while Tommy Talton played his guitar. Photographer Bill Thames was talking to me backstage before the show and remarked that Tommy played with the same touch and feel as the late Skydog. I have to agree.

Tommy Talton, one of the founding members of Cowboy, a member of the recently reunited Capricorn Rhythm Section and leader of his own Tommy Talton Band, is simply an amazing talent. Talton is the full package, an astounding guitarist, a great singer, and a magnificent creator of songs.

The gig at Cox Capitol Theatre in downtown Macon was a kickoff for the town's annual Bragg Jam, an all-day Saturday event. Bragg Jam always draws a lot of Middle Georgia acts, many who were friends with Brax and Taylor "Tate" Bragg, the brothers the event commemorates.

The Bragg brothers were driving back from Texas in July 1999 when they died in a car accident. They were supposed to perform a gig at the Rookery that weekend.

Other musicians performed a jam in tribute to the brothers, and the proceeds from the night went to the Ocmulgee Trail. That was the modest beginning of Bragg Jam, which had grown more ambitious every year.

The Talton gig brought out all of the Macon music family from Kirk West to John Charles Griffin and Mama Louise Hudson from the H&H Restaurant. I was happy to finally meet Alan Walden's daughter Jessica, and it was great seeing Terry Reeves of Music Matters Entertainment again.

Tommy had invited me to perform a couple of my original songs with him on acoustic guitars, and it was very cool rehearsing in the hotel room with him and his buddy Dave in attendance. The stars must have really been in line because it all fell together well and quickly.

We joined Tommy and his wife Patti and a group of Tommy's friends for dinner at Logan's Roadhouse before heading back over to the Theatre for the show. Having expounded upon the talent that is Tommy Talton, I need to also say that Talton's band is great as well. His youthful bass player Brandon Peeples (whose parents we sat with at dinner, a great couple) is a top-flight musician, as is drummer David Keith. Now, Tommy's keyboard man Tony Giordano is one of the best key men in the country, but he wasn't able to make this show. As a substitute Talton brought in this guy named Paul Hornsby. You may have heard of him. Played with Duane and Gregg Allman in Hourglass and produced the Marshall Tucker Band, the Charlie Daniels Band, Cowboy, and Wet Willie, among others. The master of keys.

Talton and his band rocked through two jam-packed sets of great music, including mostly Talton compositions, TT Band numbers, Cowboy tunes, and a few select covers.

Great songs like the rocking "Getaway Cars" and the R&B warning to men who want to keep their lady happy, "Wake Up Ready." "All Roads Lead Back Home" is a great song about eternal love and hope.

"Color My Sleep" is one of my very favorite Talton tunes, reminiscent of Van Morrison, and tonight the band played it with buckets of soul.

Other great Talton tunes included "God Bless Everyone" and "Someone Else's Shoes," along with a brand new, as of yet untitled, tune that was ethereal and haunting.

For us old Cowboy fans, Tommy pulled out the beautiful "River to the Sea, " as well as "Where Can You Go?" and "Time Will Take Us."

During the show Talton played a couple of tunes by Stephen Stills, "For What It's Worth" (with a funky new arrangement by Talton) and a rocked-up "Love the One You're With."

Dylan's "Leopard Skin Pillbox Hat" was a real treat, and Paul Hornsby was just ripping on the B-3. Hornsby is a joy to listen to and watch. His "producer's ear" helps him play just the right riffs at the right time and lay back and leave some "white space" as needed. Amazing.

214

I just have to say that I was honored to play a couple of my own tunes at the beginning of the second set with Talton. Both of us played acoustics on "Into the Light" and "Painting Her Toenails." I had a stone-cold blast and will never forget pickin' with Mr. "T."

I returned to Macon again just two weeks later for the Benefit for Sid Yochim (AKA: Benefit for a Brother) on Saturday night, August 4, 2007, at Macon's Grand Opera House.

Sid was a longtime bus driver for both the Allman Brothers Band and the Charlie Daniels Band and is a friend to everyone in Southern rock. He had recently undergone extensive heart surgery and the 2007 benefit was to help pay some of the bills.

It was truly a Southern rock homecoming. I was blown away by the beauty of the old Opera House and immediately flashed back to that *Don Kirshner's Rock Concert* episode called "Saturday Night in Macon, Georgia" back in 1973 that featured the Allman Brothers, the Marshall Tucker Band, and Wet Willie. The show had taken place on this very stage, and tonight certainly brought to mind those glory days.

It was great seeing so many old friends in the house. Chank showed up for a while. For anyone who doesn't know him, he's Gregg Allman's assistant and a helluva nice cat. I was happy to see fellow Spartanburg hometowner Moon Mullins in attendance. Moon was the head of the road crew for Marshall Tucker during the glory days. Longtime Allman Brothers crewman Scooter Herring (who would sadly pass away before the end of the year) was there, as was Pam Lockhart from the Georgia Music Hall of Fame.

I opened the show myself, accompanied by the ultra-talented guitarist Donnie Winters (Winters Brothers Band) picking lead. Donnie is a true joy to work with and never fails to "hit the note."

Next was the Revival. Now, this was my first time hearing these guys, and I was quite impressed. They are not Southern rock, but they blend many influences, including reggae, into a tight musical sound with amazing vocal harmonies. Lead singer Lamar Williams is the son of former Allman Brothers bassist, the late Lamar Williams Sr. I truly look for big success from these guys.

Next up was Tommy Crain and the Crosstown Allstars delivering a red-hot set that included originals like "The Hill" and "Find Another

Lover," along with a very nice version of the Allman's "Jessica" and, a tip of the hat to Tommy's old boss Charlie Daniels, "Long Haired Country Boy." The band was cooking. These guys became one of my favorite bands to see live. Great guitar work from Tommy and Bob Rumer.

The Winters Brothers Band hit the stage locked and loaded and never once let up, playing all of the crowd favorites, all the while accompanied by Mike Causey of Stillwater on guitar. As an added treat, brother Donnie Winters joined in on "Sang Her Love Songs" and "Devil's After My Soul." Like I said earlier, it was like a homecoming.

Dennis Winters introduced the man of the hour Sid Yochim, who spoke briefly to thank everyone for coming out. Sid's daughter Sydney stepped up next to sing a beautiful country song acapella. You could have heard a pin drop. All of the musicians on stage stood mesmerized by this child's beauty and talent. She truly has "what it takes" to be a country star.

Next came the moment we all live for, the all-out jam. First to join in was Tommy Crain, who played along with the Winters Brothers on "I Can't Help It." Dennis Winters called me out, and I stepped up to sing "Can't You See" with Macon local talent Chris Patterson on guitar, our friend Weedy on slide, Bob Rumer from the Crosstown Allstars and various other members of Crain's band and the Winters Brothers. Musicians were coming and going like leaves in the wind, with Dennis bringing Lamar Williams out to sing on a couple of songs, Sydney Yochim singing backup, and her brother Tucker playing guitar on a few. Most of the time there were two drummers, Towson Engberg from the Crosstown Allstars and the great Stevie Hawkins.

We all joined in on "Sweet Home Alabama" and "Call Me the Breeze," with the assembled guitar army taking turns on lead runs.

Larry Howard of Grinderswitch made his way to the stage as Dennis kicked off "Before You Accuse Me" and the the WBB tune "Ride, Ride, Ride."

Howard stepped up to the mike to sing "Driftin'," and the show turned a corner to become a red-hot blues jam. Dennis ended the show singing the new acapella gospel song he introduced at the annual

Winters Jam in June. It was a beautiful and heartfelt close to an outstanding Southern rock summit.

I left the venue with a great big smile on my face and great music rolling around in my head. I was ready to do it again. Anytime, anyplace, anywhere. Sid clearly appreciated the benefit, but sadly he would succumb to his health issues, and passed away on November 1, 2011. That southern rock flag was flown at half mast.

# 59

## THE WINTERS BROTHERS BAND

*"We lived in a smokehouse converted into a bunk room while raising cattle for Marty Robbins on his farm near Franklin, Tennessee. You might say we were sharecroppers. That's where the initial Winters Brothers Band came to be. We also wrote songs for Marty Robbins."*
—Dennis Winters, interview with Buffalo, June, 2000

In between trips to Macon in 2007, I returned to the greater Nashville, Tennessee, area for the annual Winters Brothers jam. It had become a tradition of sorts, with Scott Greene and me road-tripping each summer to the Winters farm for a great Southern rock weekend.

Father's Day weekend is a perfect time for a festival. Just ask anyone who has attended Bonaroo, and if they can remember the weekend, they will agree. As for those of us who for many moons have been making the trek to Nashville yearly to attend the Winters Brothers Southern Summer Jam, we were all ecstatic that God had blessed us with near-perfect weather.

Scott Greene (who swears he's going to write his own book about all of our travels called *Roamin' with the Buffalo*) and I left Greenville on Friday for the six-hour ride. Slightly overcast skies coupled with a large number of traffic jams made for an unusually drawn-out trip to Music City, but all's well that ends well, as we, along with many other friends of the Winters Brothers, were invited out to Dennis Winters's home in Nolensville for a spaghetti dinner on Friday night. All of the usual friends were there, John and Tracy; Jim from St. Louis; Southern George and Cici from Vienna, Austria; Patti; all of the Winters family; Dennis and Linda and their daughters, Casey, Cody, and Carly; Uncle Zak Tucker and Mrs. Tucker; and many others. The food was great and the conversation even better. A great time was had by all.

On Saturday, June 16, we left the hotel to drive back out to the farm. I had made plans the day before to interview Uncle Zak Tucker, a jam legend and brother in law of the late Papa Don Winters. We discussed Zak's early days playing music in Miami, Florida, where he backed up folks like Lefty Frizell and Hank Snow.

The jam got underway beneath sunny skies at about 5 PM, and at one point Dennis brought his grandson onto the stage Dennis sang a beautiful acapella gospel song he recently wrote. He had sung it for us at the Friday dinner as well, and it was amazing.

Billy Hester and Donnie Winters did a great set that included Donnie's acoustic version of "Shotgun Rider."

Tommy Crain and the Crosstown Allstars blew the roof off of the barn, beginning with the Allman Brothers' "Jessica" and playing a great set of originals that included "Find Another Lover" from their debut album. Tommy on guitar, Bob Rumer on guitar, Towson Engsberg on drums, and Kerry Creasy on bass burned up the stage with electric blues, Southern rock, and some serious dynamic enhanced jamming. Tommy called me up to sing on "Long Haired Country Boy," which was great fun.

Next up was an acoustic set from yours truly. I was accompanied by Donnie Winters on lead guitar, and we were joined by Tommy Crain for a couple of songs. We closed out with "Will the Circle Be Unbroken," bringing out Dennis Winters, Eddie Stone (on B-3), and the Southern Belles to take it on home.

The kings of the party, the Winters Brothers Band, were next. Tonight they had two additional members sitting in for the whole set. Eddie Stone from Doc Holiday on keyboards and Mike Causey from Stillwater on guitar really added layers to the sound. The band stood and delivered in every way, and Southern Belles Casey, Cody, and Carly sang and danced their hearts out during the whole show wearing matching outfits.

At the tail end of the show, Dennis announced the jam and brought members of Tommy Crain's band and others onto the stage for an hour of smoking jams, including "Sweet Home Alabama," "Fooled Around and Fell in Love," "Roadhouse Blues" (featuring Casey Winters on vocal), and "Can't You See," among others. The band never sounded better.

I know I say this every year, but it still holds true. The jam was just over way too fast, even in its extended, hour-longer format. It was hard saying goodbye to all of my friends for another year, but we all left with a head full of music and some great memories of another outstanding Southern Jam.

In June 2009, Scott, Steve, and I made our way back to the Winters family farm for what was being billed as the "last ever jam." I've said it before and I'll say it again. I can hardly believe this was the final Winters Brothers Southern Summer Jam. But man, oh man, was it ever a good one. I can truthfully say I have never seen a bigger crowd at the jam, and I have never heard the Winters Brothers sound better than they did on that Saturday night. But I am getting ahead of myself.

We spent Saturday chilling at the motel, talking to friends like Tom Whitten, who drove in from Cleveland, and my buddy Don Swensen and his wife Molly from Washington. Don was bassist of the band Rebel Storm, which *GRITZ* named as the best new group of 2002.

We headed out to Dennis and Lynda's farm at about 4:30, and from the time we got there, it was a constant line of meets and greets with old friends and new. Lots of "grip and grins." That's what we used to call them in the newspaper business when folks would pose for a photo shaking hands or presenting an award.

John Ryan introduced me to a band I have been enjoying for many years, the Dublin City Ramblers. These guys came from Ireland to join the final jam. They are great friends with the WBB.

I was running around trying to assemble my "high-tech pickup band" for an impromptu rehearsal. I had Don "Big D" Swensen with me, and Mark McAfee; I just couldn't find Donnie Winters. I eventually did. It seems everyone was wanting to see Donnie and chat with him. It ain't easy being a Southern rock star!

There were so many great folks to talk to, I felt like a spinning top. It was just good ol' Southern-fried fun, to be sure.

The music started out with Dennis and his wife Lynda taking the stage to welcome everyone out to the 30th Winters Brothers Southern Summer Jam. Then Dennis played a new song he had recently written. From what I heard, the tune has all the earmarks of a real country hit.

Throughout the day, various bands and songwriters performed, including a certain Buffalo. Rather than just do my usual solo acoustic set, I invited some top-flight musicians to join me in a set in memory of George McCorkle and Toy and Tommy Caldwell.

Just before we played, I was thrilled to debut my friend Scott's son Steve Greene on sax, who has joined us at these jams since he was a little kid. He was just fifteen at the time, but he looked older. Big kid. You oughta see him eat. I strummed the guitar as he played a magnificent version of "Amazing Grace," which I dedicated to my pal Doug Gray, who's wife had passed away the week before.

Our set was all Marshall Tucker and Toy Caldwell and began with "This Ol' Cowboy." Then Mark McAfee sang "Midnight Promises," and we ended with "Fire on the Mountain." The guys were just great. We did pretty well for a band who had never played together and never had a single rehearsal.

The band was billed as Hash a Plenty, named for Toy Caldwell's favorite plate at the "World Famous" Beacon Drive-In in Spartanburg, SC. Band members included myself, Donnie Winters of the Winters Brothers Band, Mark McAfee, WBB drummer Chad Booher, and Don Swensen from Washington, of whom I spoke earlier. We had a blast and those guys just ripped it up with style. Like a BBQ rib with a shot of Jack.

The Dublin City Ramblers featuring the legendary Sean McGuinness played a simply amazing set of Irish folk rock that had everybody dancing. There's a reason why they are the number one Irish vocal group in the world. They are great.

The Winters Brothers Band sounded better than ever. Along with current members Dennis and Donnie Winters, Chad Booher, and Ricky Burke, the band welcomed back longtime WBB guitarist Jamie Laritz and original WBB band member, keyboardist David "Spig" Davis. As always, background (and some lead) vocals were provided by Dennis's daughters, the lovely Casey, Cody, and Carly.

The band hit the ground running, with Jamie and Donnie teaming up many times on some awesome solos. Jamie was having a blast and really reminded me of Eddie Van Halen back in the eighties.

Dennis Winters is always the consummate showman, and he was giving it all, pouring buckets of sweat and playing to beat the band. Of course the apple don't fall far from the tree, and the Southern Belles danced and sang the whole night like fighting fire. I did take note that Casey Winters should get the award for "most intense physical workout." That girl danced, jumped up and down, and swung her hair around for the entire show. I turned to a guy beside me and remarked, "If I only had half that young girl's energy!" He agreed.

The band played all the favorites, including "Smokey Mountain Log Cabin Jones" and the jam-laden "Sang Her Love Songs" and "Devil's After My Soul." Sean McGuinniss joined in on mandolin. Amazing stuff. You should have been there.

Cody joined her dad onstage for "Seven Bridges Road," Casey sang a couple of good rockers, and the band wrapped up the set with a version of "I Can't Help It" that must have been at least forty-five minutes long. It was stellar. Off the scale. The crowd went nuts.

The end jam was great as usual, with various musicians joining in to play the standards we all know and love. The final Winters Brothers jam was great. We made our way back to the hotel and crashed. Sunday we would converge on Cracker Barrel for breakfast with our friends Don and Molly Swensen and Tom Whitten before driving six and a half hours back home.

# 60

## SLINGBLADE, THE BOXMASTERS AND
## BILLY BOB THORNTON

*"Essentially I grew up with a real wide musical taste, and then of course came the Allman Brothers, and that changed my life. They became, and still are, my favorite band of all time."*
—Billy Bob Thornton, interview with Buffalo, June, 2006

I have been a fan of movies my whole life. If anyone ever asks me to name my favorite film, I will always say *The Wizard of Oz*. After all, *Oz* was a major influence on me as a child. The whole fantasy element. And of course there was Margret Hamilton, who scared the living hell out of me. I mean, the Wicked Witch of the West was creepy, but I really believe Mrs. Gulch the teacher was much scarier.

All through the seventies I went to movies every weekend, everything from Mel Brooks and Steve Martin comedies to sci-fi galore. As the years rolled on, I took a job as a movie critic and suddenly I was seeing almost every movie that came out. There were a few stars I became such a fan of that I made a point of seeing every film they ever did. People like Peter O'Toole, Dustin Hoffman, Al Pacino, Meryl Streep, Robert Duvall, and perhaps my all-time favorite, actor/director/ screenwriter of my second favorite movie of all time, *Slingblade*, Billy Bob Thornton. You can imagine how I felt when I finally met him in person.

I drove down to North Myrtle Beach on Wednesday, August 15, 2007, to cover the Billy Bob Thornton concert at House of Blues the following day. I had met Billy Bob on the phone during a long and quite fun interview (during which he told me my voice reminded him of Johnny Sandlin, which of course made me grin like a stuck pig), and we had spoken a few times on the phone after that. He invited me to come down and check out his show in Myrtle Beach, and when the day arrived I was locked and loaded.

Thursday morning I got up early and made my way to the beach. I was bound and determined to get in a beach walk, so at 8 AM I was virtually alone on the sand walking in the surf and feeling the cool breeze blow through my hair. I found myself walking with my eyes closed. It felt great. After a bit I turned to find the marker I had established in my mind to remind me of where I had parked. It was a good 2 miles back down the beach. I had lost all track of time and reality and had effortlessly made my way down the beach. I turned around and made the return trip, enjoying every minute of it.

Next, I would go looking for the KISS Coffeehouse, something I just had to see for myself as an old-school KISS fan. The coffeehouse is located at Broadway at the Beach in the center of the biggest tourist trap (and there are many) in Myrtle Beach. Just down from the Hard Rock Cafe.

I enjoyed watching some kids feed the ducks from the footbridge that leads into Celebrity Square. It reminded me of bringing my own kids to this same spot years ago.

I found the KISS Coffeehouse easily, and since it was a little past lunch time, I decided to have lunch at Johnny Rockets, across the sidewalk right in front of the coffeehouse. The food was good, and I enjoyed the 1950s styles, attitudes, the jukebox, and the staff dancing to Aretha Franklin's "Respect." The patty melt sandwich was very tasty. I really wanted to drink a cherry smash but, following doctor's orders, opted for unsweet tea. All good.

After lunch I made my way to the KISS Coffeehouse. Just when I thought Gene Simmons could never take another dollar of my hard-earned money, I found myself buying a baseball cap and a frozen Rockuccino (French KISS Vanilla) and an Ace Frehley postcard for my wife. She never liked KISS but finds Ace fascinating. That whole "outer space" thing, I guess.

I left Broadway at the Beach and headed back to the Holiday Inn for a little R&R prior to meeting Billy Bob and company.

I made my way over to the House of Blues and got there right on time. Sound check was set for 5 PM. I parked backstage and the very first person I met was Michael Bruce, AKA "Bubba," the drummer for the band. Bubba is a fine Alabama boy and would later become a friend. I then made my way over to a group of crew folks who pointed me to Kristen Scott, Billy Bob Thornton's personal assistant. Kristen is a sweetheart, and throughout the night I would become more and more aware of how vital her role is in the whole scheme of things. The lady is always at work.

She led the way to the dressing rooms and told me to make myself at home and that Billy Bob would be up to see me shortly. The first guys I met were Mike Shipp and Brad Davis. I had seen Brad before at the Americana Music Conference. He played guitar with Marty Stuart for a number of years. Brad was very cool, and I thoroughly enjoyed meeting him.

Michael Shipp spent quite a lot of time with me, and I really like the guy. Not only is he a super guitar and bass player, he is also a lifelong friend of Billy's who played with Billy Bob back in the day in a ZZ Top cover band called Tres Hombres. Mike and I talked about a whole bunch of stuff during the course of the evening, and he told me he is working on a solo record as well, which I cannot wait to hear.

After about fifteen minutes, the familiar figure of Billy Bob walked up to me to shake hands and gave me a big hug. After first meeting him during our interview over a year ago, it was great to finally meet face to face, and I was really happy to get in a great deal of face time with this rock-and-rolling movie star, who has not a single ounce of ego. It's amazing. Hollywood has not taken the heart from this Arkansas Southern rocker.

Sound check was fun. The guys have two bands. The Boxmasters, which Billy describes as a "hillbilly band," dish up country and rockabilly. They open for the Billy Bob Thornton band, the rock group.

They did a Boxmasters sound check, and while Billy doesn't play drums during the show, he did sit on the kit and jam during sound check. He is quite the drummer, too, by the way.

After a break, they returned to sound check for the rock band. This is when I started to realize that I was in for one hell of a show that night.

After sound check, everyone was eating dinner provided backstage. I was so excited, I chose to eat like Billy, just a banana and an apple and a lot of cold bottled water.

During the dinner break someone exclaimed that it was "feeding time" for the alligators, so we all made our way to the deck to watch as dozens of alligators were hand-fed from a pier 50 yards out. Lots of people were right there on the boardwalk to view the feeding, but I was fine viewing from a distance as these absolutely huge gators rose up out of the water to get their fish dinners. It was amazing. Billy Bob and the others seemed to really enjoy it, and Billy made a few funny comments. He is a great host and seems to be a limitless entertainer, even offstage.

After a while, it was time for the band to get dressed in Boxmasters gear. Pompadour haircuts, wigs, sideburns, and tonight's costumes—British mod—were donned. Apparently they dress out differently at various gigs, sometimes even wearing sparkling outfits.

I was sitting on a sofa and looked up to see Billy Bob walking toward me, dressed in his suit and skinny-neck tie. "I can't hear because I have these ear phones in," he said. "But you'd better get down there. We start in two minutes."

I thanked him and hit the stairwell. I found a perfect vantage point at stage right just behind the sound man, complete with road cases to sit on. Best seat in the house.

The general admission audience were all pushed to the front of the stage, ready for a show, and boy howdy did they ever get one!

I really had no idea what to expect of this concert. I love all of Billy Bob's records, and they are usually Americana- and country-flavored, but I had no idea he and the band would deliver such a balls-to-the-wall rock and roll show. But I am getting ahead of myself.

The band consists of: Billy Bob Thornton—lead vocals; Teddy Andreadis—keyboards, harmonica; J. D. Andrew—guitars (acoustic and electric) and bass; Mike "Bubba" Bruce—drums; Mike Butler—electric guitar and slide; Brad Davis—guitar (acoustic and electric); and Mike Shipp—guitar and bass.

The Boxmasters opened the show, dressed like 1960s British Invasion mods and playing like honkytonk rockabillies. Billy Bob dominated center stage, and I swear there were times when the spotlight and his ever-present cigarette made him look like a young Frank Sinatra.

The Boxmasters kicked it off with a country-fried "Better by the Minute" and without missing a beat moved into the Michael Nesmithpenned (and Nitty Gritty Dirt Band recorded) "Some of Shelly's Blues." It was clear immediately that Billy and the band had this Myrtle Beach audience in the palm of their collective hand.

Billy explained from the stage that they were two different bands. "We open for ourselves," he said. "We treat ourselves badly as openers. We turn off a couple of power amps and don't allow any special lighting." Funny.

The fabulous Boxmasters pulled off a hillbilly cover of Mott the Hoople's "Original Mixed Up Kid" that caught everyone off guard. Mike Shipp thumped a Paul McCartney-style bass and Teddy played accordion. It was my kind of band, with pedal steel and accordion.

The show included original Boxmasters tunes from the band's upcoming album, as well as eclectic covers. "Shit List" was a fun and witty song to be sure, as was "The Last Place They'd Look" and "Build Your Own Prison."

After the Boxmasters set there was a scurry of activity in the dressing rooms as the guys switched from sixties mod to hippie rock and rollers. I sat in a chair and stayed out of the way. When there's this much going on, the last thing an artist needs is somebody getting in their way.

We all went back down for the show and it just plain kicked ass.

After a short intermission the guys returned, decked out in their rock and roll regalia. Billy Bob was all Southern rock, and Mike Shipp donned a hippie shirt, shades, and headband, chomping on a cigar and playing the daylights out of a Gibson SG. Bluegrass star turned rocker Brad Davis was sporting a fake tattoo sleeve for the thug look, and the rest of the band members were decked out for rock and roll.

The set kicked off in fifth gear with "Emily," "Hitchin' a Ride," and "Wanna Be Your Boyfriend." I was hoping to hear more from the new album, *Beautiful Door*, although they did perform "Hope for Glory," which Billy dedicated to "all of the innocents dying in the war."

While the new album is more laid-back Americana style, the band was more full-on rock and roll. No complaints from this writer. It was like the Beatles meet Black Oak Arkansas at an Allman Brothers Band concert.

Thornton is a rocker, but he is also the kindest and downright sweetest front man I have ever seen, speaking directly to audience members and at one point carrying on a conversation with a couple who had their child up on their shoulders. Billy told them it made him miss his own daughter Bella.

At one point Billy took a drumstick and was hitting the accents on the drummer's crash cymbal, giving the people a real show. Then he took the stick and handed it to the child in the audience.

"That Mountain" was a great song, dedicated to the memory of Billy's good friend Jim "Ernest" Varney. (By the way, for a while both Billy Bob and Jim Varney were managed by Capricorn Records' Phil Walden.)

When the band left the stage the crowd went nuts. I remarked to one of the guys that I'd not seen a crowd demand an encore like that since the heyday of 1970s Southern rock and roll. It was amazing.

The band threw caution to the wind as the encore opened with Teddy pulling off an organ solo reminiscent of Emerson, Lake & Palmer, followed by a smoking lead guitar solo, which led into a blazing hot cover of the Ozark Mountain Daredevils' "If You Want to Get to Heaven."

Since it was the thirtieth anniversary of the death of Elvis, Billy Bob called for thirty seconds of silence in memory of "the King." Then he followed with, "Now scream your asses off for Elvis!" They did.

Billy announced the last song as one written by his late brother, called "Island Avenue." What a great song. The jam at the end of the song was like Led Zeppelin on steroids. Wow.

There's some kind of weird thing in the entertainment industry whereby people automatically disrespect a famous actor who tries to also be a musician. Well, sir, that rule or stigma is out the window in the case of Billy Bob Thornton. He was a rocker before he was an actor, and it shows. The show was fantastic, and you'd be hard pressed to find a single naysayer in the packed-out house. As for myself, consider me officially rocked and rolled over. Killer.

Following the show we all went back upstairs and hung out and talked for a long time. Billy had to meet and greet and sign some autographs. After another hour or so I decided to head out. I said goodbye to all of my new friends and thanked them all for being so kind and generous with their time. I walked in on Billy Bob as he was changing into some comfortable traveling clothes. They were about to head out for Huntsville, Alabama, quite a drive. He told me I should ride down with them, but my schedule would not allow it. Rats. They would perform two back-to-back shows in Alabama, four sets in all. Wow. I gave Billy a big ol' handshake and hug.

I was in the wind back to the Holiday Inn and would leave out the next morning to drive back with some great memories of one of the most fun nights of my life.

I may have missed 'Bama that week, but during summer 2008 I was once again invited to a Billy Bob/Boxmasters show. But this time it would be two magical nights in a familiar stomping ground, Huntsville, Alabama. I set sail for 'Bama ready for some real fun.

Once in Rocket City, I rode over to Merrimack Hall so I'd know where it was, then I checked in at the Hilton with plans of taking a nap. My three hours of sleep weren't gonna get it. Oddly enough, I never met up with that illusive nap. I was making calls, doing e-mail, and blogging, and pretty soon I got a message from Billy Bob's manager Lisa Roy that we were meeting around 4:30 for sound check, so I hit the showers, dressed, ran down my checklist, and was in the wind.

Upon arrival I pulled to the back of Merrimack Hall, where the two tour buses were parked, and several cops were hanging out. Just like at Myrtle Beach, the first person from the band I saw was Bubba Bruce, the drummer, and we shook hands and said our hellos. Then I met Alan Jenkins, the owner of the hall. What a nice cat. (His wife Debra is equally Southern sweet.) And he's a rock and roller just like me. He pointed me in the right direction and I was off and up the back stairs to the dressing room area.

Merrimack Hall was built in 1898 and was the company store for Merrimack Textiles. It was purchased in 2007 by Alan and Debra and made into a theater and concert hall. A very nice one.

Inside the dressing room area I ran into band member Brad Davis, and very soon all of the band guys were in there. I was happy to see Billy Bob's assistant Kristen Scott and to finally meet his manager Lisa Roy, who was just as kind and sweet as I had imagined from our countless e-mails. All night long she was introducing me to everyone. It was great.

My pal Dick Cooper came in with "The Leaning Man of Alabam'" Donnie Fritts, and we hung for a few minutes. Then it was time for sound check. I stood front and center, leaning on a guard rail while the band ran through a song. At the end, Billy Bob put his hand over his brow to squelch the spotlights, and to see me standing there. "Buffalo!" he said, shooting a peace sign. "How are you buddy?" "Great, I said. Except your Cardinals really put a hurtin' on my Braves." I knew that would make him laugh, and it did. The band was tuning and Billy Bob stepped up to the mic and, in a voice as strong as a baseball announcer, said, "Ladies and gentlemen, Columbia recording artist, Michael Buffalo Smith!" I laughed, "Thanks for the record deal, Billy Bob."

They ran through another song, and then I got the thrill of a lifetime. Billy Bob said, "Buffalo, you want to jam one with us?" I was blown away. "Come on up, man." Then he sat down at the drum kit. Hell yeah.

Mike Butler handed me his baby-blue Telecaster, and I kicked off "Can't You See." I looked at Billy Bob and he was grinning. The man loves Southern rock as much as I do. It was great fun singing and playing Toy Caldwell's signature song with the Boxmasters. Venue owner Alan Jenkins was grooving it seemed, and he later thanked me and said, "I love that song." All of the band made me feel like one of their own. An honorary Boxmaster was born. An experience for the books. Billy Bob came down from the drum riser and said, "That was fun, Buffalo. You sounded great." All I could muster was, "So did you, bro."

I must have been introduced to a hundred people, all of them great. Crew people with Billy Bob, venue personnel, fans and friends—Lisa, Kristen, and Billy Bob were introducing me left and right, and it was just a great, large time.

We all sat down to dinner. I sat beside pedal steel master Marty Rifkin, another really nice, really talented cat. I was excited to learn of his work with Bruce Springsteen on several albums I have been enjoying for many moons.

Billy Bob joined us and was having some good ol' pulled pork. Later he said to me, "Buffalo, next time you see me with a plate full of BBQ pork, slap that shit out of my hand." We all laughed. While the food was great, the combination of eating a pork plate and the back-to-back live sets didn't quite sit well. Of course, you couldn't tell by his performance, which was great.

As a part of my "no sleeping allowed" policy, I got up at 8:30 after sitting up talking to my buddy Sonny Edwards until late-thirty. Let me see, I went to bed at 3:30, so that was my five hours. Not my usual quota.

I did a lot of writing, went down for a nice omelet breakfast there at the Hilton, and did some more writing. Soon it was time to hit the road again.

At 4 PM, Merrimack Hall hosted a Q&A similar to *Inside the Actor's Studio* with Lynn Hoffman of the A&E Network. The Hall was packed with fans, and Billy Bob gave them 100 percent as always.

Lynn is a great moderator, and the whole session was fun and informative, funny and insightful. Billy talked about growing up poor in Arkansas, eating squirrel and possum, and he did an impression of his old preacher at the Methodist church. ("We're semi-Catholics," he said. "They started the church because they wanted to be Catholics but didn't want to do confession.") The pastor had only one arm, and Billy stood to do a hilarious take on the preacher. All in fun, of course.

He talked about his mother and her psychic abilities and how she predicted his Oscar win. He told the packed house that the character Kate Blanchet played in the movie he wrote, *The Gift*, was based on his mom.

Folks from the audience were brought down one by one to a microphone front and center by Lisa Roy to ask questions. Inevitably one guy asked, "Would you tell us about them biscuits and mustard?" The crowd went nuts. Billy explained that he rarely does the Karl Childers character in public, but for Huntsville he'd be happy to. So there he sat on the sofa, in sunglasses and smoking a cigarette, and transformed into his most famous character, doing a brief monologue about killing Doyle. He got a standing ovation.

After the Q&A I got to spend a little time with Billy Bob, talking music and stuff. I always enjoy our chats. The guy is well-read and brilliant and could beat anybody at Trivial Pursuit, the Music Edition. We all had dinner together and this time Billy had some good Southern fried chicken. He really seemed to enjoy that real food. I don't think he gets much of that in California. Lots of granola.

As show time came around, Donnie Fritts was back and I had a blast talking with him. Then came guitar slinger Kelvin Holly, and pretty soon my friend Sonny Edwards.

I really got to spend more time with the members of Billy Bob's band, all of whom are awesome talents and just great folks.

The show was just as good Saturday as it was on Friday. Both nights were simply rocking, and at the end of the show Brad Davis and Mike Butler were shredding on those guitars, Teddy was blowing harp, Marty was thumping and jumping on bass, and J. D. held down a tight rhythm. Sonny leaned over to me while Billy Bob was on drums and said, "That man right there is in the pocket son. What a drummer!" (Bubba was on tambourine and dancing his ass off. The real Alabama wild man. And if you haven't read his Southern fiction novel *Show Bidness*, by all means do so. It is hilarious.) Billy Bob rarely sits behind the kit during shows, but when he does, watch out.

After the show we all mulled around talking and shooting the bull.

I headed back to the hotel worn completely out. I was already missing my friends, especially Lisa, Kristen, and Billy Bob. Good people, them is.

I finally hit the sack at 2 AM. At 3 AM, the fire alarm went off, and everyone was evacuated. About thirty minutes later, we were allowed to return. Seems there was water leaking on an alarm and that set it off. There were firemen everywhere, as I stood there stylish in my black undershorts and Black Crowes "Remedy" T-shirt. When I did get back to bed, I was out cold. I would awaken Sunday at 11 AM, ready for the party at Dick Cooper's house. But that's another story, the details of which have been lost in the sands of time and beer. All I remember is that the music was great. Jason Isbell played; so did Shawna P and Scott Boyer Jr. Lots of friends were there. Kevin "Kahuna" Plemmons, David Hood, so many—and the man himself, do I have to say his name? Dick Cooper.

My fifty-fourth birthday was one for the books. It was June 24, 2011.

The night before, I had gone to hear Silver Travis rock the weekly Music on Main event in beautiful downtown Spartanburg, SC, and even managed to kick out a jam or two with my old buds and Justin McCorkle, son of the late George McCorkle from the Marshall Tucker Band. It was a large time.

The next morning I packed up the car, and along with my buddy Tim Shook headed due west for a special visit with Billy Bob Thornton and other friends on the set of his latest film in Cedartown, Georgia. If you are looking for it on the map, it's close to Rome.

Now, I can go no further without giving the hugest shout-out possible to a man among men, an amazing musician, a fantastic humorist and author, and one of the kindest souls to ever come out of the fine state of Alabama—the aforementioned Bubba Bruce, the man seen pounding drums behind Billy Bob, the Boxmasters, Unknown Hinson, and many others, and a man who had picked me up just a few weeks prior at my house to ride with him to Anderson, SC, to pick up a 1960s Shure Vocal Master PA system Billy wanted for his movie. A man who goes out of his way to see to it that everybody is happy, including one grateful Buffalo. Bubba is the man. Just sayin'.

We met up with Bubba somewhere near Cumming, Georgia, and followed him another gazillion miles to Cedartown and straight to the set of the movie, *Jane Mansfield's Car*. The movie takes place in 1969, and the film crews had rebuilt Cedartown's Main Street in true sixties chic, with a cool record store (advertising the new Kingston Trio record in the window), hardware store, a wedding shop, and a keen-looking movie theater. The classic cars lining the street had me drooling like a kid in a candy store.

When we first got there, Bubba introduced us to a few folks right quick like, and then we hopped on a golf cart and were driven out to the set. Bubba's wife Joani, a sweetheart who does all the hair for the movie stars, was doing a cameo role as a waitress in the diner and had just finished filming when we got there. I followed Bubba into the heart of the beast. Dozens of lighting folks, audio folks, gaffers, and all were hard at work. I am sure there was a "best boy" somewhere. Ever see that on movie credits? Wonder what you have to do to be a "best boy?"

With a "Quiet on the set" direction, we all got as quiet as Marcel Marceau at a golf tournament. One of the audio guys I recognized from his work with the Boxmasters handed me his headphones. I put 'em on, and there was Billy Bob, on a monitor, filming a live scene. I was grinning like a stuck possum. Billy was in a conversation with a British chick, and she was cussing to beat the band. His character, Skip Caldwell, was telling her, "Honey, you're gonna have to quit talking like that. People around here don't go for that kind of talk." Hey, it was the deep South in 1969. I believe he hit the nail on the head.

Just moments later, Billy Bob came dashing out from the restaurant set onto the street and darted right up to me, smiling and shaking my hand. I introduced him to Tim, and he asked if we wanted to ride over to his trailer. We all got into the truck with his driver. I heard the driver talking with Billy and kind of ascertained that he was a local cop. He was a great guy, and when he heard we were from South Carolina he told me that he used to work in our area and loved it. I wanted to talk with him some more, but we were quickly out and over to the trailer.

A bad storm had hit and it was lightning and raining. Billy Bob made the comment, "Well, it's a bad wind storm; at least we're in a trailer." We all chuckled.

Inside, I was so pleased to see the one and only Chuck Leavell and his lovely wife Rose Lane. Apparently Chuck had played piano in a street dance scene the night before. Oh, and Bubba had played the role of a cop, arresting some hippies. Boo! I know, Bubba, it's a character. That's why they call it acting, right?

Now, I may lose the chronological order of the sequence of events at this point, as there was a lot happening all at once. One thing that stands out most is my daughter Hannah calling me from Hawaii right in the middle of this mayhem of Hollywood and lightning and rain to wish me a happy birthday. Made my day. I love that kid. And to hear my granddaughter Zoe say "Happy birthday" tickled me to death.

At certain points during the night Billy would have to ride back to set, do the actor thing or the director thing, and return to home base. At one point he and Chuck left to shoot a scene in the barbershop with Robert Duvall. Now, *there's* another gem of a man. I have met Duvall twice in the past, but tonight my meeting him would be short and sweet.

All I can say is Bobby Duvall is not only one of the finest actors ever, he is also a kind and humble man. I like that.

While Chuck was gone with Billy, I spent a good deal of time talking with Rose Lane about the old Capricorn Records days. She had worked there, and actually, that's where she met her husband. They married in 1973. And boy have they had a life so far. From Chuck playing as a member of the Allman Brothers Band, to his many years as musical director for the Rolling Stones, Rose has been there. Chuck and Rose have also done major work in forestry and conservation, and Chuck had given me a copy of his new book called *Growing a Better America*. I am totally in their corner on this one. Chuck also cofounded the definitive website for conservation, which I highly recommend—the Mother Nature Network (www.MNN.com).

I was also happy to see J. D. Andrew and his wife there. J. D. is Billy Bob's partner in the Boxmasters as well as a great songwriter, producer, engineer, and musician.

At some point we walked down to the set, where a beautiful catering spread was laid out. The food was excellent, from the brisket to the green beans and some really good salad fixins. Mighty fine.

Another thing that happened was that J. D. came in with a box of fifty T-shirts advertising the movie for Billy to sign. He whipped out the Sharpie and sat there and signed them all. They would be auctioned for charity. I swear, this guy never turns anyone away. Just this day I saw him sign God knows how many autographs and pose for God knows how many photographs. What a trooper. Anyone who thinks this movie business is all glamour and easy should follow—or *try to follow*—Billy Bob Thornton around for a day. Good luck with that.

Like I said before, there was a whole lot happening in a short period of time, and at one point I was in Billy's trailer while he changed out of his movie costume and into his regular BBT duds. I got a little one-on-one time with the man of the hour, which is always cool.

There was another time when Billy brought in an actor who was starring in the movie. A tall gentleman with a strong Irish accent. Billy introduced him as Ray Stevenson, and the three of us had a nice visit, talking about movies and even more about the important things, like enjoying the "moments" that just happen in life. Those that are not and never could be planned. They just are, and you have to grab them as they come by. All I could think was, I am having one right now. I recognized Ray from somewhere, and when I asked where I had seen him he said maybe *The Book of Eli*. Sure enough. I loved that one. Denzel Washington and Gary Oldman. Ray played a skinhead with a bad attitude. He was a badass. It wasn't until I googled him later that I realized he had just appeared in the recently released *Thor* movie (he was great) and had starred as yet another comic book hero, *The Punisher*. Wow. He didn't look like the badass in his 1960s garb and huge smile. What a nice guy. It was a joy to meet Ray.

We had so many great conversations, enjoyed lots of laughs, saw old friends, and made new ones. Then, somewhere around 1:30 AM, it was a wrap. Billy's significant other, Connie, and daughter Bella were in town, so he had plans with them for Saturday. Me and Tim would stay in a motel near Cedartown before driving back home the next day. The people of Cedartown were great. Met some local law enforcement and they were too kind. One officer expressed to me just how thrilled they were to have had the crew and stars in town. But the circus was now over, and the film crew would move to LaGrange for more filming on Monday.

We said our goodbyes and put the ol' Honda in the wind. It had been a great birthday for me. One I won't forget.

Billy Bob continues to make movies and the Boxmasters continue to record and tour. In 2010, I wrote the cover story for the debut issue of *Twisted South Magazine*, which featured an interview with Billy Bob, a man who remains one of my all-time favorite actors and musicians and a man I am happy to call my friend.

# 61

## STARVING FOR AIR

In December 2007, I lost my breath. Actually, it began in November. I began to notice I couldn't get my breath when I would lie down to go to sleep. After a few minutes, it would all level out and everything would be fine. I ended up in the emergency room on the morning I was scheduled to drive down to Alabama for the Cowboy reunion at Johnny Sandlin's Duct Tape Studios. My breathing was bothering me, so I just drove over to the ER instead.

In the ER, I was put through several tests including a chest x-ray, blood tests, and more. I stayed in the ER from 10 AM until 5 PM, and by the time it was all over, I didn't know much more than I had known when I came it. They did assure me that I was "okay," so I went on to Alabama for the next few days, feeling badly the whole trip and trying to decide just what was wrong.

The day before Thanksgiving, I went in to the doctor and was immediately sent to the hospital for three days of tests. Again, I didn't get any real answers besides the pat verdict, "You need to lose weight." Wow, I had never heard that one before.

After getting out of the hospital, I was told I needed to have an oxygen machine at home and sleep with it on, so I did. I took a portable unit with me when Scott and I drove down to Tampa for the Angelus. Again, I felt badly for most of the trip, but the doctors didn't have any solutions for me.

Just a few days later, I was sitting on the sofa when I lost my breath. I could barely get air at all. I was in a panic. My step daughter Hannah drove me back to the ER. My oxygen level was impossibly low, and they rushed me into a room and started a breathing treatment.

I was in the ER from 11 PM until 7 AM, when the ER doctor came in to tell me I had a chronic lung infection. Okay, that made sense. He put me on a high-grade antibiotic and a rescue inhaler. I went home and got to work taking the antibiotic. I will spare you the details, but there were a couple of weeks of serious sickness that followed, during which time I was forced to sleep sitting up on the sofa, which caused edema to set in and my legs and feet to balloon to massive proportions. After being put on a low-sodium diet and given water pills, the swelling went down, but I was left with a cracked open heel and an infected right leg. It was time for another round of antibiotics and a whole new health-and-life plan to be drafted. After all, I didn't want this to be the final chapter in my book. Not by a long shot. This is just part one. I plan the follow-up in fifty more years.

# 62

# A DEATH IN THE FAMILY:
# BACK TO THE ANGELUS, 2008

Scott Greene and I had been talking about our annual pilgrimage to the Angelus for months. He was about as excited about it as I was. This would be Scott's fourth trip and my eighth.

We headed out in Scott's Dad's minivan with some great CDs playing the best of our collections all the way from point A to point Z. Bands like Gov't Mule, Marshall Tucker, Casting Crowns, Silver Travis, Bo Bice, Jackson Crossing, and, of course, the Charlie Daniels Band.

It was a beautiful day for a drive, and Scott and I caught up on everything from sports to music, politics to family, with good ol' Southern rock as background music.

After many hours on the road we stopped in Lake City, Florida, and hit the sack. We always break the trip up into two sections; it just makes it easier. Especially since I usually have to do a solo gig shortly after we arrive each year.

On Thursday we drove on into Tampa to the Seminole Hard Rock Hotel and Casino, and the party was officially on. Well, that is, after we waited two more hours until the room was ready.

I was to play in the lobby bar at 5:15. By the time the room was ready, I had all of fifteen minutes to get dressed in my Buffalo clothes and get ready for the stage.

Downstairs I met country singer-songwriter Amanda Martin, who would be sharing the stage with me for a songwriter's circle. We originally were set to be joined by our old friend Donnie Winters, but he was unable to be there. I had asked Tommy Crain if he and bassist Kerry Creasy would join us like they did with me the year before, but Tommy said Kerry had not yet arrived. We would have to wait to jam.

Amanda and I had a pretty nice crowd, including longtime friends and Angelus supporters Tom and Ann Bell. The problem came when I plugged in my Washburn acoustic. We couldn't get any sound out of it.

Sound man Pete McCaffrey tried every trick in the book and then we realized it wasn't his cords or PA, it was a short inside my guitar. Oops. I played my first song on Amanda's axe, and then one of the other performers loaned me her acoustic.

Amanda and I swapped off, me playing songs like "Natural Born Cowboy," "Smell All the Roses," "Into the Light," "Painting Her Toenails," and "I Want Paris Hilton to Be My Friend." Amanda sang several of her originals such as "Whiskey Makes Me Cry," "I Don't Think So," and "You Can't Help but Love Me." A good time was had by all, and I continued to see many friends I had not seen since last year's event.

Pretty soon it was time for the Pairing Party in the grand ball room. When we came in, there was a young country cover band playing, and we all mulled around and spoke to old friends and new ones. As usual, there was a wide variety of buffet finger foods, as well as chefs carving roast beef, lamb, ham, and other vittles.

I found myself hanging out with old friends such as CDB members Charlie Hayward and Pat McDonald, B. B. Borden, Pat Elwood, and various members of the MTB. I finally met their newest addition, sax/flute/key man Marcus Henderson (husband of Georgia Music Hall of Fame director Lisa Love)—a great and funny guy. I also fulfilled the plan set forth during one of my recent interviews by meeting Bo Bice and, as he said during the interview—"I look forward to meeting you and putting hand in hand." Which we did. Bo is a great kid. An old Southern rock soul in a young body.

Longtime Angelus supporter, cartoonist Guy Gilchrist, came over to speak and asked me to run up to his room with him; he had me a gift. As a former cartoonist myself, I was thrilled when he presented me with the original drawings of three of his daily Nancy comic strips, each with a different Southern rock theme. How cool is that? Now, this is the first year I knew that Guy was also a songwriter and singer, and he gave me his new CD, which includes some help from mutual friend Tommy Crain. Guy sat down and played me several of his originals, and I loved them all. I also liked being the recipient of a private concert. Cool factor number two.

Soon it was time for Tommy Crain and the Crosstown Allstars, and they came out of the chute locked and loaded with a brilliant cover of "Hot 'Lanta" by the Allman Brothers Band. They followed that with one of their own, "Find Another Lover," with Bob Rumer singing his heart out. I've said it before and I'll say it again, Bob has one of the best blues voices on the scene. Towson Engsberg locked in on drums with Kerry Creasy on bass, and Bob Jones just wailed on the B-3. The cherry on top was Tommy Crain, dressed in tie-dye, wielding that famous Les Paul goldtop, smoking the fret board like it was a filterless Camel.

Charlie Daniels joined the Allstars for a blistering mini-set that included "Further On Up the Road," "One Way Out," "Stormy Monday," "The Legend of Wooley Swamp," "Trudy," "The South's Gonna Do It Again," and, of course, "The Devil Went Down to Georgia," with Charlie playing the song faster than ever. It was seriously hot.

The set was all that and more, and when it was over, Scott and I and a few others made a beeline to the hospitality room for an adult beverage or two. There I met my pal Rick Broyles, the videographer and photographer, as well as Fast Fred Cole, a fellow traveler and picker. We were joined off and on by various and sundry brothers and sisters of the road, including MTB bassist Pat Elwood and his significant other Linda. Toward the end of our conversation, one of Ginger Ambrose's friends came by walking his bulldog, and we had some fun playing with him. That old boy loves dogs as much as the Buffalo does.

Scott had already headed in for the night, and I said a temporary goodbye to Broyles, Fred, and the others. As I walked into the hotel I saw Kerry Creasy and his wife Donna headed for the hospitality room. I told them goodnight and told Kerry how great he had played and sang with Charlie. I had no way of knowing it would be the last time I would see my friend alive.

Friday morning after due showers, me and Scott headed down to hit the breakfast buffet in the grand ballroom. As I exited the elevator and rounded the corner, I ran right into Tommy Crain. I noticed he looked a bit distressed. "Michael, we lost Kerry last night," he said. Well, I was like, "What, did he go home?" I was not even awake yet. "He died," said Tommy. There was a group of friends there, although the only person I can remember is Crain. I totally lost it and hugged Tommy as we let the emotions and shock wash over us. I just couldn't believe Kerry had died. He was so full of life.

After a while, Scott and I made our way to breakfast. One of the first folks I saw was Tommy's keyboard man Bob Jones. I gave him a Buffalo hug and shook his hand and spoke briefly. He too was in shock.

I called Mike Proctor, the guy who has the High Lonesome in Rome, GA, an invited guest of Angelus this year, and told him the news about Kerry. It nearly floored him. He said he was on the way down to meet us. We ate a little eggs and bacon and then headed back toward the room with Proctor. All along the way we were running into folks who were just hearing the sad and tragic news. On the second floor, just outside Kerry and Donna's room, stood Towson and Bob. We spoke for a while and then Donna asked to see me. I went in and spoke and held her and let her cry her heart out. I felt so much for her. Such a loss.

The next few hours are a blur. I didn't do much of anything until time to go down for my 4 PM set with Amanda. Arriving in the lobby bar, I found it filled with a whole lot of folks, including CDB/Bonnie Bramlett fan club boss Ginger Ambrose, Danny Shirley from Confederate Railroad, and Doug (MTB) and Rene Gray.

Ginger's friend Taylor Henry was doing some fine acoustic tunes and sounding mighty excellent as his mother watched from the front lines. It only got better when Tommy Crain stepped up during a song, plugged in his Chet Atkins acoustic guitar, and started playing lead fills. This is one reason why my web magazine almost always votes Tommy "Most Valuable Player."

Tommy offered to let me play his guitar for my set since mine was broken. Bob Rumer has loaned me his resonator, but I chose to play Tommy's because I had never played a steel-body resonator guitar before.

Amanda started off with a cover of "Suspicious Minds," and I dedicated "Fire on the Mountain" to Doug Gray and in memory of George McCorkle. Amanda did a mix of covers and originals, as did I, and the hour-long set seemed to just fly by.

I retired to the room for a while after the set, knowing that the banquet and auction would soon begin in the ballroom. We sat with our friends Tom and Ann Bell at a table right beside the Marshall Tucker

Band table. Throughout the evening I kept making my way over to sit and speak with the now long-haired B. B. Borden ("I just noticed one day that everyone in the band had long hair except for me, so I grew it out," he told me.), bassist Pat Ellwood and Linda, Clay Cook and his girlfriend, Doug and Rene Gray, and new guy Marcus Henderson, whom I was glad to finally meet. It would be the next day before I heard him rock, and boy howdy, he is good.

Charlie spoke to the crowd and led in a prayer. He played a video of Jodell singing "The Twelve Days of Christmas" with the kids from the Angelus home. It was very touching.

The Sweeny Family returned for their second year, mixing *Andy Griffith*-style (G-rated) comedy with some super-tight mountain music pickin'. They played a lot of the old songs and asked Charlie Daniels to join them for "Rollin' in My Sweet Baby's Arms" and a couple of others.

Jimmy Hart, "the mouth of the south," now the man in charge of pro wrestling in Florida spoke and introduced a table full of new up-and-coming young wrestlers. Then they showed a hilarious film clip of Charlie Daniels at his new job as a pro wrestler, doing a "clothes line" on two hulking wrestlers at the same time. Pretty doggone funny.

Lots of awards were handed out, including several for years of service to Ginger Ambrose, the Marshall Tucker Band, and Confederate Railroad.

There was a live auction that began with a heated bidding war between a fan and singer Bo Bice. It was for a "golden" fiddle signed by Charlie Daniels. Bice eventually won the fiddle for a whopping $3,000. Of course, it was all for the Angelus.

Over the next few hours, I spoke with so many great people, including Angelus event organizers Gar and Tammy Williams as well as Ginger and Bobby Ambrose, Charlie and Hazel Daniels, Brad "the Animal" Lesley, and many others. The fellowship is a big part of the fun each year.

Finally, we were all filled with prime rib, tea, and coffee and ready for Tommy Crain and the Crosstown Allstars with guest Charlie Daniels. Charlie Hayward filled in for Kerry and even played Kerry's bass. Tommy wore Kerry's hat, which we had all signed for Donna. Charlie spoke about Kerry, and the jam began.

The Allstars, Tommy in particular, were on fire. I know it had something to do with working the emotions out on the instruments, but you should have been there. It was amazing.

Daniels joined in for "The South's Gonna Do It Again," the classic that brought myself and Guy Gilchrist to the stage to sing backup alongside CDB regular Carolyn Corlew. The band played "Sweet Home Alabama," with Chad Brock standing in.

Charlie and Chad left the stage, and Crain kicked into "Hot 'Lanta," "Jessica," and, in dedication to Kerry, "Can't You See" with me singing. Then came "Whipping Post" for what seemed like forty-five minutes. I told them later that, although I have been fortunate enough to hear the Brothers play it live many times, the song never sounded better than on this night as these fellas played it in tribute to their fallen brother. The people watching knew they had witnessed a major event.

On Saturday morning we hit the breakfast room pretty early, where I sucked back far too many cups of Joe. The big outdoor concert was moved from the old location to the actual back parking lot of the Hard Rock Hotel, and I must say, I think it worked out better overall.

We ran into Tom and Ann on the way out, and our friend Mary Wilson had just driven in. She's a dear and one of the CDB's biggest little fans.

Hanging out backstage and running back out front to snap pictures was an aerobic workout and I enjoyed every minute of it. Throughout the afternoon I found myself in conversations with everyone from Rick Broyles and Bo Bice to Doug Gray; Chris and Jenny Hicks; the boys from Confederate Railroad, including Danny Shirley; Charlie Hayward and his wife Pat; Taz DiGregorio and his wife Donelle; my buddy Mike Proctor; all the Crosstown Allstars and Marshall Tucker band cats; and many others.

We got there in time to catch Confederate Railroad's smoking set, which ended with a half-dozen or more young girls onstage for the band's hit "Trashy Women."

Because he had to catch a plane later, former American Idol and fulltime Southern rocker Bo Bice hit the stage next, backed by the N-Kahootz Band. Bo mesmerized the audience with several tunes from his latest album *Let It Shine*, including my personal favorite, "You Can't Take the Country Out of Me." He is also one heck of a nice guy. He simply rocked the yard with his closer, a familiar little Skynyrd tune called "Sweet Home Alabama."

Next up were the Crosstown Allstars with special guest Dangerous Danny Toler. It was great to see the former Allman Brothers/Dickey Betts guitar-slinger again, and Tommy seemed really happy to have him join in. They played dual leads and smoldering versions of "Hot 'Lanta" and "Jessica," along with a funky take on the right Rev. Al Green's "Take Me to the River." It was amazing, and the Angelus kids in the front row were dancing in their seats.

Next came the Marshall Tucker Band, beginning with "This Ol' Cowboy" before bringing Chris Hicks to the mic to deliver the title track from his new solo album, "Dog Eat Dog World." The MTB turned in a blistering, extra-long jam on "Ramblin' on My Mind," featuring guest jammers Tommy Crain, Dan Toler, and soon-to-be MTB member Ric Willis. The set closed with a stage full singing "Can't You See" and the ol' Buffalo accepting Doug's kind invite to sing. At one point there were no less than five guitar players lined up across the front of the stage. If I didn't know better, I would have thought they were the Outlaws.

The Charlie Daniels Band closed out the show with a set of great tunes including "Drinkin My Baby Goodbye," "Wooley Swamp," and many others. At one point Charlie brought Kerry Creasy's wife Donna onstage and held his arm around her as he sang "Amazing Grace." Of course it all ended up with a huge jam on "The Devil Went Down to Georgia," and everybody left the show satisfied. You could not have asked for more. No way.

After the show I joined Doug Gray and Rene, along with young singer, friend (and soon-to-be American Idol Aaron Kelly) and his mom Kelly for dinner. Scott would join us later in the Garden Restaurant on the second floor.

The sponsor appreciation party wrapped things up in style with the Crosstown Allstars delivering the goods on "Standin' on Shakey Ground," "Jessica," and a guest appearance from myself to sing and play my George McCorkle model Copley guitar on "Can't You See," as well as to sing "Crossroads." It was a stone blast, baby. Also joining in was Big Mike from the Trunk Band, who can play like nobody's business.

Tommy cleared the stage of all but his band to dedicate the beautiful Tony Joe White tune "Rainy Night in Georgia" to Kerry's memory.

After the show, some of us hung out for a while. The Angelus has long been my charity of choice. We will always support the cause. They do great work, and they have heart. The next morning we would say our goodbyes and Scott put the Dodge in the wind. By the time we arrived home at around 7 PM, the 2008 Angelus was just another great memory— albeit it a little bittersweet. We'll miss you, Kerry.

The Angelus would feature more great fun the next year in December 2009, although Tommy Crain's band was not in attendance. The recent passings of Kerry Creasy and Rene Grey were on everyone's minds the whole weekend, and a cold rain plagued the event relentlessly. Of course, the Angelus always manages to keep the fun alive, and by the time the Charlie Daniels Band closed the country concert on Saturday night, we all knew we had been rocked like only the Angelus event can rock us. Southern rock style.

## CAN'T YOU SEE? *GRITZ*FEST II

On February 25, 2010, I was staying at the Hotel Preston in Nashville with my new friends Gig Michaels and Mark Carlyle of the band Swampdawamp. We had driven in through cold rains and heavy fog the night before, and by the time we got to the Preston we were all dead on our feet.

Mark and Gig had business meetings all day on the 25th, so I hung at the hotel. I did have a nice business lunch with videographer Rick Broyles and his friend, but the rest of the day was spent writing and chilling out. After all, my recent laser eye surgery had not yet healed, so I was not at my full potential and needing some rest.

You see, I had been battling eye issues brought on by diabetes for a couple of years, and had recently undergone a series of these outpatient laser surgeries in an attempt to correct the extremely poor vision in my right eye, the same eye that in 2004 had once been brought up to 20/20 after cataract surgery. As fate would have it, diabetes crept in and my vision took a tumble in 2008. Just a week before our trip to Huntsville via Nashville, I had undergone a pretty massive preventive laser surgery in the left eye, my quote "good eye." So here I was, traveling out and about with still blurred vision, and doing it much too soon following the surgery. What is it they say about hindsight?

The Swamp guys went out that night for a show at the Wild Horse Saloon downtown. The guys invited me to have dinner on them at the Preston while they were gone. They told me to ask for Chef Danny, which I did. Chef Danny was a great guy and hooked me up with what may have been the best ribeye steak I ever had. It was amazing. No wonder the hotel Preston attracts so many music stars. All of this and a staff that is just great. Everyone is friendly and helpful.

Mark and Gig came in at about 2 AM and we sat up and talked about their excellent night with their rep from Jagermeister, who had been sponsoring the Swampdawamp Tour. Fellow Jager tour artist Eric

Church was providing the show tonight, and the guys had a blast. Gig even ended up on CMT. As the stories wound down, we were all ready to hit the sack. *GRITZ*fest II was the next day.

Mark put the big Ford truck in the wind and by early afternoon we were pulling up in front of the Space and Rocket Center Marriott in Huntsville, Alabama. Immediately things began to hop and they didn't slow down until the end of the day at 3:00 AM. I met my coconspirator Sonny Edwards in the lobby, and we began to unload the truck. The next person I met was Karen Blackmon Caldwell, with whom I had just reconnected via Facebook.

Karen was lead singer in the APB (Artimus Pyle Band) back in 1983. They had a deal with MCA Records and released an album called *Night Caller*. My friends and I used to see them a lot in Spartanburg. When the band broke up, I never heard from Karen again. It was really terrific to see her again after twenty-nine years.

After tossing my luggage into my room, I got a call from Tommy Talton telling me to come downstairs to the restaurant. When I got there, all my buddies were there, seated around a table. Talton, his former Cowboy partner Scott Boyer, Tommy's wife Patty, and the Queen herself, Bonnie Bramlett. After a lot of hugs, Karen Blackmon and her friend joined us, and I stepped over to the adjacent table to meet another longtime phone and Internet friend for the first time. Peter Cross had flown all the way from England for *GRITZ*fest, and he introduced me to his friend Jeannie Greene—a popular singer from the seventies Muscle Shoals scene—and her family. Everyone was extremely kind.

Our time chatting and sipping coffee was short-lived, and it was soon time to get dressed and head to the Crossroads Music Hall. I caught a ride with Tommy and Patty Talton, and we arrived just in time to hear the sound check.

I was running into one old friend after another. From former Crawlers singer Thad Usry to my friend and songwriting pitchman Joe Meador, who drove in from Nashville. It was great. I only wish I had more time with each one.

Dennis from US Legends Guitars was set up for his silent auction, and I saw Terry Reeves and her intern Willie from Music Matters Entertainment helping the fine folks from Bandito Burrito set up the food in our green room. What a spread it was, all sorts of Mexican food, individually wrapped burritos, tacos, etc. along with great trays of raw veggies, sandwiches, and much more.

I felt like a spinning top. Every way I turned I was greeted by familiar smiling faces. Sonny, who was perhaps the hardest working man in show-biz by this point, was running all over, trying to be sure every "t" was crossed and every "i" dotted.

Tommy Crain and the Crosstown Allstars had finished setting up their gear. Crain's excellent band would serve as backup band for all of the acts. Bonnie Bramlett had her sound check first. She sounded as great as ever. Tommy Talton sound-checked next, followed by Jimmy Hall. Mere minutes after sound check was over, stage manager Dick Cooper told me the doors had opened. In minutes it was time for an acoustic set from my Angelus buddy, Nashville songwriter Guy Gilchrist, best known at present for his "other" job as cartoonist of the world famous Nancy comic strip.

As a special treat, Guy brought along world-class fiddler Greg Holt, a superb player who has worked with artists such as Billy Joel and Bo Bice among others. The two turned in a fantastic set.

Bonnie had been feeling a bit poorly, so she asked to go on early. She took the stage next along with the Crosstown Allstars seated in a straight-backed wooden chair. The divine Ms. B proceeded to set the bar extremely high during a short set, beginning with "Strongest Weakness," a song she proudly introduced as being penned by her daughter Bekka. The crowd moved closer to the stage as Bonnie delivered the title track from her latest album, "Beautiful." Now, I have called this one of the most beautiful ballads ever written, and her version with the Crosstown Allstars was breathtaking. At the end, Bonnie found herself wiping away her own tears, much like a few audience members standing around me. She closed her set with "Only You Know and I Know," a classic she performed countless times with her late husband in Delaney & Bonnie & Friends.

The audience was mesmerized. Now it was time for the Crosstown Allstars to rock their own stellar set.

It's no secret that Tommy Crain is true Southern rock royalty, having spent over fifteen years on the road and in the studio as a member of the Charlie Daniels Band, cowriting many of Charlie's best-loved song, including the zillion-seller "The Devil Went Down to Georgia." While Crain is the point man in the Crosstown Allstars, his band is made up of a group of truly top-flight musicians, including Towson Engburg on drums, Bob Rumer on guitar, Bob Jones on keyboards, and the most recent addition, famed Wet Willie bassist Jack Hall, who replaced Kerry Creasy following his passing. The band is tighter than Jack Benny's hat band, and its members have become masters at backing their fellow Southern rockers while shining like the harvest moon on their own material.

The Allstars blazed through a forty-five-minute set that included smoking blues and high-octane Southern rock, like their crowd favorite, "The Hill." Of course, Tommy never fails to pay tribute to the man he calls "my old boss," by playing "Long Haired Country Boy." I was happy to be invited onstage to sing, along with Guy Gilchrist and fiddler Greg Holt. We had a blast. Following on the heels of that one, I took over lead vocals for a tribute to our host club, singing the blues staple "Crossroads" with the Allstars and Sonny Edwards on guitar. For my second song, I led a full stage of jammers on Toy Caldwell's "Can't You See." Bob Rumer and Sonny Edwards rocked on guitar, and Bob Jones wore out the B-3. It was great having a fiddle on hand to sing a verse. Backing vocals were also added by Donna Hall and Terry Reeves.

During a short break in the action I made my way backstage, where old friends were having a great time catching up. Tommy Talton stood playing an acoustic guitar, rehearsing with Donna Hall and Karen Blackmon Caldwell.

Tommy Talton was on deck next, bringing along friend and guitarist Kelvin Holly (Little Richard) to join the Allstars band. Now, Talton is always great, but tonight he was just over-the-top good, shining on guitar and making jaws drop with his stellar slide playing. Talton treated the crowd to an amazing set that included many of his best-loved songs, including several old Cowboy tunes. He was joined by Jimmy Hall on sax for a simply bombastic rendition of Alan Toussaint's "On Your Way Back Down." The interplay between Hall on sax, Talton on slide, and Tommy Crain on lead was a huge crowd favorite.

Without skipping a beat, Jimmy Hall took the center stage position and the church of Southern rock was in session. Joined by sister Donna Hall Foster and Allstar brother Jack Hall, it was an impromptu family reunion—there was little doubt we were about to see some serious Wet Willie action.

Jimmy Hall is a consummate showman. This Southern rocker has been going strong for forty-something years and hasn't lost a thing. Fact is, like a fine wine, he has only gotten better with age.

Jimmy rocked the joint from the get-go, delivering the goods on classics like "She Caught the Katie" and his own "Rendezvous with the Blues." Jimmy's vocals, considered by many (myself included) to be the best in Southern rock, were at their peak this night, and his sax and harp work only served to enhance the whole Wet Willie style experience.

Jimmy turned lead vocals over to his sister Donna, who nailed Delbert McClinton's "Every Time I Roll the Dice." Before one could gather back the breath that Donna had knocked out of them, Jimmy took us all to church with a rocking "Swing Low, Sweet Chariot" that brought screams and applause from the crowd.

Of course, Hall saved the best for last, closing with his biggest hit, the eternally optimistic "Keep On Smilin'," which ended several times only to kick back in like the best James Brown live performance.

Sonny Edwards and Guy Gilchrist took the stage for a live auction of goodies donated by Charlie Daniels, Billy Bob Thornton, Randy Poe, and Guy himself, among others. The winner was then selected and received a guitar signed by all of the GRITZfest performers, donated by US Legends Guitars.

Shawna P. closed out the show with a set of amazing acoustic tunes. Although an all-star jam had been scheduled, the show ran long and we just ran out of time.

Now, somewhere in the middle of Jimmy Hall's set, I went blind. Seriously. As I said earlier, I had been having laser treatments in my eyes, and something went wrong. I had a retinal bleed in my good eye and everything went completely dark.

Needless to say, the next few days were some of the most frightening of my life. It would take weeks, months actually, before I would be able to see clearly again. Retinal bleeds, followed by surgery, followed by cataracts, followed by more surgery. I spent ten months legally blind. I am thankful to so many people who came to my aid during those scary times. So many friends. Never take the gift of vision for granted.

# 64

## THE TRAIN TO GRINDERSWITCH

*"We [Southern Rockers] used to be a brotherhood. Now it seems like we are split into different factions, and the ones who have maintained their popularity just aren't willing to lend a hand to their old friends. Used to be we were all for one and one for all. It's sad that it ain't that way now."*
—Dru Lombar, interview with Buffalo, December, 2004

The first time I met Dru Lombar face to face was when his band Dr. Hector & the Groove Injectors played at Occasionally Blues in Greenville, SC, several years ago. Dru and I had been talking a lot on the phone, and I had done a story on him for *Hittin' the Note* magazine. I was a huge fan of all things Capricorn Records, still am, and Grinderswitch was one of their best bands.

I showed up to the gig early with my *Honest to Goodness* album cover in tow. Dru sat and talked with me a good while and wrote some really nice words on my LP cover that made me feel like someone very special. Dru was a great guy.

He and I started talking a lot on the phone. Dru was going through a bit of a rough time dealing with the way things were as opposed to the way they were during the seventies.

"We used to be a brotherhood," he said. "Now it seems like we are split into different factions, and the ones who have maintained their popularity just aren't willing to lend a hand to their old friends. Used to be we were all for one and one for all. It's sad that it ain't that way now."

Dru and I would talk for hours about his dreams of reuniting the Southern rock community. We spoke of a great tour with the Winters Brothers Band, Grinderswitch, Tommy Crain and the Crosstown Allstars, and myself, perhaps featuring additional guest jammers on each date.

One really great show I did with Grinderswitch was down in Spirit of the Suwannee Music Park in Florida, a biker event called Rock and Wheels. A really rocking band called Big Engine played right after I did my solo acoustic set. Original Molly Hatchet bassist Banner Thomas was handling bass duties in Big Engine.

Grinderswitch rocked the blues like crazy that night, with Dru singing and playing to beat the band, and Eddie Stone wailing on keyboards. I was thrilled when Dru asked me to do a couple of songs with them. I sang "Stormy Monday" and "Crossroads." Original Hatchet man Steve Holland was also in the house and played guitar with us. It was a large time.

In 2005, I staged the first *GRITZ*fest in Greenville, SC at the Handlebar. We had a ball. Tommy Crain and the Crosstown Allstars, Bonnie Bramlett, Donnie Winters, Denny Walley, Silver Travis, Mark Emerick from Commander Cody Band, Tony Heatherly and Mark Burrell from the Toy Caldwell Band, Mark McAfee, Darren Brothers, and the capper, Dru Lombar leading a stellar blues jam.

Dru refused to take any expense money. He rented a car and drove all the way up from Jacksonville and donated his time and talent in full to the charity we were helping out. Man, he smoked "Kiss the Blues Goodbye" and a couple of others, each song stretching beyond the twenty-minute mark. Real Southern rock jamming.

It was only a day or two later that I heard Dru had suffered a heart attack and was in a coma. He died a couple of days later, and again we all wept. There was a lot of that going on in 2005.

In months to come I would finally meet Grinderswitch original Larry Howard at a gig in Macon, as well as Judi Petty, widow of Grinderswitch bassist Joe Dan Petty. Both great folks. I still have a hard time wrapping my head around the fact that Grinderswitch can never play another gig. God works in mysterious ways. But I will never forget Dru.

# 65

# A FRIEND NAMED TOMMY CRAIN

As I was wrapping up the writing of this book, I got the news that yet another Southern rock friend had passed in the night. It was January 2011, and at first I just didn't believe it. There must be some mistake, I thought. After all, other than needing hip surgery, Tommy has been fine—well, at least as far as I knew.

I have been a fan of Tommy's since 1975. He joined the Charlie Daniels Band right after the *Fire on the Mountain* album came out, and the first time I saw a CDB concert Crain was on the Les Paul. He blew me away with his Southern-fried leads, and the dual leads between him and Charlie in concert were just amazing. Stuff like "Caballo Diablo" and "Saddle Tramp," and a few years later "In America" and "Still in Saigon."

It wasn't until 2001 that I actually met Tommy. My very first trip to the annual Angelus Golf and Country Concert benefit. At that time it was being held in Clearwater, Florida, before moving to Tampa.

It was an absolutely beautiful day, and the concert venue was right on the edge of the water. Seagulls and pelicans flew all around, and there was a cool wind blowing in across the water. There were tents set up in the backstage area, and Jill and I were sitting and talking with all sorts of great folks. I had just met Bonnie Bramlett the night before at the pairing party, and today she came across the yard in her tie-dyed T-shirt and sat down with Jill and I and talked for the longest time. I truly feel our friendship was forged in Southern steel that very day. Same with me and Tommy Crain.

When Tommy showed up at the tent wearing a huge cowboy hat, I could hardly wait to meet him. It was actually Bonnie who introduced us. I spoke to him a few minutes and had my picture taken with him, and at the time I had no idea just how good a friend he would soon become. That day I watched Tommy sit in with virtually every band that played, from Wiley Fox to Marshall Tucker, Confederate Railroad to

Molly Hatchet. I was still running *GRITZ* magazine at the time, and when I listed my "Angelus Superlatives" in the magazine, Crain was my "MVP," a title he went on to receive every year that he came to the Angelus event.

I looked forward to returning to Angelus annually and most every year Tommy was there as well. There's no way I could ever say what happened in what year, but some random memories include: the year Scott Greene and I had just arrived at the Hard Rock Hotel to find I was scheduled to perform an acoustic set in less than one hour. I ran into Tommy Crain, who had also just arrived, and he asked me when I was going to perform. I told him that apparently I was to go on in fifty minutes. He asked if I wanted him to sit in, and of course I said yes. He had soon recruited Crosstown Allstars bassist Kerry Creasy to join us, and I basically threw my set list out the window and turned it into an acoustic jam. Great fun. Also, at one of my first Angelus events I ended up onstage in a jam with Tommy, Charlie Hayward, and Sparky of CDB and Doug Gray of Marshall Tucker. There are a lot of funny memories from the green room involving alcohol, but I only recall Tommy being involved once, and that was when he walked by followed by Charlie Daniels while Bonnie Bramlett was sitting in my lap. We were acting silly and having fun. Tommy looks over and says, "Now, be careful, Michael." Charlie grinned and shook his head, saying something like "You kids." Doug Gray invited me to play with Marshall Tucker Band many, many times at Angelus, and most of the time Tommy was onstage as well. Always a stone-cold blast. There were so many late-night jams and so many opportunities to just sit around and talk, and I have nothing but good memories.

The only sad one came in 2008. The first day of the event, there was a late-night jam that found Tommy Crain and the Crosstown Allstars backing Charlie Daniels on a set. I ended up onstage, along with Guy Gilchrist and a handful of others, singing backup on "The South's Gonna Do It Again" and "The Devil Went Down to Georgia." This was the night Tommy's bass player Kerry Creasy died during the night, which I told you about earlier in the book.

Tommy was always the first to sign on for a benefit concert. When Tim Shook and I did the Archangel Benefit in Huntsville, Alabama,

Tommy was there with an all-star cast including Jakson Spires, Ray Brand, and JoJo Billingsley, all of whom have now passed on.

When I was recording my *Southern Lights* album in Huntsville, Tommy drove down from Nashville in his big pickup truck. It was literally filled with a bed full of musical instruments, from his goldtop Les Paul to a beautiful Gibson acoustic, a Dobro, a pedal steel, and a few other stringed instruments. Tommy joined the Crawlers, Bonnie Bramlett, Pete Carr, John Wyker, Stephen Foster, and others to help make what I feel is my best CD. We had a real ball with Tommy in the studio, and he seemed to have a great time reconnecting with old friends. One song we recorded was "Ride on, My Friend," written by Tony Heatherly in memory of Toy Caldwell. Tommy helped arrange the song, and at the end he and I improvised a lead jam with me on his Gibson acoustic and Tommy on the Les Paul. I remember him talking about how stupid he had been years earlier when he attached a midi device to the body of his Les Paul, and it would soon disappear. Then he blew me away by asking me to autograph his Martin acoustic guitar. I was shocked, especially since I was the first to sign it. He had a way of making me feel special, for sure.

A short time later I returned to Huntsville for a CD release party in the bar at the Space and Rocket Center Marriott. We had some major talent there to perform, including Tommy. He would return to play my *Something Heavy* CD party a few years later in the same place, as well as to perform at the memorial concert and jam we put together to honor our friend Ray Brand after he died of cancer.

When I was organizing the first ever *GRITZ*fest in Greenville, SC, at the Handlebar, Tommy and his band were the first to sign on for the benefit show. Then five years later, when we were planning *GRITZ*fest II, this time in Huntsville, Alabama, Tommy and his band were again first in line, and that night they played their own set and backed up virtually everyone else.

Man, we had so many great jams together. I will probably forget a couple. In 2007, when another friend of ours died, a bunch of us did a Jam for George McCorkle in Spartanburg, and Tommy was again front and center.

I spoke to Tommy just a few days before his passing, and he was feeling great. He was really excited about the Crosstown Allstars new live album they were putting out, and has asked me if I was still writing the liner notes for it. Of course I said yes. When I hung up the phone I had no idea whatsoever that I would never speak to him again. How could I? But I know one thing. As long as I am drawing breath, I will cherish the memories of making music and having some laughs with Tommy Crain. I feel blessed to have known him.

# 66

# THE OUTLAWS, BEKKA BRAMLETT, AND MY MAGICAL NIGHT IN NASHVILLE

I had really had a rough couple of years health wise, and I have no idea where I would be now had it not been for my friends. A series of benefit concerts had been staged in 2011, and on November 3, my buddy Rick Broyles put together a show in Nashville at the legendary 3rd and Lindsley that simply blew me away.

Me and my friend Tim Shook rode up to Music City with Roxanne Lark and Colleen Knights, having loads of fun and laughs along the way. From the time I walked in it was like…remember in *The Wizard of Oz*, when Dorothy opens the door of the house and it goes from black and white to color? It was like that the whole night for me. So many friends, so much great music.

I cannot begin to say how many great friends showed up or describe how full my heart was all night long.

First up on the stage was my dear friend Donnie Winters from the Winters Brothers Band, a man who never fails to show up for a friend and never fails to play his heart out. From his timeless "Shotgun Rider" to his yodels and his beautiful songs in the style of his father Don Winters and mentor Marty Robbins, Donnie sounded amazing, as always.

Next up was former Outlaw, current Ghost Riders member Steve Grisham with fellow Ghost Rider and former Pure Prairie League bassist Phill Stokes. The boys sounded great, playing acoustic versions of one of Grisham's Outlaws songs, "Keeping Our Love Alive," and a great tune he wrote called "Roots." Steve and Phil were excellent. Then they brought up drummer Don Kendrick for the blues number "Handy Man." So nice.

I went backstage to the green room, where the Outlaws were pouring in, getting their guitars out of their cases and tuning up. The room by now was just packed with folks. Friends, old and new. It was then that Tim told me Bonnie Bramlett was in the house. I went out and hugged my friend and sat with her while The Outlaws did their magic. And magic it was. I had not yet seen this lineup, and this was my first face–to-face meeting with Billy Crain, brother of my dear friend Tommy. Henry Paul is a great guy and an amazing talent, as are the rest of the guys.

The Outlaws started off with "There Goes Another Love Song" and didn't let up. Bonnie and I were both having a ball as Henry Paul sang to beat the band, with fellow original Outlaw Monte Yoho on drums, Randy Threet on bass, and Billy Crain and Chris Anderson on lead guitars. The twin leads of Chris and Billy were nothing short of stellar. The band rocked through "Freeborn Man," "Hurry Sundown" (my favorite), and many more, including a great new Outlaws song. I was happy to hear them play the Henry Paul Band Skynyrd tribute "Grey Ghost," and the jam at the end had me (and Bonnie) on our feet screaming. Southern rock the way God intended it to be played. Of course they closed with a ten-minute-plus rendition of "Green Grass and High Tides," and I was fit to be tied.

After their set, I joined everyone in the green room for photos, and somewhere around this time Bekka Bramlett showed up backstage wearing a shirt she had decorated with my name, "Buffalo." It was the sweetest thing. Now, I had met Bekka only once, down at the annual Angelus event in Florida, but after I had her as a guest on my radio show, we started talking a bit. Then on Christmas eve, 2010, we got on the phone and started talking about music and stuff and ended up talking for hours. We quickly became friends, and she was among the first to sign on for this benefit show.

Bonnie walked in and we were just having a ball talking and taking pictures. Roxanne was the consummate professional photographer, and I was having serious fun for the first time in a while.

Soon Bonnie and I returned to our seats to sit and listen to Bekka sing. Tonight she was joined by the great Jon Coleman on keys. Currently a member of the Trace Adkins band, John was once a member of the Outlaws as well. Just a top-of-the-line musician.

Throughout Bekka's set, Bonnie kept expounding her pride in her daughter. Bekka, in turn, gave more than one shout-out to her Mommy from the stage.

Bekka's set included "What Happens in Vegas," "One," "Used," and "When It Rains," a simply beautiful tune. Her songwriting is impeccable, and her voice—well, she is after all the daughter of Delaney and Bonnie. But she sings from the gut, from the depths of her soul. She feels the music, and therefore, so do we.

Jon sang a couple of his great songs as well, which were showstoppers in and of themselves. Then they brought up drummer Don Kendrick and harp man Coconut Harley for a blues jam before Bekka managed to talk her mom into coming to the stage for one song. Bonnie had just had oral surgery and was not supposed to sing, but she did. Did she ever! The ladies dueted on Sam Cooke's "You Send Me" and it brought the house down. So good.

After a break, my old friends from the band Old Union came out to jam. Chuck and Spotty treated the audience to a few songs, and they rocked. I had not seen my friends since Angelus several years ago, but they have gotten even better with time. Good stuff. Toward the end of their set, they were joined by Outlaw county rocker Kara Clark, who sang "Honky Tonk Women." Kara's new husband Eerie Von (of Danzig fame) joined in on backing vocals.

Next, Kara brought her entire band to the stage for a short set of original songs that included "Whiskey and Cigarettes." The kids rocked. By the way, Kara is the future face of outlaw country music. Mark my words. And just like that, the show was over. It was time to hang out with old friends and chat a while before venturing out in search of late night/early morning foodstuff.

There was a little sleep, a lot of late-night text messaging, and then it was morning and time to drive back. All I knew was that the events of that weekend would remain with me the rest of my life. I have been very lucky to have so many magical musical moments in my lifetime, and now the "3rd on 3rd" benefit sits high up toward the top of the list, one for which I am forever grateful.

# 67

# THE ROAD GOES ON FOREVER

My career as a writer and musician has afforded me more blessings than I could have ever imagined. It's been a thrilling rock and roll joyride, and I hope it just keeps on a-rocking along. I will certainly continue to write about my love of the music, and as long as I draw breath, I will write and play my songs.

To all of the musicians I have worked with, jammed with, recorded with, or simply interviewed, you all have my deepest gratitude and respect. To the music fans and readers of *GRITZ* and my other writings, I thank you all. Hopefully I will meet each and every one of you at some point along my journey down the road. I sure hope so.

People have asked me about the title of this book, *Prisoner of Southern Rock*. Some have speculated that I was implying something negative. Truth be told, I did find myself somewhat pigeonholed as the "Southern Rock Ambassador" after so many years. I felt I was losing touch with all the other great music out there. I did begin to feel trapped, kind of like a prisoner. All that being said, I would not trade those years with *GRITZ* for anything. They were a blast. And as I continue, writing about music of all types, Southern rock will always, I repeat, *always*, hold a special place in my heart.

Moving forward, perhaps my biggest dream is to see our nonprofit organization Hearts of the South become fully realized. It is a longtime dream of mine to establish an entity that can provide assistance for uninsured Southern rock musicians when needed. We are currently hard at work on Hearts of the South, as well as the music website UniversalMusicTribe.com. Meanwhile, I am working on at least five other books, three of which are Southern-rock related. Kind of shows you where my real love lies. So, if you will excuse me, I am going to kick back and listen to some Marshall Tucker, Allman Brothers, and Lynyrd Skynyrd for a while. After all, as much as I love my Springsteen, Boston, and Aerosmith, there comes a time when I have to crank out some sweet Southern rock.

# ACKNOWLEDGEMENTS

It's been several years since I first started writing this memoir, and there have been literally hundreds of people I want to thank. You all know who you are. Many thanks to all the great bands and artists, as well as to my family and friends.

A special thank you goes out to the following folks for help and inspiration along the way: Billy Bob Thornton, Robin Duner-Fenter, Lisa Roy, the Boxmasters, Kristen Scott, Benjamin Greene, Hannah Jane Maxey, Tim Shook, Richard "J. R." Smith, Scott Greene, Charlie Daniels, Doug Gray, Gar and Tammy Williams and the Angelus, Michael Mullendore, Mitch Lopate, Rick Broyles, Rebyll and Ms. Rebyll, the Southern Rock Society, Jody Weisner, Jeff Bannister, Jay Taylor, Dr. Nick McLane, Tom Coerver, Roxanne Lark, the team at New Horizon—Dr. Malvern and her nurse "T.J.," and Hal Stewart; Dr. Bowden, Dr. Tommy Bridges, the South Carolina Commission for the Blind, and all those who helped me through the eye issues of 2010; and the bands who gave so much to play benefits for me—and there are a lot of you!

In loving memory of Tommy Crain, Taz Digregorio, Barney Barnwell, Frankie Toler, Jakson Spires, Ray Brand, Delaney Bramlett, Robert Nix, Bobby Lowell, Eddie Hinton, Toy Caldwell, Tommy Caldwell, George McCorkle, Ronnie Hammond, JoJo Billingsley, Ronnie Van Zant, Steve and Cassie Gaines, Allen Collins, Leon Wilkeson, Billy Powell, Ean Evans, Hughie Thomasson, Duane Allman, Berry Oakley, Allen Woody, Lamar Williams, Dru Lombar, Steve Miller, Joe Dan Petty, Donnie McCornick, Wayne Sauls, Duane Roland, and Danny Joe Brown. And of my friends James Irwin, Bill Hudson, Tony Pearson, and Patsy Smith Harvey.

# APPENDIX I

## THE TOP SOUTHERN ROCK ALBUMS OF ALL TIME
## (JUST MY OPINION...)

1. *At Fillmore East*—The Allman Brothers Band

This has been my favorite record since the very first time I heard it in a motel room at Myrtle Beach in 1972. A girl had a stereo in the room and turned me on to this and *Layla* in one great week.

2. *Layla and Other Love Songs*—Derek & the Dominos

Yes, it's the British Clapton, and yes, it's still Southern rock to me. Southern rock is all about a certain vibe, and with Duane Allman way up in the mix, the vibe is there in spades.

3. *Where We All Belong*—The Marshall Tucker Band

Those of you who know or read me know, I am a die-hard Tucker fan. If I had only one MTB album (I can't imagine that...), it would be this brilliant Capricorn classic. One studio record, one live. Toy just blazes across the fret board on the live stuff.

4. *Fire on the Mountain*—The Charlie Daniels Band

Never forget unwrapping my copy and finding the bonus Volunteer Jam EP inside. Blew me away. And every song here is classic. As Paul T. Riddle would say, "It's Cadillac, man."

5. *5'll Getcha Ten*—Cowboy

Every record Scott and Tommy did was a classic, but *this one is my favorite* because it featured "Please Be With Me," with Duane Allman on dobro.

6. *Highway Call*—Dickey Betts

Brother Dickey, the country element that made the Brothers what they were. Here, he really got to stretch those country wings and soar freely.

7. *Brothers and Sisters*—The Allman Brothers Band

The favorite record of my high school years. "Pony Boy" still resonates with me, and I never tire of "Jessica" or "Ramblin' Man."

8. Any Volunteer Jam album

That includes *Volunteer Jam, Volunteer Jam III* and *IV, Volunteer Jam VII,* and the more recent *Best of the Volunteer Jam* volumes 1 and 2. The Volunteer Jams were/are the epicenter of Southern rock.

9. *The Wetter the Better*—Wet Willie

Every record brother Jimmy Hall and the band recorded is a living, breathing work of sweat-soaked soul. This one is my favorite. Truth be told, that cover art may have a little something to do with it. Just kidding. I am all about the music.

10. *Second Helping*—Lynyrd Skynyrd

"Curtis Leow" is my favorite Skynyrd song. Ed King is a genius. Ronnie was the man.

11. *Brother*—Cry of Love

I nearly died when they broke up the band. This North Carolina band had it going on in the 1990s, and "Peace Pipe" remains an all-time favorite song. Audley Freed a great guitar slinger.

12. *Dose*—Gov't Mule

Don't get me started. The Mule rocked my world from day one. When Woody died, my whole life changed. To me, he was the best bass player in Southern rock. And Warren Haynes? Sheesh. And Matt Abts? Please. Like I said, if I start on the Mule, this may turn into a book.

13. *Honest to Goodness*—Grinderswitch

Dru Lombar and the boys...man, do I miss Dru. We sure have lost some great Southern rockers these past few years.

14. *Eat a Peach*—The Allman Brothers Band
Nothing else like it, from "Mountain Jam" to "Blue Sky."

15. *Champagne Jam*—Atlanta Rhythm Section
What a great band. My buddy Robert Nix wrote some great tunes, and the whole band just played like nobody's business. The best harmonies. Wow. All good.

16. *Ladies Choice*—Bonnie Bramlett
No, she wasn't a Southern girl, but by God she is now. And this, one of her Capricorn releases, finds her surrounded by Dickey Betts, Chuck Leavell, and a slew of Southern royalty. Not to mention, Southern Soul Sister Number One can wail.

17. *Strikes*—Blackfoot
Speaking of heroes who have passed, Jakson Spires wrote some great songs, and perhaps his finest is right here. "Highway Song" is as timeless as "Free Bird." Love you, Jak. (And Greg, Charlie, and Rick.)

18. *Raunch 'n' Roll Live*—Black Oak Arkansas
I saw this band perform live several times, and boy howdy, did they ever entertain. Jim Dandy Mangrum has a one-of-a-kind voice, and on this live record he works it to beat the band.

19. *Flirtin' with Disaster*—Molly Hatchet
Danny Joe Brown—yet another loss. What a singer and entertainer. If you look up Southern rock in a dictionary, there should be a picture of Danny there, smiling that wicked grin.

20. *The Winters Brothers Band*—The Winters Brothers Band
Dennis and Donnie delivered an album of country-fried Southern rock that is as good today as the day it was recorded. A classic.

21. *The Outlaws*—The Outlaws

Okay, I am getting sick and tired of all the greats dying off. Billy Jones and now Hughie. Damn, we are going to miss you, Hughie. To me, the first record by the Florida Guitar Army remains the finest.

22. *Drinking Man's Friend*—Eric Quincy Tate

EQT should have been just as famous as the Allman Brothers Band. God only knows why that didn't happen. The music is fantastic. If you missed them, go back and have a listen to Donnie McCormick and company. This, their second album, may well be their finest.

23. *Point Blank*—Point Blank

Texas gave us some great music, and none better than Point Blank. Rusty Burns is simply an amazing guitar slinger.

24. *Tres Hombres*—ZZ Top

I loved all of ZZ's songs but still have a thing for "LaGrange" and "Beer Drinkers and Hell Raisers." Now that, brothers and sisters, is Southern rock.

25. The Marshall Tucker Band

The excellent debut from The MTB changed my life forever by turning me onto my hometown heroes.

# APPENDIX II

# 100 DEFINING MOMENTS IN THE HISTORY OF SOUTHERN ROCK

100. "Pony Boy" Handbone (1973)
Dickey Betts brought country music sensibility into the Allman Brothers Band, and on *Brothers and Sisters* he did a jazzy country tune called "Pony Boy" that was so country, it ends with Butch Trucks handboning against his thigh.

99. Black Oak Arkansas Put On a Show (1975)
Black Oak Arkansas was one Southern band with a straight-up hard rock show, complete with extended drum solo, light show, and the destruction of at least a couple of guitars each show, all for the audience's amusement. All of this and J. D. playing the "washboard."

98. Rock and Roll Revival Tour: Kid Rock/Lynyrd Skynyrd Together (Summer 2008)
An outrageous, rip-roaring Southern Rock extravaganza.

97. Jam 4 George (November 2, 2007)
Staged by Justin McCorkle and friends to honor his dad George McCorkle's memory, the all-day outdoor show in Spartanburg, SC, was a hell of a show, with guests that included Tommy Crain and the Crosstown Allstars; the Winters Brothers Band; Artimus Pyle; members and former members of MTB including Jerry Eubanks, Ace Allen, and Pat Elwood; JoJo Billingsley; Donnie Winters; the Southern Boys; and many more.

96. *Behind the Music: Lynyrd Skynyrd* (2000)
VH1's documentary on Skynyrd upset a few apple carts, including Artimus Pyle's, with Billy Powell's version of events surrounding Cassie Gaines' death and the plane crash.

95. .38 Special and Marshall Tucker Team Up for Schlitz Malt Liquor TV Commercial (1984)

We were all thrilled to see the Schlitz folks add a Southern rock pairing to the set of rock and roll band team ups on the "Bull" song.

94. Dickey Lends a Hand to Marshall Tucker: On the Song "Searchin' for a Rainbow" (1975)

From what they tell me, a lot of the guest appearances on various Capricorn Records releases happened on a whim, when someone, like Dickey, was in the studio, and Toy asked him to sit in. Dickey's guitar run is now a classic.

93. Tommy Crain and a Band of Demons (1980)

Remember the first time you heard Charlie Daniels' "The Devil Went Down to Georgia?" Remember the first time you heard "A band of demons joined in and it sounded something like this," followed by Tommy Crain's funky-junky rhythm and Charlie sawing the neck off of his fiddle? I sure do. And it still gets me rockin'.

92. Jaimoe Plays the "Guitcongas" on "Can't You See" (1973)

Yes, it's true. Jaimoe flipped an acoustic guitar over and played it with his hands like a conga on the Marshall Tucker Band classic. Paul Hornsby caught it all on magnet tape.

91. Gregg and Cher (1975–1977)

Brother Gregg Allman married Cher in 1975, and nine days later she filed for divorce. Then they got married again, had a baby named Elijah Blue, and recorded an album *Two the Hard Way*, produced by Johnny Sandlin. And yes, I really liked the album. Still do.

90. Chris Hicks Joins Marshall Tucker (1996)

Hicks was a former member of the Outlaws and a friend of the Tucker Band, so when Stuart Swanlund had to take time off because of a hand surgery, Hicks filled in. As fate would have it, he would later be asked to join the MTB, where for many years he remained a driving force.

### 89. The Winters Brothers Band Debuts (1976)

The Tennessee Southern rockers featuring brothers Dennis and Donnie Winters came from a musical family. Their dad, Don Winters, was a part of the Marty Robbins show, singing all the harmonies with Robbins. Their debut was produced by Taz DiGregorio of the Charlie Daniels Band and is considered a Southern rock classic.

### 88. 7-11 Offers Marshall Tucker Band ICEE Cups (1975)

Sure, you could buy a Peter Frampton or Edgar Winter plastic cup, but the one with MTB on the front and their bio on the back is a collector's item for Tuckerheads the world over.

### 87. Charlie Daniels Band in *Urban Cowboy* (1980)

The CDB rocked the silver screen with John Travolta and scored a number-one hit with "The Devil Went Down to Georgia."

### 86. Derek Trucks joins the Allman Brothers Band (1999)

Butch Trucks's whiz-kid, guitar-hero nephew Derek joined the band, where he remains to this day, playing alongside Warren Haynes and bringing some real youth to the band.

### 85. Dale Krantz Delivers on "Prime Time" (1980)

Rossington Collins Band rose from the ashes of Lynyrd Skynyrd with a great album, a hit "Don't Misunderstand Me," and a smoking Ann Wilson-meets-Janis Joplin vocal by Dale on "Prime Time."

### 84. Allmans Inducted into Rock and Roll Hall of Fame (1995)

The Brothers were inducted into the Rock and *"Rolling Stone"* Hall of Fame in 1995 and performed an amazing acoustic set at that venue that included Dickey, Gregg, and Warren trading vocals on the Robert Johnson classic "Come On into My Kitchen."

### 83. Sailcat Album Features Wyker, Pete Carr, Chuck Leavell (1972)

John D. Wyker and Court Pickett turned out a great album that scored a #12 hit, "Motorcycle Mama," in 1972. The album was produced by Pete Carr and included future Allman Brother and Rolling Stone Chuck Leavell.

### 82. Chuck Leavell's Piano on "Jessica" (1973)

The most memorable piano work in Southern rock may very well be Chuck Leavell's performance with the Allman Brothers on Dickey Betts's "Jessica" from *Brothers and Sisters*. I can't get it out of my head. Can you?

### 81. Jakson Spires Dies (2005)

The Blackfoot drummer (and former Southern Rock Allstars drummer) died on Wednesday, March 16, 2005, from a brain aneurysm suffered a couple of days earlier at home. The world lost a great talent and a good man.

### 80. Warren Haynes Annual Christmas Jam (1989)

What started as a small benefit in Asheville, NC, for Habitat for Humanity has grown from the club Be Here Now to the biggest auditorium in Asheville. Guests have included the Allman Brothers Band, Gov't Mule, Edwin McCain, Kevn Kinney, Jackson Browne, MOE, and hundreds of others. The Xmas Jam has become a regular happening for many Southern rock and jam band fans.

### 79. Cameron Crowe Puts the Allmans on the Cover of the *Rolling Stone* (December 6, 1973)

Cameron Crowe went on the road with the Allman Brothers at the age of fifteen and gave them their first ever cover story. Later, Crowe would turn his career into a semiautobiographical film called *Almost Famous*.

### 78. Tommy Caldwell Dies following an Auto Accident (1980)

After returning home to Spartanburg, SC, following a show in Long Island, Tommy was on his way to the YMCA to work out when his Jeep hit a stalled car in the rain on Church Street and flipped over. Tommy remained in a coma for several days before dying on April 28 at the age of thirty. The Marshall Tucker Band had lost its leader.

77. Jimmy Farrar Takes the Helm of Molly Hatchet (1980)

When Danny Joe Brown left Molly Hatchet to form the Danny Joe Brown Band (with future Hatchet bandleader Bobby Ingram), Jimmy Farrar became lead vocalist and recorded one of the band's biggest hits, "Beatin' the Odds." Farrar would later resurface in the Southern Rock Allstars, the Dixie Jam Band, and Gator Country.

76. Birth of the Mule (1994)

Formed by Warren Haynes and Allen Woody (along with drummer Matt Abts) as a side project of the Allman Brothers Band, the power trio became a quartet following Woody's untimely death in 2000. The Mule is a staple of the outdoor festival jam and rock band scene.

75. The Death of Hughie Thomasson (September 9, 2007)

Hughie went out to dinner with his wife Mary on Sunday, September 9, 2007, returned home, got comfortable in his favorite chair to watch football, and then passed away from a heart attack during a nap. He was fifty-five. Hughie was the leader of the Outlaws, the "Florida Guitar Army" based out of Tampa. He had just finished a brilliant new album and a great Volunteer Jam run with Charlie Daniels and Marshall Tucker.

74. Bobby Whitlock Records *Rock Your Socks Off* (1976)

Bobby Whitlock, formerly of Derek & the Dominos and Delaney & Bonnie, was a Capricorn recording artist during the seventies. One of his best releases was *Rock Your Socks Off*, an album often remembered for its awful cover art by Martin Mull (sorry, Martin!) and its great music. Joining Whitlock on the album were Jimmy Nalls (Sea Level), Dru Lombar (Grinderswitch), Ricky Hirsch (Wet Willie), Les Dudek, Jimmy Hall (Wet Willie), Larry Howard (Grinderswitch), and Chuck Leavell (Allman Brothers/Rolling Stones).

73. Allen Collins Dies (January 23, 1990)

The hard-rocking guitarist of Lynyrd Skynyrd survived the ill-fated plane crash of 1977, but in 1986 a car accident killed Collins's girlfriend and left the guitarist paralyzed from the waist down, with limited use of his arms and hands. Allen Collins died in 1990 from chronic pneumonia resulting from his earlier accident. He was buried in Jacksonville, Florida.

### 72. The Marshall Tucker Band Homecoming (1977)

During the peak of their popularity and with "Heard It in a Love Song" still riding the waves of the Top 40, the Marshall Tucker Band returned home to Spartanburg, SC, to play a benefit for the Shriners Hospital. What was supposed to be two shows ended up being one very long, very awesome jam, with special guests Charlie Daniels, Jaimoe, and Marshall Chapman.

### 71. Lynyrd Skynyrd Appears on *Old Gray Whistle Test* (1975)

One of the most beautiful available videos of Skynyrd is this appearance on the long-running British TV show. This appearance featured the two-guitar era of Gary and Allen without Ed and before Steve, and Ronnie is in fine form.

### 70. *The Midnight Special* Features Dickey Betts and Great Southern, Bonnie Bramlett, Charlie Daniels, and Elvin Bishop (May 12, 1978)

Dickey Betts and Great Southern called on Bonnie Bramlett, Elvin Bishop, and Charlie Daniels to help out with Dickey's "Southbound." Great Southern featured Dangerous Dan Toler, Rook Goldflies, Don Sharbono, David "Frankie" Toler, and Mike Workman. This is the kind of jam we all live for!

### 69. Blackfoot Smoke Monsters of Rock Festival (August 22, 1981)

The Rattlesnake Rock and Rollers burned up the stage Castle Donnington Raceway in Derbyshire, UK, along with AC/DC, Slade, Blue Oyster Cult, and more. According to personal accounts and an available film of the show, Blackfoot was on their A game, plus.

### 68. Allen Woody Dies (August 26, 2000)

Woody died in a hotel room in New York City from accidental overdose. Woody was the badass bassist for the Allmans, Gov't Mule, Artimus Pyle, and, at one time, the Peter Criss Band.

### 67. Bonnie Solos at Capricorn (1975)

After recording *Sweet Bonnie Bramlett* for CBS in 1973, Bonnie made her Macon, Georgia, debut on Capricorn Records with *It's Time* in 1975, followed by two other Capricorn catalog releases, *Lady's Choice* in 1976 and *Memories* in 1978. During this time she solidified her status as a Southern rocker, adding to a resume that included "gospel and soul diva" with Delaney & Bonnie & Friends.

### 66. Grinderswitch Is Formed (1973)

Four young musicians, Joe Dan Petty, Larry Howard, Dru Lombar, and Rick Burnett, some of whom worked on the Allman Brothers road crew, moved to a farm outside of Warner Robbins, Georgia, and for ten months the band wrote and rehearsed material for what was to become their first album on the rising Capricorn label, *Honest to Goodness*. They would soon find themselves a vital part of the whole Macon/Capricorn scene.

### 65. The Marshall Tucker Band, Bonnie Bramlett, and Grinderswitch Tour Europe (1975)

The Tucker Band flew to Europe for their only European tour ever in 1975, bringing along Bonnie Bramlett and Grinderswitch, who not only played their own sets but backed Bonnie on hers.

### 64. The Angelus Country Concerts (1990)

Charlie Daniels hosts these annual events held near Christmastime each year in Tampa, Florida. The four-day event features a celebrity golf tournament, an all-star outdoor country concert, and countless jams, dinners, and auctions. All this is for the benefit of the Angelus, a home for special needs children and adults. Regular performers include Marshall Tucker, Molly Hatchet, Tommy Crain, Bonnie Bramlett, Montgomery Gentry, Dickey Betts, and, of course, the CDB.

63. Drive-By Truckers Record *Southern Rock Opera* (2001)

A double-CD concept album loosely based on the Lynyrd Skynyrd mythology, *Southern Rock Opera* was funded by loans from friends and fans and originally self-released. In 2002 the album was professionally released by Lost Highway and has become a fan favorite in both the Truckers and Skynyrd camps.

62. Marshall Tucker Band Appear on *Fridays* (March 13, 1981)

*Fridays* was a short-lived *Saturday Night Live*-type show that featured a young pre-*Seinfeld* Michael Richards. The March 13, 1981, episode was hosted by comedian David Steinberg and featured Marshall Tucker in a skit as well as performing "Heard It in a Love Song" and "This Time I Believe."

61. The Allman Brothers at Atlanta International Pop Festival (1970)

The second Atlanta International Pop Festival was a music festival held at the Middle Georgia Raceway in Byron, Georgia. Originally scheduled for July 3–5, 1970, it did not finish until near dawn on the 6th, due in part to the jamming of one Allman Brothers Band, who played two smoking sets and invited Johnny Winter up to play on "Mountain Jam." The complete ABB sets were released on CD in 2003.

60. Donnie and Johnny Van Zant Team Up (1998)

Brothers Donnie and Johnny Van Zant teamed up to record a side project outside Lynyrd Skynyrd and .38 Special in 1998, recording a second album in 2001. In 2005 they were signed to Sony, went country, and have released a pair of critically acclaimed albums.

59. *Freebird* the Movie Premiers (1996)

Drawn mostly from Lynyrd Skynyrd's 1976 show at Knebworth Fair in England, the movie also included footage from a few smaller shows, along with rare photos, interviews, and more. The movie was released on DVD in December 2001.

58. Eddie Hinton Dies in Alabama at Age 51 (July 28, 1995)

The great Southern singer, songwriter, and guitar player Eddie Hinton went from fame to homelessness and back to popularity during his life, recording for Capricorn Records and playing with Duane Allman and as a member of the Muscle Shoals rhythm section known as the Swampers.

57. .38 Special Forms in Jacksonville (1975)
.38 Special was formed by neighborhood friends Don Barnes and Ronnie's brother Donnie Van Zant in 1975 in Jacksonville, Florida, and remains a concert draw to this day.

56. Wet Willie Forms in Mobile, Alabama (1969)
Drummer Lewis Ross assembled the musicians for a group called Fox in summer 1969, which a year later became known as Wet Willie, fronted by the enigmatic Jimmy Hall. The group was soon signed to Capricorn Records and Macon became their second home. "Keep On Smilin'" was released in 1974 and became their biggest hit.

55. *Hank Williams, Jr. and Friends* Is Released (1975)
Following a near-death accident while climbing Ajax Mountain, Bocephus changed his musical direction in what is often cited as the first move of a country artist into the Southern rock realm. Joining Hank on the record *Hank Williams, Jr. and Friends* were Toy Caldwell, Charlie Daniels, Pete Carr, Chuck Leavell, Dickey Betts, Waylon Jennings, and other greats. Hank also recorded two of Toy's songs on the record, which is considered by many to be Hank's best work ever.

54. Danny Joe Brown Dies at Fifty-Three (March 10, 2005)
Brown, diagnosed with diabetes when he was nineteen and in poor health since suffering a stroke in 1998, succumbed to renal failure and pneumonia. Molly Hatchet was formed in 1974 by Brown and lead guitarists David Hlubek and Steve Holland. Their name was taken from a seventeenth-century prostitute known for chopping off her clients' heads. Guitarist Duane Roland, bassist Banner Thomas, and drummer Bruce Crump joined the following year to complete the six-member lineup, based in Jacksonville, Florida.

53. Doug Gray Sings "Ramblin'" Live (1974)

Nowhere is the sheer vocal ability of Marshall Tucker Band's lead vocalist Doug Gray more evident than on the double album *Where We All Belong*, and of all the great vocals on the classic record, none is more intense than "Ramblin (on My Mind)," the Toy Caldwell-penned rocker that goes and goes, building to a climactic sustained note that shakes the walls and rattles the balls.

52. "In Memory of Elizabeth Reed" (1970)

Supposedly written at Rose Hill Cemetery after Dickey Betts saw the words on a large tombstone, the original studio recording is the fourth song on the Allman Brothers Band's 1970 album *Idlewild South* and appeared on their seminal *At Fillmore East* release (among others) Written in a minor key, the understated jazzy instrumental was the band's first original instrumental and the first of many classic Dickey Betts instrumental compositions.

51. "Layla" Merges Duane Allman and Eric Clapton (1970)

The story of how Duane Allman and Eric Clapton's union came to be is the stuff of legend, and Tom Dowd told us about it during our interviews with him. The addition of Skydog's guitar to this already unbelievable band was the cherry on top, creating a double album of timeless classic rock.

50. Clint Black Records a Toy Caldwell Song (1999)

The Marshall Tucker favorite "Bob Away My Blues" was given an acoustic treatment by country star Clint Black for his first ever self-produced album *D'Lectrified*.

49. The Outlaws Piece Together "Green Grass and High Tides" (1975)

Hughie Thomasson went on record saying that the original Outlaws song lasted four minutes, but after years of jamming out on the end of the song, it ended up being the new "Free Bird."

48. Marshall Tucker Band Appear on *Hollywood Squares* (1977)

Yes, the MTB (George, Toy, and Paul, anyway) were answering questions from Peter Marshall alongside Elvin Bishop, the Tubes, and others on the classic seventies game show.

47. Charlie Daniels Records Tribute to Fellow Southern Rockers (1975)

"The South's Gonna Do It Again" from the Charlie Daniels Band LP *Fire on the Mountain* is a straight-up "roll call" for all of his friends, from Skynyrd to Marshall Tucker, Barefoot Jerry to Wet Willie, Dickey Betts, Grinderswitch, and more. The song is considered by many to be the unofficial Southern rock anthem.

46. Phil Walden Signs the Allman Brothers (1969)

Phil Walden signed Gregg and Duane Allman and company to the newly formed Capricorn Records in Macon, Georgia, in 1969, a moment that arguably may be the instant Southern rock was born.

45. Lester Bangs Reviews The Marshall Tucker Band in *Rolling Stone* (1973)

Legendary rock journalist Lester Bangs was known for his rave reviews of Lou Reed and punk rock records, but he also found passion in groups like Wet Willie and loved the debut Tucker record, exposing the bands to a whole new (and huge) audience.

44. Dickey Betts Fired from The Allman Brothers Band (May 2001)

Just before the summer 2001 tour, the other members of the Allman Brothers Band sent a FAX to Dickey Betts, firing him from the band. The FAX cited alcohol and substance abuse as the primary problems, although Betts claimed at the time to no longer have a problem. He was replaced for the summer tour by Jimmy Herring and never returned.

43. 3614 Jackson Highway Opens Doors (1969)

Muscle Shoals Sound Studio was formed in 1969 when musicians Barry Beckett (keyboards), Roger Hawkins (drums), Jimmy Johnson (guitar), and David Hood (bass)—AKA: the Swampers—left FAME

Studios to create their own studio. Besides recording everyone from Aretha Franklin to the Rolling Stones, the studio is remembered as one of the first places Lynyrd Skynyrd recorded. In 1978, the Muscle Shoals group built new facilities on the banks of the Tennessee River in the abandoned Navy Reserve building, which included two then-state-of-the-art studio complexes with Neve recording consoles and Neve's automation 'flying faders' in Studio B.

### 42. Muscle Shoals Sound Studios Sold to Movie Company (2005)

The second Muscle Shoals Sound Studio closed and the building was sold to Cypress Moon, a company that makes movies. The company is headed by Tonya Holly, who maintains a deep respect for the building's history. Her husband Kelvin is a respected Shoals guitarist who performs with Little Richard.

### 41. Bonnie and Delaney Meet and Marry (1967)

Bonnie met Delaney and a few weeks later they were married, creating one of rock's most legendary pairings. The couple formed a band that at times featured everyone from Dave Mason to Eric Clapton, George Harrison, and Duane Allman. After recording several albums, the couple divorced in 1973 and went their separate ways personally and musically.

### 40. Paul Hornsby's Synthesizer on "Take the Highway" (1973)

Down at Capricorn Records Studios in Macon, Paul Hornsby was producing the debut album from the Marshall Tucker Band, a decidedly country rock group. Somehow, Paul made the decision to play synthesizer on the song "Take the Highway," and it worked like magic. Now, *that* is innovation!

### 39. Jammin' for Danny Joe Brown (July 18, 1999)

Riff West headed an all-star concert to raise money for Molly Hatchet lead singer Danny Joe Brown, who at the time was buried under piles of medical bills. The show featured almost all of the surviving members of the original Hatchet, as well as the Southern Rock Allstars,

Artimus Pyle, Pat Travers, and others. The show, held at a big club in Florida, was later released as a DVD and CD.

### 38. Tommy Caldwell's Bass Solo on "24 Hours at a Time" (1974)

When the Marshall Tucker Band put out the double album *Where We All Belong*, with one live LP and one studio record, it turned the song "24 Hours At a Time" into an extended live jam, with a remarkable bass solo by Tommy Caldwell.

### 37. Gregg Allman Acts in *Rush* (1991)

Gregg Allman stepped into the role of a kingpin drug dealer in the dark and somewhat depressing story of two undercover cops infiltrating the drug community. Stars include Jason Patric and Jennifer Jason Leigh.

### 36. Warren and Woody Join the Allmans (1989)

When the Allman Brothers Band reunited in 1989 to support the new *Dreams* boxed set, the band featured Warren Haynes and Woody Allen, as well as Johnny Neel. Haynes infused the band with an entirely new spark, and the group regained its creative magic, recording and releasing *Seven Turns* in 1990.

### 35. *Uncivil Wars* Special on VH1 (August 2002)

Creative editing and an obvious agenda made this Lynyrd Skynyrd special come off like a bad soap opera or reality show. It's on the list to remind us all of just how low the media will stoop to get viewers.

### 34. Tommy Caldwell's Last Show, King Biscuit Flower Hour (1980)

Recorded at Nassau Coliseum in Long Island, New York, it was one of the Marshall Tucker Band's finest performances, high-energy and bombastic. "Cattle Drive" sounded like the heard was being driven right through your head. The next day, Tommy would have a Jeep wreck in his hometown and die a few days later. The show was remastered and released in early 2007 as a two-disc set called *Live on Long Island*.

33. Ol' Waylon Cuts "Can't You See" (1976)

Waylon Jennings and Toy Caldwell had struck up a friendship, and in '76 Waymore did a great version of Toy's signature tune on his album *Are You Ready for the Country?*

32. *Volunteer Jam: the Movie* (1975)

This full-length film was shown in theatres in 1975, sometimes as a double feature with a John Wayne western or other similar film. The footage is from the second ever jam and includes a smoldering set by the Charlie Daniels Band, along with the Marshall Tucker Band, Dickey Betts, Grinderswitch, and more. The movie eventually made it to home DVD.

31. Mama Louise Feeds the Brothers (1969)

In their early days, the Allman Brothers Band didn't have any money. They were in Macon recording and playing free shows in the park, trying to make it. Along comes the angel known as Mama Louise Hudson and her diner the H&H in Macon, now known as the soul food capital of the South. Mama Louise fed the Brothers many times on credit, many more times for free. No small wonder she is looked upon as a saint by the Peach Corp.

30. The Southern Rock Allstars Release Double Live CD (2004)

The SRA began life as the Dixie Allstars and at one time included Billy Jones, Greg T. Walker, and more. Drummer Jakson Spires and guitarist Jay Johnson were core members, and the band enjoyed a successful run and two studio albums. The live CD was full of covers by Hatchet, Skynyrd, and Blackfoot, as well as SRA originals, and featured guest guitarist Mike Estes. When the live album hit, the band included Johnson and Spires, Charles Hart on bass, Dave Hlubek on guitar, and Jimmy Farrar on vocals. Around the same time, Hlubek left and Duane Roland came in. Later, with the death of Roland, Scott Mabry became guitarist. Jakson died in 2005, and the band all but disappeared.

29 Volunteer Jam Tour (2007)

The Charlie Daniels Band, the Outlaws and the Marshall Tucker Band toured the United States in 2007. The Nashville show scheduled for May 19, 2007, was cancelled due to the closing of Nashville's Starwood Amphitheater due to its age and size (it was called a "first generation amphitheater"), but the other cities. Other cities, however, witnessed a jam unlike anything they had seen in years, with members of all three bands sitting in with their friends and the whole show wrapping up with all three bands onstage together.

28. *Stompin' Room Only* Released (2003)

The "holy grail" for Marshall Tucker Band fans, these live recordings from the mid-1970s have been sought after for years. Originally slated to be released by Capricorn, the album took twenty-eight years to see the light of day. In 2003, Shout! Factory released the Paul Hornsby-produced album, and Toy and Tommy fans rejoiced. I was honored to be asked to write the liner notes.

27. Duane at FAME (1968)

Duane Allman asked FAME Studios exec Rick Hall if he had any session work. Hall said not right now, and Duane said okay, that he would just pitch a tent in the parking lot and when some work came up, Rick could let him know. It wasn't long before Duane got his shot, playing on Wilson Pickett's *Hey Jude* LP. The rest is history, as Allman played on many great records by Aretha Franklin, King Curtis, Delaney & Bonnie, Boz Scaggs, and many others, cementing his legacy.

26. Kid Rock Brings Dickey Betts on Tour (2008)

Kid Rock's Rock and Roll Revival tour of January 2008 featured Rev. Run from Run DMC, Peter Wolf from J. Geils Band, and Dickey Betts from the Allman Brothers, bringing Dickey's great music to a whole new audience.

25. Toy Caldwell Dies at Home (Feb 25, 1993)

The legendary guitarist and primary songwriter for the Marshall Tucker Band died at home in Spartanburg, SC, at the age of forty-five from respiratory problems. The world lost a one-of-a-kind guitar picker and human being.

### 24. Shorty Medlocke (1970s)

A Florida musician and the grandfather of Rick Medlocke of Blackfoot and Skynyrd, Shorty was a major influence on the Blackfoot Band. He played harp at the opening of "Train, Train," a song he wrote. He also cowrote "Fox Chase" and "Rattlesnake Rock and Roller."

### 23. "The Swampers" Immortalized in a Skynyrd Song (1974)

The Muscle Shoals Swampers, the studio band during the sixties and seventies that dominated Shoals recordings, received a shout-out from Ronnie Van Zant and Lynyrd Skynyrd in the band's ever-popular song.

### 22. *One More from the Road*—Lynyrd Skynyrd (1976)

The now legendary live Skynyrd double LP produced by Tom Dowd gave us the definitive live version of "Free Bird."

### 21. *Fire on the Mountain*—The Charlie Daniels Band (1975)

The Paul Hornsby-produced album that put Charlie over the top, with hits "Long Haired Country Boy" and "The South's Gonna Do It Again," also included a bonus disc of live music from the first Volunteer Jam, an item that is highly sought after by collectors today.

### 20. The Marshall Tucker Band First Album Debuts on WORD Radio (1973)

Growing up in Spartanburg, SC, our local AM rock station was the main source of rock and roll entertainment. Billy Mac followed up his January 1, 1973, countdown of the top 100 songs of the year with the debut playing (by anyone) of the Tucker album and an in-studio chat with the band members. They guys were off and running.

### 19. Duane and the Dead (Feb 11, 1970)

The Grateful Dead rocked the Fillmore East with some heavy special guests. The jam on "Dark Star" with Duane Allman, Peter Green of Fleetwood Mac, and Arthur Lee from Love is legendary. During "Turn On Your Love Light," Butch Trucks got on Mickey's drum kit, Mickey played percussion, Barry Oakley played second bass, Peter Green and Duane Allman played guitar, and Gregg Allman joined in on organ and vocals. Pigpen and Gregg traded off vocals. Classic.

18. *Highway Call* (1974)
Dickey (as Richard) Betts put out a classic album filled with country music that remains one of the Buffalo's all-time favorites, featuring Vassar Clements, the Rambos, Johnny Sandlin, and more. The perfect bookend with Gregg's *Laid Back* that same year.

17. Bonnie Bramlett's Run on *Roseanne* (1991)
Bonnie (then known as Bonnie Sheridan) shows up as a waitress in a diner and a friend of Roseanne in both the third and fourth season of the comedy series. She even sang on a couple of episodes.

16. Toy Caldwell Sits Down Behind the Pedal Steel (1973)
Besides being the fastest thumb in the South and one of our finest guitarists, Toy was also a master of the steel guitar, adding his Marshall Tucker magic to classic songs like "Fire on the Mountain" and "Desert Skies."

15. The Allmans Play MTV *Unplugged* (December 9, 1990)
What a band! This version of the Brothers featured Warren Haynes, the late Allen Woody, Gregg, Dickey, Jaimoe, Butch, and Mr. Johnny Neel on keys, and they sure sounded great acoustic, especially on the Robert Johnson classic "Come On into My Kitchen." With the recent *Dreams* boxed set and a new studio album out, the revamped Brothers were smokin'.

14. Lynyrd Skynyrd Enter the Rock and Roll Hall of Fame (March 13, 2006)
And the Southern rock world rejoiced! Ronnie and his band were honored at long last, as Kid Rock read the induction just before the

current band reunited for two songs with Ed King, Bob Burns, JoJo Billingsley, Leslie Hawkins, and Artimus Pyle.

13. *Hotels, Motels and Road Shows* (1978)

The ultimate live compilation from Capricorn. Two LPs featured live tracks from Stillwater, the Dixie Dregs, the Marshall Tucker Band, Bonnie Bramlett, Grinderswitch, Elvin Bishop, Wet Willie, Richard Betts, Gregg Allman, and the Allman Brothers Band.

12. "Dreams" Times Two (1970, 1979)

"Dreams" was a hell of a blues tune by the Allman Brothers Band, then it became a rocker in the hands of Florida's Molly Hatchet, creating two very distinct versions of the same Gregg Allman-penned song.

11. Hank Williams Jr.'s "All My Rowdy Friends Are Comin' Over Tonight" Video (1985)

Hank rocked the country with a killer all-star video that featured tons of babes as well as Paul Williams, Jim Varney, the Oak Ridge Boys, Little Jimmy Dickens, George Thorogood, Waylon, Grandpa Jones, Cheech and Chong, Kris Kristofferson, Porter Wagoner, Willie Nelson, Merle Kilgore, Dickey Betts, Jimmy Hall, Ronnie McDowell, Bobby Bare, Mel Tillis, and more.

10. Jimmy Carter Rocks the Vote (1976)

Democratic presidential nominee Jimmy Carter from Plains, Georgia, brought out all his own rowdy friends to support his campaign, including close friend Phil Walden of Capricorn Records, the Allman Brothers, Marshall Tucker, and many others who played fundraisers for the Southern presidential candidate, himself a huge fan of Southern rock.

9. Willie Nelson's Fourth of July Picnics (1972)

Willie's annual shows featured many of our favorite performers over the years, including Lynyrd Skynyrd, Toy Caldwell, Stevie Ray Vaughan, Billy Bob Thornton, Neil Young, Townes Van Zandt, Waylon, and, in 2007, the Drive-By Truckers.

8. *The Midnight Special* Features the Marshall Tucker Band, the Charlie Daniels Band (January 24, 1975)

A major advance in Southern Rock, MTB hosted the show and played their hit "This Ol' Cowboy," as well as "In My Own Way" and "24 Hours at a Time," with Charlie Daniels on fiddle. The CDB rocked on "The South's Gonna Do It Again," "Long Haired Country Boy," and "Caballo Diablo." The show also featured Olivia Newton John and Poco.

7. Duane Allman Dies in Motorcycle Crash (October 29, 1971), Berry Oakley Dies in Motorcycle Crash (November 11, 1972)

The founder of the Allman Brothers Band died in a motorbike wreck in Macon, Georgia, in 1971, rocking the music world. A year later, his brother in arms, bassist Berry Oakley, died in a similar bike crash only three blocks from where brother Duane died.

6. Internet Groups and Chat Rooms (1996)

As the Internet began to grow, music fans began to find one another, and Southern rock was no exception. Yahoo groups, before they were called Yahoo Groups, were cropping up in the mid to late nineties, including Rebel Rock, Skynyrd Frynds, and many others as well as band specific chat rooms where fans meet to discuss their favorite music and talk about what adult beverage they might be drinking that night. All of this was prior to the Myspace and Facebook craze.

5. *Saturday Night in Macon, Georgia* (1975)

A special episode of *Don Kirshner's Rock Concert* filmed on location in Macon, Georgia, featured an outdoor afternoon set by Wet Willie before moving indoors for the Marshall Tucker Band, comedian Martin Mull, and the Allman Brothers Band. A pivotal moment in Southern rock history, to be sure.

4. *At Fillmore East*—The Allman Brothers Band (1971)

The double live album by the Allman Brothers Band, produced by Tom Dowd, is universally regarded as their breakthrough success. Released in July 1971, *At Fillmore East* is hailed as one of the greatest live recordings in the history of rock music. It was number 49 among *Rolling*

*Stone* magazine's 500 Greatest Albums of All Time and is consistently named the favorite Southern rock album of all time by fans and fellow rockers alike.

### 3. Capricorn Records Opens Doors (1969)

Backed by Jerry Wexler at Atlantic Records, Phil Walden, Alan Walden, and Frank Fenter opened the Southern record label based in Macon, Georgia, in 1969. The label was the home of the Allman Brothers Band, the Marshall Tucker Band, Elvin Bishop, Bonnie Bramlett, Eddie Hinton, Grinderswitch, and many others. Capricorn went out of business in 1979, reopened in the early 1990s (with Lynyrd Skynyrd signing on), and closed for good in 2002.

### 2. Volunteer Jam (October 4, 1974)

The Charlie Daniels Band hosted their first jam at the War Memorial Auditorium in Nashville, Tennessee, with band members Barry Barnes (guitar), Taz Digregorio (keyboards), Mark Fitzgerald (bass), Gary Allen (drums), and Freddy Edwards (drums). This was the beginning of a tradition and featured the Marshall Tucker Band, Dickey Betts, Grinderswitch, and many more.

With a new band lineup that featured guitarist Tommy Crain and bassist Charlie Hayward, the second jam was held in 1975. It was released in the form of a movie, billed as the "first Southern rock movie," and even appeared in theaters across the US. The movie was re-released on DVD in 2007. The jam featured the Marshall Tucker Band, Jimmy Hall, Dickey Betts, Grinderswitch, and many others.

In 1979, Lynyrd Skynyrd reunited for the first time since the 1977 plane crash with several members of the Charlie Daniels Band. CDB keyboardist Taz Digregorio took lead vocals on "Call Me the Breeze," followed by an extended instrumental version of "Freebird."

Over the years, each of the Nashville concerts featured a long list of special guests appearing onstage with Charlie and his band, including Ted Nugent, the Allman Brothers Band, the Marshall Tucker Band, Molly Hatchet, the Winters Brothers Band, Billy Joel, Elvin Bishop Garth Brooks, Billy Ray Cyrus, Stevie Ray Vaughan, Tammy Wynette, Little Richard, James Brown, Roy Acuff, Carl Perkins, Alabama, Don Henley, and many more. Many of these concerts were broadcast live on the radio. The *Volunteer Jam* on nationwide TV included a live broadcast on the Jerry Lewis Telethon and a Dick Clark-produced network special.

Lynyrd Skynyrd reunited for Volunteer Jam 1987, and Toy Caldwell played a blistering set on the same show.

Beginning in 1999, Charlie took the Volunteer Jam on the road for almost yearly tours, featuring bands like the MTB, Molly Hatchet, the Outlaws, Hank Williams Jr., Edgar Winter, Jimmy Hall, and more. The 2008 tour featured Shooter Jennings and .38 Special.

1. The Lynyrd Skynyrd Plane Crash (Thursday, October 20, 1977)

Just three days after the release of *Street Survivors* and three days into their most successful headlining tour to date, Lynyrd Skynyrd's chartered Convair 240 developed mechanical difficulties near the end of their flight from Greenville, South Carolina, to LSU in Baton Rouge, Louisiana. Though the pilots attempted an emergency landing on a small airstrip, the plane ran out of fuel and crashed in a forest near McComb, Mississippi, just short of its goal.

Singer-songwriter Ronnie Van Zant, guitarist-vocalist Steve Gaines, backing vocalist Cassie Gaines, assistant road manager Dean Kilpatrick, pilot Walter McCreary, and copilot William Gray were all killed on impact. Other band members were injured, some seriously.

Drummer Artimus Pyle crawled out of the plane wreckage with several broken ribs but still went for help, along with road crew members Kenneth Peden Jr. and Mark Frank. The three injured men hiked some distance from the crash site, through swampy woods, and finally flagged down farmer Johnny Mote, who had come to investigate.

The Southern rock world was devastated, but this was only the beginning of the Skynyrd Legend, which is bigger now than ever before. The tragedy of the airplane crash is our number one defining moment in the history of Southern rock. Many have suggested that Southern rock died that day, but the rumors of its death have been greatly exaggerated. Souther rock is alive and well in 2012.

# APPENDIX III

## PRISONER SOUNDTRACK

*Prisoner of Southern Rock* was written over the course of several years, during which time I listened to hundreds of hours of music as I wrote. Still, there were certain albums that kept popping up more frequently than others. I have listed them below, in no particular order, as my way of showing that, although Southern rock is a major love of mine, at any given moment music of all types is flowing through my consciousness.

*Layla and Other Love Songs*, Derek & the Dominos (1970)
*The White Album*, the Beatles (1968)
*Eat a Peach*, The Allman Brothers Band (1972)
*Beautiful Door*, Billy Bob Thornton (2007)
*Motel Shot*, Delaney & Bonnie (1971)
*Big Lonesome*, Marshall Chapman (2010)
*Ain't Love Strange*, Paul Thorn (2000)
*Discreet Music*, Brian Eno (1975)
*Low*, David Bowie (1977)
*Device, Voice, Drum*, Kansas (2002)
*Modbilly*, The Boxmasters (2009)
*Greatest Hits*, The Jackson Five (1971)
*Reach for the Sky*, Cowboy (1970)
*Someone Else's Shoes*, Tommy Talton (2008)
*Brothers and Sisters*, The Allman Brothers Band (1973)
*Letters from Mississippi*, Eddie Hinton (1987)
*Fire on the Mountain*, Charlie Daniels Band (1975)
*Tres Hombres*, ZZ Top (1973)
*Saints & Sinners*, Johnny Winter (1974)
*Just Another Band from L.A.*, Frank Zappa & the Mothers (1972)
*Still Alive and Well*, Johnny Winter (1973)
*Beautiful*, Bonnie Bramlett (2008)

*Not a Word on It*, Pete Carr (1976)

*Highway Call*, Richard Betts (1974)

*Toy Caldwell*, Toy Caldwell (1992)

*The Best of Merle Haggard* (1972)

*What's In It for Me?* Bekka Bramlett (2002)

*Where We All Belong*, Marshall Tucker Band (1974)

*At Fillmore East*, The Allman Brothers Band (1971)

*Southern Rock Opera*, Drive-By Truckers (2001)

*Pimps & Preachers*, Paul Thorn (2010)

*American Street*, George McCorkle (1999)

*Saddle Tramp*, Charlie Daniels Band (1976)

*Drinking Man's Friend*, Eric Quincy Tate (1972)

*Old Five and Dimers Like Me*, Billy Joe Shaver (1973)

*Tapestry*, Carole King (1971)

*1812 Overture*, John Williams and Boston Pops Orchestra (1996)

*Dog Eat Dog World*, Chris Hicks (2008)

*Honest to Goodness*, Grinderswitch (1974)

*Pulse*, Pink Floyd (1995)

*Roadwork*, Edgar Winter's White Trash (1972)

*Dose*, Gov't Mule (1997)

*Stardust*, Willie Nelson (1978)

*5'll Getcha Ten*, Cowboy (1971)

*Uncle Charlie and His Dog Teddy*, Nitty Gritty Dirt Band (1970)

*Sweet Bonnie Bramlett*, Bonnie Bramlett (1973)

*They Only Come Out at Night*, Edgar Winter Group (1973)

*The Kick Inside*, Kate Bush (1978)

*Born to Run*, Bruce Springsteen (1975)

*Unearthed*, Johnny Cash (2003)

*Reckoning*, Grateful Dead (1981)

*On Tour with Eric Clapton* boxed set, Delaney & Bonnie (2010)

*Hurry Sundown*, The Outlaws (1977)

*The River*, Bruce Springsteen (1991)

*Keep On Smilin'*, Wet Willie (1974)

*Sweet Baby James*, James Taylor (1970)

*Killer*, Alice Cooper (1971)

*Brothers and Sisters*, Thomas Wynn and the Believers (2012)

*The High Road*, Silver Travis (2009)
*The Year I Grew Up*, Clay Cook (2008)
*Works Vol. I*, Emerson, Lake and Palmer (1977)
*Joe's Garage*, Frank Zappa (1979)

To name a few...

# AUTHOR'S BIOGRAPHY

Michael Buffalo Smith is a writer and musician from Spartanburg, South Carolina. He founded *GRITZ Magazine*, the magazine of Southern rock, in 1998, and has since met and befriended countless legends of the genre, from Charlie Daniels to Dickey Betts, from Bonnie Bramlett to the late Jakson Spires of Blackfoot. Smith has become known as "the Ambassador of Southern Rock" and has written thousands of articles and reviews for various music magazines as well as two books on Southern rock. In 2010 he left *GRITZ* and started the online magazine Universal Music Tribe, and in 2011 he realized a true dream in forming a nonprofit corporation to help uninsured Southern musicians in need called Hearts of the South. He is also a performer, recording artist, songwriter, screenwriter, and actor.

Author's websites:

www.michaelbuffalo.net

www.universalmusictribe.com

www.heartsofthesouth.org

# INDEX